Urban Planning and Politics

Urban Planning and Politics

William C. Johnson

PLANNERS PRESS

AMERICAN PLANNING ASSOCIATION
Chicago, Illinois   Washington, D.C.

Second edition
Copyright 1997 by the American Planning Association
122 S. Michigan Ave., Suite 1600
Chicago, IL 60603

ISBN (paperback edition): 1-884829-14-7
ISBN (hardbound edition): 1-884829-15-5

First edition published as The Politics of Urban Planning
Copyright 1989 by WIlliam C. Johnson

Contents

Preface

I address this book to three groups of readers. First, I have in mind students in college and university courses in planning, public administration, and urban politics and policy. Whether of traditional college age or more mature years, they are looking ahead to roles that will allow them to participate in planning or to influence it in some fashion. For these aims, they need to link urban planning with all else they are learning—in politics, economics, sociology, business management, architecture, or human services.

Second, I think of those who are professionally active in urban decision making. These individuals may include city transit specialists, county engineers, or state environmental protection officers. Some may work in the private sector as Realtors, attorneys, or chamber of commerce directors. Planning has not been the central focus of their education, yet they realize the need to know how it happens, who participates, and what policies have emerged from it.

A third group consists of attentive and concerned citizens who recognize that planners make choices that affect their quality of life and property values. Some may seek to protect the open space remaining in their suburban communities, while others deplore the city's neglect of vacant lots and deteriorated buildings in their neighborhoods. Citizens have many ways to influence the planning process, but they require some knowledge of the system and the ability to communicate their views constructively.

In this decade of widespread public distrust of government and large business enterprises, planning attracts its share of that distrust. It is seen, sometimes rightly, as an elite process, magnifying the power of the politicians, bureaucrats, developers, and attorneys who pursue their selfish ends at the expense of ordinary citizens. Indeed, planning is, like many policy realms in our technological society, the domain of experts. This book challenges that view by showing that planning can be, and often is, penetrated by citizens with a broader public concern and interest.

This book is not an apology for planners and their choices, however. I regard planning as an essential function for urban areas and argue that it can be done well by both technical and democratic standards. Yet I show that it has also been done badly and in undemocratic ways. Readers should seek to discern "good planning" from its less laudable forms, keeping in mind the many situational and political factors that sway choices in one direction or another.

I hold three basic concepts that have inspired and directed this book. First, *politics* stands as the essential self-steering enterprise of a complex pluralistic society. It is the choosing mechanism of a democracy, reflecting all of its faults as well as its strengths. Such politics must be inclusive, calling diverse interests into the public arena and balancing them satisfactorily. Yet it must also be guided by an overriding concern for a *public* interest, promoting the good of all, even while it reconciles the drives for private gain.

Planning must be an element in that political process when it chooses how cities will grow and change. It is a holistic, ordering activity that gives political decision makers a coherent point of view. Planners specialize in depicting the choices that a community can make about its future and how to assess them intelligently. Thus it provides a "first word" about how cities can be made more humane, livable, and just, though properly not the final decision.

The third concept is *justice,* which sets a norm for the products of planning politics. In this context, it is a pursuit of the fair distribution of the benefits and costs of urban society. This effort entails a special concern for those who are currently disadvantaged by some condition of life—age, race, ethnic identity, personal disability, income, or family status. Planning politics cannot remedy injustices arising from these inequities, but it can mitigate some and avoid worsening others.

This book links the general values and concepts of planning with concrete policies and contemporary events. In the first chapter are four brief case studies of planning politics, from San Diego, New York City, the Minneapolis-St. Paul metropolitan area, and Tigard, Oregon. I refer to these in later chapters to illustrate key points.

Many other current situations also appear; in fact, nearly one-third of the references are to 1996 or 1997 publications. While each example is unique, it has some features that typify a larger group. One case never makes a rule, but many cases form significant patterns. These examples allow readers to learn inductively, leading them to concepts and hypotheses that they can test against further evidence. It is important that they pay close attention to ongoing issues and developments in their own communities and in the nation at large in continuing their own education.

The 11 chapters fall logically into four parts. In the first part, chapter 1 introduces the basic concepts and themes in addition to the four cases. Chapter 2 surveys American planning history to identify the central values and experiences that make up the collective memory that guides our system today. It also describes the affective meanings that geographic places have for people and how they express and defend those meanings.

The second part portrays the cast of participants in urban planning. Chapter 3 focuses on governments and their officials—national, state, and local—and the role each plays. The nongovernmental participants appear in chapter 4, from the profitmaking businesses and nonprofit institutions to individual citizens and their voluntary organizations. Together these players define the scope of cooperation and conflict and the interests at stake in each decision.

Specific planning practices and policies make up the third and largest part. Chapter 5 describes the methods and tools that planners use in the stages from intelligence gathering to plan implementation. Included are such basic techniques as comprehensive planmaking and zoning. Chapter 6 takes up economic development as a key purpose of planning, from the sources of funds to the choices of locations for industrial and commercial enterprises. Housing is the theme of chapter 7, including the control of residential environments and the provision of homes for those who would lack them without outside intervention. Chapter 8 turns to transportation, the means of mobility and access, whether by providing avenues for private vehicles or supplying public transit service. The urban environment, with the means of protecting air, water, and soil from pollution, appears in chapter 9, as do policies for controlling urban growth in agricultural and other sensitive areas. Finally, chapter 10 examines planning for several aspects of the "cultural environment," from historic preservation and the arts to education, parks, and crime prevention.

Chapter 11 constitutes the final part. Here, the view is into the new century and the new or intensified challenges it will present to planners. These range from the vast potentials for information technology to basic demographic trends in age and cultural diversity. I do not offer a single vision for what can or ought to be, but rather a span of options for deliberation within an open process.

Readers should notice several other aids to learning. Each chapter concludes with several questions for review and discussion. These come in pairs; the first is relatively factual and can be answered from the text, while the second calls for additional thinking and judgment. The appendix provides, first, an annotated list of 25 of the better case studies on urban planning. Students can find in them further illustration of the many themes in this book. A brief essay follows on how to research and write cases in planning, on the as-

sumption that one learns best while examining the activity first hand. Finally, a glossary defines selected major terms that appear in the book. The language of planning is not highly specialized, but its concepts are fairly precise.

I owe thanks to more people than I can remember or name who have contributed to my understanding of urban planning. But I express special appreciation to the planners, planning commission colleagues, and concerned citizens who have been part of my experiences in Shoreview and Lino Lakes since 1979. These individuals provided an education on the political and personal aspects of this subject that no book could convey. Most of all I thank my wife, AnnMae, for her constant encouragement to bring this work to print.

William C. Johnson
Lino Lakes, Minnesota
1997

1

Perceptions and Politics in Planning

1.1 PLANNING AS VISION AND IMAGINATION

Planning for cities begins when we look around us and say, "This could be different!" We see what is there and think about it. We then construct in our minds what ought to be in its place. The most basic "tools" of planning are our eyes and imaginations. We stand atop the Sears Building in Chicago, for example, and look westward at a vast stretch of vacant ground. That land once provided many jobs and homes in an economy that depended more heavily on human labor. Those jobs and homes are now out beyond our vision in suburbs like Hoffman Estates and Elk Grove Village. And so we ask, "Couldn't that abandoned space again be used to provide jobs or homes or better schools?"

We might fly over a Los Angeles freeway (see Figure 1.1) and view the 5 o'clock gridlock. We ask, "Isn't there a better way to move people than that?" We realize that a crowded freeway is a planning success, in a way, since its vast expanses of concrete never lack for

wheels. And the drivers in those cars are no doubt quite comfortable with their air conditioning and stereo CD players. But we are not sure that this is what makes city life healthy or fulfilling.

Or we watch a bulldozer clear away a stand of Connecticut woods to make room for another upscale residential tract. It obviously sold for a good price and is another acomplishment of the free market in real estate. But we could ask, "Why can't the homes that people need be built on lands that are already cleared? Or at least clustered together so they don't have to destroy all that forest?"

What we see interacts with what we value. Our questions, and their answers, depend on the goods and bads we see in urban life and the prospects for change. They grow out of our experiences with blighted city lots, congested freeways, and lost woodlands. If we try to act on our answers, we follow the guidance of our eyes and imaginations and those of fellow citizens and the planners whom we employ.

Planning is done by many people, whose

1

Figure 1.1 A Los Angeles freeway interchange at one of its less crowded times. Reprinted with permission of the California Department of Transportation.

eyes and imaginations guide them in different directions. They perceive those cityscapes through their own values and so pursue conflicting dreams. Certainly the entrepreneurs who build factories in Chicago's suburbs rather than in the city view their options from the hard-eyed perspective of the market. And the bulldozer operator takes out trees at the orders of a developer who envisions half-million-dollar homes as the best of all worlds, even though a nature lover despises them.

As we view our cities and suburbs, we consistently see several things, if we are alert to them. There are *boundaries* and *walls*—the features which insulate people and activities from one another. Some are natural. The rivers that bisect most metropolitan areas are obvious. Others are there by human choice, and we do well to examine why they are there. Traveling north from Chicago's Loop on the CTA elevated train, one sees on the right side the apartments of the affluent residents of Near North and the Gold Coast. But windows on the left side reveal the Cabrini-Green public housing project, both symbol and reality of an urban failure soon to be replaced. The "El" structure itself is a tangible boundary between alienated communities.

Boundaries and walls may produce good neighbors as well. Residents seek buffer zones between their bedrooms and nearby shopping centers, freeways, and factories. Waste recycling and treatment facilities and other LULUs ("locally unwanted land uses") require broader separations due to the noises, odors, and visual clutter that even the cleanest of them produce. Indeed, nearby citizens may press for boundaries so wide as to exclude them altogether.

At the same time that we see boundaries, we also view *paths* and *corridors*, the "free ways" that move people and goods for all kinds of purposes. These are sidewalks and streets, expressways and boulevards, railroads and waterways. We see the terminals of invisible corridors in the form of airports and the teleports that catch and send electronic signals. Urban life has grown around these pathways and often defines their endpoints. In turn, cities are cut by new corridors when the market for movement wills. Each land use adjoining these corridors depends on the access they provide.

People view city locations as places of *security* or *danger*, places of adventure or quiet. From New Orleans's French Quarter to a quiet suburban playground is an incalculable distance. There is every incentive to preserve Bourbon Street's ambiance for those attracted to it, just as surrounding residents want their playground to be kept safe for their children. Since danger and security arouse emotions, decisions about such locations invite controversy, whether made by private developers or government bodies.

Our older cities are artifacts of past values and choices. Their "time-depth" reveals what long-gone generations wanted their cities to be. Philadelphia's center-city street grid was laid in the 17th century, when the good Quaker developers wanted to subdivide it easily for buildable lots. Boston's more random street pattern reflected an incremental approach to growth. Washington, D.C., was designed to be a grand capital in the European mode, and its Pennsylvania Avenue today may do for the imaginative visitor what the Champs Elysees does for Paris. The monumental city halls, post offices, railroad stations, schools, and libraries portray the dignity that planners of those days wanted to endow on the public activities in them. The current drive to preserve those historic structures and communities is a call to respect the investments that past generations made for our benefit.

Urban places are, in short, arenas for life. Some are deliberately private, reserved for homes that are protected from intrusions. Others provide space for voluntary social activities—churches and temples, fraternal halls, health clubs, and community centers. Still others are more public, accommodating jobs, students, shoppers, and sports fans. Often the boundaries we demand between these uses are intended to admit only their "owners" and rightful users and to prevent activities that take place in the public spheres from intruding into the private.

Another factor which makes these places targets of controversy is that they are constantly changing. Urbanization spreads rapidly over the countryside surrounding San Antonio, Phoenix, and Seattle. Inner-city and suburban neighborhoods around Los Angeles and Miami experience dramatic changes in their ethnic makeup. A new airport for Denver, amusement complexes ringing Orlando, and a megashopping mall close to Minneapolis spill their effects far and wide. Even more stable residential communities undergo changes in income levels, housing quality, and intangible "atmosphere" that are not readily noticed by outsiders. The experience of such changes, and the expectation (often becoming fear) of more change, is also a planning stimulus. As Jacobs [1985, p. 12] indicates, "City planning involves managing the process of change," and it is particularly important to "identify who might benefit by changes and who might be hurt."

1.2 CASES ON URBAN PLANNING POLITICS

Let us consider four recent cases in which urban development became a point of contention between groups who saw their surroundings differently and thus had conflicting preferences for them. These controversies are atypical of planning politics only in that they received wider than usual attention from scholars, the judicial system, or the news media. The issues they highlight—growth limitation, commercial redevelopment, location of a major public infrastructure, and control of private property—arise frequently in urban communities. These cases set the stage for more systematic discussion of the basic concepts of *urban, planning,* and *politics.*

Case 1: A hold on San Diego's growth

San Diego, like most California cities, has grown explosively during the 20th century. It spread with little restraint over its surrounding mesas and valleys, leaving few gaps in its urban landscape. Many of its residents feared that such sprawl was destroying the amenities of clean air and open vistas for which they moved to San Diego in the first place. In 1974 these citizens, spearheaded by the Sierra Club, began to press for legal measures to slow and channel their city's growth. Their efforts advanced a step five years later when the city council enacted new growth guidelines. It designated large areas in the scenic northwest sector either for "planned urbanizing" uses, where gradual development would be allowed, or for "future urbanization," to take place only after 1995. Figure 1.2 shows these areas on a city map, updated to 1996.

This plan moved political conflict into a new stage. As developers sought to open up parts of the reserved area, they aroused opposition from the "slow-growth" partisans. The latter took their case to the voters in the form of ballot initiatives, widely used in California to decide land-use questions. A 1985 vote added some restrictions on removing land from the future urbanization districts. However, two complex and somewhat contradictory initiatives that appeared on the ballot in 1988 would have further curbed development but lost by decisive margins. Yet another set of measures, two sponsored by pro-development interests and one that would have purchased land for parks, were defeated in 1990 [Caves 1992, ch. 6].

The debate over growth management continues in the San Diego City Council and other arenas, treading a fine line between the well-financed, pro-development forces and the highly motivated preservationist voters. By 1996, a development plan had been approved for part of the reserved area which included a golf course and a high-priced residential community on four-acre lots. One observer predicted, "Most of the urban reserve will eventually become an exurban enclave for the rich and super-rich" [Calavita 1997, p. 21].

A new challenge for growth management was added in 1991, when the state of California mandated local government cooperation in preserving the habitats of endangered plants and animals. The region contains 24 species considered "endangered" and hundreds more that are "sensitive." The San Diego Association of Governments responded with the Multiple Species Conservation Program, which includes segments of the city as well as its suburbs and unincorporated parts of San Diego County. This effort, mandated by federal and state policies, augments a slow-growth policy, but calls for extensive study by conservation biologists and negotiations with landowners and developers to determine which areas should be protected and which left open for development [Stevens 1996].

This case illustrates the delicate and often unstable balance of power that shapes such choices. Planners and public officials must heed many vocal publics, outside the com-

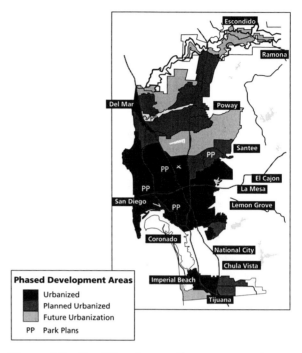

Figure 1.2 San Diego's growth management system is based on tiers of phased development within its sprawling boundaries. Map by Susan Deegan; source, San Diego Planning Department.

munity as well as inside. A vexing problem is how to finance the necessary public land acquisitions, with minimal federal and state dollars available. This issue also raises substantive questions about who benefits from growth limitations and habitat protection. As in all planning situations, there are winners and losers, but the line separating them usually is not sharp.

Case 2: Rebirth of Times Square

Many visitors to New York City have come to know Times Square as a place of celebrations and sex. Anchoring the south end of the Broadway theater district, 42nd Street has a reputation for bawdy and dangerous entertainment. That reputation has been its undoing: By the 1980s few of the businesses operating there were not sex-oriented, and property values plummeted. Crime, prostitution, and drug abuse abounded on its streets and in its peep shows and cheap hotels.

In 1984 a partnership came together, comprised of city officials, New York State's Urban Development Corporation, and private developers, to renew the four blocks centered on 42nd Street and Broadway. Their plan envisioned four high-rise office buildings, a wholesale mart, and a 550-room hotel, along with rehabilitation of the derelict 42nd Street theaters. This would, they promised, bring a "new class" of people into the area and expand tax revenues. They even pledged to keep the bright lights that signal the area's entertainment offerings, well illustrated in Figure 1.3.

A lengthy environmental impact study followed this public proposal, to examine how it would affect land values, employment, criminal activity, pollution, and traffic. Skeptics and opponents of the project emerged. Some questioned the extent of the public subsidies required, arguing that the city had pressing needs for housing in other neighborhoods. Others held that extensive demolition would ruin the historic character of Times Square and turn it into another sterile office complex, of which Manhattan already had enough. Residents and business owners in nearby neighborhoods anticipated detrimental spillovers into their living and working areas. As a result of this opposition and the financing roadblocks that appeared over time, the original developers withdrew and that plan was shelved.

In 1992, the Urban Development Corporation generated a more modest plan to renew the block of 42nd Street from Broadway to Eighth Avenue, not necessarily to purge it of its sex-oriented entertainment but to enlarge

Figure 1.3 Lively signs have always been a Times Square landmark, and new ones are appearing with the encouragement of the area's design guidelines. Photo by Todd W. Bressi.

its clientele with a variety of theaters, restaurants, book and music stores, and jazz clubs. Some of the groups that had opposed the "grand plan" pledged their support [Fischer 1995, ch. 5]. As of early 1997, this second public-private partnership was bearing fruit: New businesses were gradually occupying the 42nd Street strip, including the reopening of the New Victory Theater for children's arts programs. One of its biggest investors, in fact, was the Walt Disney Company.

Case 3: Finding an airport for Minnesota

Among the most difficult locational choices that could face a major metropolitan area is the placement of a large airport. When Denver began such a process for the airport that opened in 1995, it had to choose a rural site far from the city's center. The state of Minnesota contemplated this prospect with one additional variable: the option of enlarging the existing facility rather than building an entirely new one. The present airport is convenient to the centers of both Minneapolis and St. Paul. Intensive residential and commercial development surrounds it, including the Mall of America, the nation's largest indoor shopping center. This location has little room for airport expansion, however. Further, homeowners in the vicinity have long complained of the noise of jets departing and arriving.

In 1989, the Minnesota Legislature took charge of the issue by mandating a two-track planning process. On one track, there would be surveys of potential locations for a new airport and studies on how to reuse the present site. On the other track, planners would examine whether and how to enlarge the existing field's capacity. This approach kept the lawmakers' options open but confronted planners with an ambiguous task. The job was handed to the Metropolitan Council, the region's planning body, and the Metropolitan Airports Commission (MAC), the independent airport operating agency. A final recommendation was mandated by 1996.

In 1991, the study group on the first track selected an agricultural area in Dakota County, southeast of both city centers, as the preferred location for a new facility. It followed with an assessment of how orderly development could take place around the site, not only road and utility access but also the offices, hotels, freight terminals, and other accessories for a major international airport. Controls over the development would be exerted jointly by the Council and the local governments in and around the area. At the same time, MAC proposed the total redevelopment of the present airport, and second track planners showed how a new runway could be built, the current runways extended, and the terminal enlarged. This choice may require additional controls on surrounding land to minimize noise and the dangers posed by flight paths. In addition, discussions with the neighboring cities' officials were held to explore how new land use controls could cope with increased flights.

Needless to say, intense pressure accompanied both planning tracks. Dakota County residents were adamantly opposed to loss of their rural way of life, and Northwest Airlines, the airport's largest user by far, did not want the expense of a new facility. Major commercial interests, on the other hand, argued that a new airport is essential to promote the economic development of the region well into the 21st century.

The matter was settled early in 1996, almost as an anticlimax. The MAC and Metropolitan Council went on record recommending that the existing airport be expanded, and were quickly backed by Governor Arne Carlson and the legislature. Several factors were responsible. First, sufficient business support for a new airport never emerged, and no prominent political leader endorsed it. Regular travelers were not enthusiastic about having to drive a much longer distance to catch a plane. Above all, economics drove the choice: The new airport would cost an estimated $4.5 billion, compared with $2.8 billion for an expansion plan which would suffice for expected air traffic through 2020. Public budgetmakers, facing mid-1990s constraints, needed no prompting on that comparison, particularly in view of the cost overruns that Denver experienced.

Planning efforts after the legislature's decision focused anew on the region surrounding the airport, and its ability to attract additional development. Everything from flight patterns and noise insulation for homes to expansion of the Mall of America must be dealt with in a holistic manner by the MAC, the Metropolitan Council, and the six nearby municipalities.

Case 4: Property rights in Oregon

The Dolan family owns the A-Boy Electric and Plumbing Supply store on the banks of Fanno Creek in Tigard, a suburb of Portland, Oregon (see Figure 1.4). In 1989, John and Florence Dolan applied to the city for permission to replace the shop with a building twice its size. There was no problem with the zoning, but municipal authorities, realizing that the larger roof area would increase the water runoff rate from the property, insisted that they deed to the city about 10 percent of the site along the creek for drainage improvements. Further, the Dolans would have to allow the construction of a bicycle path through their land, extending from a park area on the south. The Dolans balked at this, asserting that the city had not shown that their expansion really necessitated either the drainage area or the bikeway, and that they should be compensated for the loss of land.

The dispute passed up through the Oregon courts and finally reached the U.S. Supreme Court. The justices, by a 5–4 margin, found for the Dolans in 1994. The majority opinion, written by Chief Justice Rehnquist, stated, "The city must make some sort of individualized determination that the required dedication is related both in nature and extent to the impact of the proposed development." Sending the case back to state court, the ruling

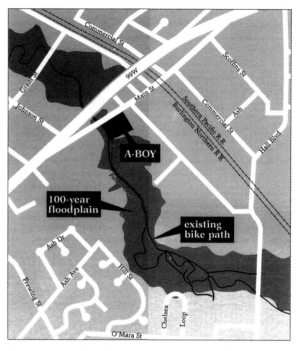

Figure 1.4   The Dolan property, containing the A-Boy hardware store, adjoining Fanno Creek, in Tigard, Oregon. Map by Dennis McClendon; source, City of Tigard.

called on the city to show conclusively that its "taking" of property for environmental purposes is specifically required by the building's expansion [Walters 1994].

The *Dolan* case stands in the center of a national controversy. The Fifth and Fourteenth Amendments to the U.S. Constitution forbid government from taking private property for public use without fair compensation. Taking land without payment is permitted by law when the land is necessary to provide essential public services. Subdivision developers dedicate part of their land to cities for streets and utilities, for example. But the voices of the current "property rights movement" argue that governments have been overly aggressive in restricting land use for environmental reasons and thus have denied owners the financial return to which they are entitled. The decision in *Dolan v. City of Tigard* gave further support to this movement. Planners throughout the nation are on notice that their plans must show a "rough proportionality" between the impacts of a proposed development and the amount of space they claim for use without compensating the owner [Kraus 1995]. Chapter 9 explores this issue further and suggests how planners can avoid the major legal pitfalls.

1.3 THE BASIC CONCEPTS: PLANNING, URBAN, FUTURES

This book has thus far used the terms *urban* and *planning* in a very generic way. But these terms have more precise meanings that form the boundaries for this work. Further, since all planning is by definition aimed at futures, defining that concept is also necessary.

A classic sociological definition of an *urban* area is "a relatively large, dense, and permanent settlement of socially heterogeneous individuals" [Wirth 1938, p. 1]. Although this concept identifies some major roots of planning challenges, it doesn't draw a clear line between "urban" and "nonurban." How dense must settlement be on the fringes of any metropolitan area before it is urban? Is a popular vacation region such as Cape Cod, Massachusetts, or Vail, Colorado, an urban area?

The U.S. Census Bureau, needing a precise definition of urban places, designated as a Metropolitan Statistical Area a single city or twin cities with a population of at least 50,000, the county or counties in which it or they lie, and all adjoining counties that are economically linked with the core. Such an area may include rural portions, but the great bulk of its population is urban by Wirth's criteria.

For this study's purposes, urban places are those that present more intense and complex planning choices than typical rural areas. A large and dense settlement poses a steady stream of options about how its land is to be used. Whether a particular parcel accommodates high-rise offices, low-cost homes, or open space concerns a great many people who live, work, or own land in the vicinity. The American market and political system provide multiple opportunities for them to influence such decisions, and a complex pattern of conflict and cooperation emerge. Thus we can include the planning for any place that is experiencing conflict over population density or nonagricultural land use, whatever its formal classification. Many parts of California's coast and Vermont's mountains could fit this standard, therefore, in addition to Cape Cod and Vail.

Planning for urban places is the process of making and implementing decisions about their land use and their space-dependent social and economic policies. This definition excludes the long-range decision making that focuses on human services, for example. Yet it is not sharply limited to the physical uses of land and such tangible public facilities as roads and sewers, as was the focus of much of the planning profession in the first two-thirds of this century.

To speak of "space-dependent social and economic policies" takes into the planning process responsibilities for housing, recreation, and social-benefit facilities that depend on specific land uses. The location and design of a juvenile corrections center or a group home for persons with disabilities is a planning issue, even though the treatment within the facilities is decided by other specialists. Likewise, a new factory that expands job opportunities in a depressed area is a planning concern, while a training program therein would not be. Yet, as chapter 11 will show, the scope of planning by this definition is gradually broadening as more and more social and economic concerns have locational and land-use implications.

Planning entails choices and controls. "Plans are designed to create predictable, orderly relationships and so to establish control. The power to make and carry out plans is therefore the power to control" [Marris 1982, p. 58]. Ideally, it is done by making at one point in time, and in accordance with one set of criteria, decisions that would otherwise be scattered across time and made by different standards. To the extent that these decisions are implemented as intended, the planning is successful. The redevelopment of a large inner-city neighborhood, for example, is a permanently ongoing endeavor, yet would best proceed according to a holistic plan that allocates spaces to meet every resident need. If a new apartment complex lacked a school and shopping facilities nearby, it would be less successful for its residents.

We could think of planning for a given geographic area as a cycle with three major stages. In the first stage, governmental and private planners set goals and criteria to guide the succeeding steps. They may choose to preserve an older residential area that is threatened by deterioration, or to draw new industries to an abandoned railroad yard. Goal setting is basically a valuing exercise: One determines the overall good of a community and how the area under consideration contributes to it. The challenge is to set goals that respond adequately to needs, are financially and technically realistic, and have public support.

In the second stage in the cycle, planners select actions that give the goals tangible form. To preserve an older neighborhood

calls for investments in the homes that have not been kept up as well as they should, street and park improvements, and perhaps replacement of obsolete buildings. While building codes and street repair are the responsibility of the city government, funds must also be secured from banks, foundations, state and federal governments, and the homeowners themselves. On the other hand, industrial development typically occurs when firms decide to locate on sites in the selected area; yet government and private funds often combine as incentives to such decisions.

Third, planning leads to implementation of the choices. There is a point at which a development leaves the realm of planning, perhaps the breaking of ground for a new plant. But planning must give attention to follow-up actions, such as traffic management in the vicinity of the factory or transit service for a renewed neighborhood. Many cities have drafted elaborate master plans but ignored them when specific projects were on the table, particularly when political forces steered development in another direction.

Since this is a cycle, the path back to the first stage is essential. Goal setting and choice making must be continuously informed by what is "on the ground" and the results of past efforts to program it. Planning can be a school for social learning, where successes and failures are analyzed and better methods selected. For example, many housing complexes for lower income families have failed as living environments because of improper design and location. Planners who attended this "school" were able to avoid repeating those mistakes.

The futures with which planners are concerned are multiple. On the one hand, they realize that much of what they build will still be on the ground many decades hence. Boston's downtown streets were once 17th century cartpaths. Yet time horizons may also be short, because markets insist on immediate uses and profits. Thus, planners must keep several "futures" in mind: The near term of one or two years, the medium-term of 3 to 10 years, and the long term of decades and even centuries to come. Each choice of a future opens and closes doors to other futures. While no one can forecast the farthest futures with great confidence, planners need to be sensitive to their many potentials.

1.4 POLITICS OF PLANNING: MARKETS AND GOVERNMENTS

Urban development is both private and public in scope. Thus it takes place in individual choices and those of voluntary groups, in larger market places, and in governments. A major choice in itself is the extent to which each participant should control a given decision.

All of these values, perceptions, and visions become organized among groups of people, who then act them out. Land developers share their economic views of urban futures, which are likely to be different from those of apartment dwellers or environmentalists. Organized attempts to change cities soon generate conflicts. This is because each change alters the distribution of advantages and disadvantages, of benefits and costs. A new urban freeway makes commuting easier for some while it disrupts settled ways of living and doing business for others. Nature lovers lose access to a forest when affluent residents claim that land for their homes. Prospective "winners" and "losers" compete for funds, and ultimately for governmental endorsement of their preferred futures.

There are two basic ways of resolving the conflict between planning preferences and competing values. The market is one: The contestant who pays the most gets to decide. Occasionally a group of nature lovers manages to save a forest by buying it away from a developer. A Japanese company chooses a Kentucky location for a new factory, and rare is the local market that would refuse such an economic boon. When only the private parties that are materially affected are involved, their freely made agreements can properly settle routine differences in a short time.

The second means of conflict resolution is government, whether by legislative, executive, or judicial authorities. Ordinarily this is a last resort, adopted when a market outcome arouses controversy or infringes on the legal rights of a party to the matter. But our society has defined certain types of planning choices as inherently subject to governmental control—uses of land, provision of transportation facilities, supply of utilities, and safety of buildings. These affect many parties who cannot participate in the market choices. The market is permitted to operate only within limits on such matters. No one can locate a waste processing site in an urban area without conforming to a host of requirements and to a political process that could well say "no!" even if the facility meets those formal standards.

As defined in this book, urban planning is the interplay between imagination and regulation, between free individual will and collective choice as expressed in law codes and master plans. There is inevitable tension, breaking out in public hearings, lawsuits, mass demonstrations, hotly contested elections, and competing public relations campaigns. We call this interplay *politics*, the process of managing and steering the common life of a society. The boundary between market and government (itself drawn from the Greek and Latin term for the pilot of a ship) is not self-evident or inscribed in stone for all ages to come. Rather, it is renegotiated by each generation as it encounters specific challenges.

The governments on which this planning process is centered are predominantly local. Incorporated cities and villages and many counties have land-use control powers bestowed on them by their states. School boards and special purpose districts responsible for such public facilities as sewers, airports, transit lines, parks, and harbors plan create and implement their own plans. In some metropolitan areas, regional agencies and councils of local governments have limited planning roles but cannot override the local units in their area. These local governmental forms are discussed in chapter 3.

State and national authorities intervene in local planning at their discretion. State legislatures can mandate, permit, or prohibit planning actions by their local units—perhaps to protect sensitive environments or expand the supply of modest-cost homes. They may also intrude on local choices in the location of a highway or prison. Federal agencies likewise enter the planning process when they locate an office building or veterans' medical center in a city. In abandoning military bases, the U.S. Department of Defense created many new opportunities for local enterprises. As chapter 3 also relates, both state and federal governments supply financial aid to localities for land-use related projects. As a result, major planning choices nearly always are intergovernmental, calling for negotiations and cooperation between officials who have no formal obligations to one another.

The "private" side of planning has several kinds of participants as well, to be detailed in chapter 4. Most prominent are the profit making landowners, developers, and prospective

users of new projects. Most urban land is in private ownership and while zoning may bar certain uses from a given parcel, the decisions of how to use it belong to the individuals or firms that hold the title. Their financial resources buy them seats at the decision making tables in government and the market alike.

Other nongovernmental participants include charitable and religious institutions, unions, foundations, homeowners' associations, environmental protection leagues, and other voluntary citizen groups of all kinds. Some groups promote a certain kind of development, while others arise to block a proposal. Groups often form coalitions and alliances, and one might see a neighborhood association joining city planners to oppose a project that is favored by a state development agency and the city's chamber of commerce.

The political relationships in planning differ according to the type of decision made and the scale of public impact and participation. The broadest choices consist of comprehensive goal setting and detailed choices in advance of actual development. A plan could be a master design for an entire city, a redevelopment scheme for a blighted area, or a specialized program for transportation or waste management. San Diego worked out such a plan for its undeveloped area. This type of plan is distinctive in that it contains a package of interrelated choices, intended to steer development well into the future. A plan is often initiated by local government planners, but may be spurred or even drafted by a business or civic group. Since its implementation is not immediate, it may spark little conflict unless a participant challenges one of its provisions.

Most planning decisions focus on the near future. The most common decisions on local agendas are on the smallest scale: A private applicant proposes to alter a building or parcel of land in a way that requires government approval. That proposal may consist of dividing one lot into two, placing a convenience store on a vacant corner, or converting a large home into a duplex. The decision in such a case has little or no impact on the community as a whole, though it may arouse concern from the immediate neighbors. The outcome ordinarily can be guided by existing policies and standards, although each case must be judged on its merits to some extent. However, if the local agency fails to uphold those standards consistently, they could be undermined over time. The Dolans' application would have required this type of decision if their store had not been located next to Fanno Creek.

On a larger scale are choices about shopping centers, apartment complexes, and industrial parks. Concerns about noise, traffic, drainage, and visual impacts may raise questions and opposition among citizens in the surrounding area. The process of decision making becomes more intricate and time consuming as more participants realize what is at stake and offer their views. The many choices about Times Square are of this scale and level of controversy.

Governments also undertake development projects on their own. Many of these are infrastructure investments, the basic support facilities that are the traditional province of the public sector. These include waste treatment plants, parks, libraries, educational facilities, sports stadiums, convention centers, and museums. Cities, counties, special authorities, and states all provide these facilities. While they are public facilities, they are also of benefit to various private interests, from neighborhood associations to professional athletic teams. which makes decisions about these facilities political. The Minnesota

Legislature's decision about the airport was of this type.

Another form of larger scale planning consists of joint projects undertaken by government units and private interests. These are formal partnerships in which city and state governments, businesses, banks, foundations, and nonprofit associations each contribute funds, authority, and expertise to make a complex project successful. These partnerships have played a major role in renewing many central business districts and depressed neighborhoods. The initiative for an individual project may come from either the public or private side, but a complex working relationship must be formed in the goal-setting stage and continue through implementation. Times Square's renewal is guided by such a partnership.

All such planning choices distribute benefits and costs, advantages and disadvantages, unequally to various participants and to other citizens who don't take part. Even those who seek democratic solutions most passionately find that there is usually no way to treat everyone equitably. As later chapters in this book demonstrate, the best practical goal is a system of ongoing choices in which no group's or individual's interests are excluded, and which is always seeking to remedy prior injustices. Yet even the criteria for fairness and the means of reaching it are constantly open to political dispute.

1.5 THE PUBLIC GOALS OF PLANNING

Urban planning both creates and implements public policy, but as we have seen, it is not exclusively *government* policy. Most planning decisions involve the private sector to such an extent that its choices have public effects. Thus "private policy" can be binding on the persons affected by it when government either endorses it or does not act to the contrary. For example, when lending institutions refuse to extend credit for purchase or improvement of homes and businesses in depressed areas ("redlining"), they effectively condemn these areas to further decline.

Because planning policies are complex bundles of public and private efforts, participants must take care that they are indeed compatible and mutually supportive. Many policies fail because not all of the relevant efforts moved toward the same purpose. Cities have invested large sums in renewal of industrial districts only to see major employers close their plants later.

What public policies depend on urban planning, as defined here? Recall that the term focused on the use of land and space-related aspects of other efforts. While all of the following are governmental responsibilities, the market and voluntary actions also affect their success.

1. Secure orderly use of the community's land resources. This is a central purpose of planning, so intensively practiced in most urban areas as to become "land budgeting." As a community contemplates the future use of vacant space and possible changes in the already built areas, it must choose what areas to devote to residences, industry, business, transportation, recreation, and other applications. It must also ensure that no use unduly harms or inhibits one in an adjoining area.

2. Provide for mobility of persons and goods. This planning concern encompasses the location and design of public streets and highways, airports, transit facilities, ports, truck terminals, and vehicle storage. How people and goods travel and where they stop affect all other uses of land, so planners have learned they must integrate these issues in a single perspective.

3. Protect and enhance natural resources. Many policies are necessary to relate the built environment to the natural in order to prevent degradation of wetlands, wooded areas, steep slopes and shorelines; to maintain water quality in lakes, streams, bays and underground aquifers; and to protect scenic views and require landscaping in new developments.

4. Assure satisfactory residential environments. The allocation of most homes is left to the private sector, operating within building and zoning codes. Much of planners' time is taken up with proposals for new dwellings and modification of existing ones. However, the planning process must at times address the housing needs of low-income households and others with special needs.

5. Promote economic development and employment opportunities. This is of growing importance to the governmental sector as cities try to retain and nurture their employers and attract new ones whose tax payments are vital to support public services. To do this, cities establish industrial parks with necessary support facilities, reserve choice sites for desired newcomers, and finance land acquisition and new buildings.

6. Assure safety of life and property. While the planning process does not take in police and firefighting operations, it is concerned with the safety-related features of development, such as vulnerability to fires and floods, access for emergency vehicles, and reduction of opportunities for crime. This is also an aspect of street and highway design, which seeks to reduce accidents.

7. Isolate or recycle wastes safely. This activity becomes a planning concern when a choice must be made about whether to extend a sewer line to serve a new development or where to locate a facility to process household refuse or hazardous wastes. Landfills are increasingly unacceptable in cities, and long-term plans must deal with what past generations simply threw away.

Other responsibilities of governments in urban areas relate to planning in various ways: location of parks, schools, libraries, and health care facilities; drinking water supply and quality; and energy supply and consumption. The typical comprehensive guide plan that a city or county adopts is intended to integrate all of these policies within its land budget.

1.6 GLOBALISM AND URBAN PLANNING

Urban planning has a global dimension, as the events of the past decade amply demonstrate. The economic well-being and social demography of American metropolitan areas depend on, and in turn influence what all other cities do, from London to Tokyo, Mexico City to Manila. A global culture is making them alike in many ways even while their internal differences grow. They form nodes in the communication webs that link bankers, engineers, marketers, and immigrant families across miles that have been erased electronically. Vice President Albert Gore has publicized the nation's need for an "information highway," but the on-ramps can only be local. Technological developments are so rapid that only the well prepared will grasp the opportunities.

Among the many specific impacts of globalism, we can discern four. First, urban development is increasingly initiated and financed by international firms and banks (Toyota, Daiwa Bank of Tokyo), and by domestic firms active in world markets. They often provide high-wage jobs and can demand public subsidies and incentives: thus they exert significant political power. They participate in planning not only in New York and Los Angeles but also in Marysville, Ohio, Vance, Alabama, and Georgetown, Kentucky.

Second, global technology and competition alter local economies. Steel plants close or downsize while electronics and biotechnology firms flourish. This trend has reduced the demand for inner-city space and spurred suburban expansion. Social groups that lack sufficient education and training lose in the race for jobs, and their unemployment has spawned a wide range of ills.

Demographic shifts, the third factor in globalism, impact urban neighborhoods as immigrants compete for jobs, create new businesses, and introduce diverse cultural norms. Some Los Angeles suburbs have become largely Asian-American, and two blocks of Argyle Street in Chicago give a visitor the feel of Hong Kong or Hanoi. Their norms gradually penetrate planning choices just as those of earlier European immigrants did.

Fourth, the global information economy and networks enable much "work" to be done anywhere—small towns, suburbs, individual homes, or on the road—and not necessarily in the United States. Teleconferencing, electronic mail, the Internet, and distance education can eliminate miles as a cost factor wherever fiber optic cables are laid. Virtual corporations, libraries, and even banks offer services unconfined by a specific location.

The challenge to planners is to develop their own urban regions' capacity to participate most effectively in this network, giving attention to the communication links and local access points that this endeavor requires. This task is partly technological, concerned with locating fiber-optic cables and high-capacity data terminals. It is also a social imperative to provide access to such nets for lower-income neighborhoods, small businesses, and educational institutions. As work and commuting patterns change, perhaps decentralizing to homes and remote job stations, demands on highways will shift. Chapter 11 gives further attention to these global, demographic, and technological trends and forces.

This diversity of challenges shows both the potential for conflict and the need for cooperation. Planning is so multifaceted that it requires the collaboration of governmental and private specialists in all functions listed above, but they do not automatically agree on ends or means.

The political process is thus central to planning, as it ought to be. This democratic system has harnessed conflict and cooperation, rather than the centralized decision making of authoritarian regimes, as the engines of policy making. Conflicts over policy are not simply roadblocks to wise and timely decision making, as some might claim. Land is the common heritage of all citizens, and the "stakeholders" have the right to be considered in choices about it. Public and private planners must marshal the knowledge and expertise of their trade to inform the public and enlighten the process. Civic and business leaders have the task of blending these views with the wider perspectives of other stakeholders. No one can predict how this synthesis will emerge in any given case, nor will it always be the most just, efficient, or popular choice. But in the long run, a community must guard its political process if it wants to retain control of it.

People who disagree or cooperate on planning have set ideas of what it should produce, and often an image of what kind of city should develop. These mental images are individual, but when they are shared by many influential people, they can dominate the choices. American cities embody in their visible presence a host of intangible values to which we have given such names as beauty, efficiency, productivity, community, and opportunity. To understand how these values have shaped the built environment and been shaped by it is the goal of the next chapter.

FOR REVIEW AND DISCUSSION

1. What features of cities do people see when they look around them? What happens when people view the same features differently?

2. What is the basic distinction between *urban* and *nonurban* places? Where would you draw the line between them in actual places with which you are familiar?

3. For what reasons is *politics* an inescapable feature of urban planning? How can this politics be conducted in the most democratic fashion?

4. How does *public* policy differ from *private* policy in urban planning choices? In what ways are they interdependent?

5. In what ways does globalism affect the planning choices of local communities? How can those communities best respond to the challenges and opportunities that globalism presents?

2

Planning Values and Memories

2.1 CITY BUILDING AND PLANNING VALUES

City building has always served human ends, whether of the mighty who hold the society's power and money or of the ordinary citizens who locate their homes and shops where they can afford to. The shapes of cities are mirrors of people's ambitions and of the civilizations that constructed them.

This chapter surveys the experience of American urban planning, with emphasis on the past century or so, and examines the values and purposes that guided those uncounted decisions. This history is not simply a story of the past but a living public memory. It is a collection of images of how things have been done, for better or worse, and of how American cities evolved in a chain of choices that began in far distant time. It is living memory because it is embodied in the laws of governments, in procedures for making decisions, in popular expectations, in the norms of professional planners, and above all, in the built environment itself.

Cities' "presents" are the sum of past plans and choices and the starting points for all futures. Futures always build on these foundations, indeed are constrained by them. These presents are not just the built environments, but the achievements and failures of society, the human relationships shaped by those environments, and the values people hold because of experiences with them. A proper understanding of urban planning begins with clear insights into these pasts and presents. Schultz [1989, p. xiii] asserts that cities are

the manufactured containers, the physical expressions, of human culture. In that sense all cities are planned environments. They are the results of cultural decisions about the most appropriate physical uses of land and the residential distribution of people...... At any moment in time, the physical landscape of the city reveals the countless decisions of bygone days about the 'best' uses uses of space—'best' means those individual or collective values and judgments about the quality of life made by citizens in the past, judgments that affect the lives of those in the present—and the future.

We also infer from this that much urban planning is a reaction to the perceived evils of existing cities. This planning does embody visions of ideal cities, but those visions are deliberate corrections to or departures from current realities. Thus, much of the early 20th century planning literature is a reaction to the ills of the 19th century city. But as the current century wore on, cities became more diverse in their character and spread and grew more "evils" to discern and remedy. The accomplishments of one generation became, to some degree, the problems that the next generation strove to correct—suburban sprawl and congested highways, for example. We now have a huge stock of unsolved problems for future planning work.

A *value* in this context is a good that people seek, a quality in an object or situation that makes it valuable. In the context of urban development, a value is a benefit that can be drawn from the built environment and the activities it supports. Cities embody many such "goods," as chapter 1 identified: security, economic opportunity, esthetic beauty, accessibility, and so on. Likewise they contain such negatives as danger, ugliness, and stressful conditions. What is on the ground today provides visual evidence of many intertwined planning values. A luxury office building or hotel that overlooks a cheap hotel inhabited by destitute families, for example, poses the question of which interests are to be served within a city's land budget.

Because urban areas contain so much social and cultural diversity, planners and developers who think on the largest scale must also be sensitive to the personal values that people hold about the locations in which they live, work, shop, and play. This divergence between the "macro" and "micro" perspectives could be expressed as the space/place dichotomy. *Space* is abstract; it is an area viewed by an outsider as a location on which to put a condominium, airport, or factory. It can be described as "blighted" or "a prime commercial site." An appraiser catalogs it by its size, zoning, market value, soil type, and distance from the nearest freeway.

A *place*, on the other hand, is a unique location with which a person has established an emotional connection, a meaningful identification. Each place has qualities to a person that no other place has. Tuan [1974, p. 9] refers to this relationship as *topophilia*, "the affective bond between people and place or setting." When understood as personal experience, this concept is vivid and concrete, including "all of the human being's affective ties with the material environment." [Tuan 1974, p. 93]

For example, the deepest such relationships are often with the places one lives in. "Home" is a place in this sense; contrast that with the impersonal spaces called "housing" [Ravetz 1980]. Home may be a single room in a decaying hotel, but it can be the only source of security a low-income elderly person has. That home is often extended to one's neighborhood, perhaps a single block, a district of several hundred residents, or an independent suburban village on the edge of a large city. It has meaning because one grew up there, one's friends are there, or it is beautiful, safe, or congenial.

The concept *valued environment* designates a place that holds such meaning for a group of people.

An environment can be considered "valued" if its residents can show recognition of an empathy with their local social and physical environment, a milieu that in turn serves to buttress their own preferred life-styles. In a sense, the word "value" acquires a mirror-like quality in which residents recognize attributes in their local environment which are themselves reflections of the residents' own scale of preferences [Hall 1982, p. 172].

These values are not static; they change with the residents' life situations and condition of the area. Yet enough people hold them in common to act to protect them when a threat appears.

Place-based values are important to planning in two ways. First, actions that change cities also manipulate valued environments for better or worse. Plans not only organize space but also arrange important facets of human lives: their use of time, whom they are likely to communicate with, and the meanings they find in their built environment [Rapoport 1977]. If Minnesota had chosen to plant an airport in the Dakota County farmland, it would have had large-scale impact on the meanings of much of that county's territory, not to mention the lives and livelihoods of the surrounding region. This is not to claim that localist place values are superior to the benefits that a larger area might gain from a facility like an airport, but rather that the planning process should be open to weigh them fairly.

Planners and developers must be sensitive as well to creating place values as they redevelop areas. When whole neighborhoods were demolished and new dwellings rose in their place, the residents had to form new environmental identities. But it was difficult for many of them, especially families with small children, to regard the new high-rise apartment structures as "home" and acquire a sense of responsibility for them. The characteristics of the buildings themselves, designed more for economy than liveability, frustrated these residents. As a result, those who were able to leave did so and left behind the poorest and most antisocial elements,

who were then free to turn the projects into battlegrounds. One result of this unfortunate process was the 1976 demolition in St. Louis of the Pruitt-Igoe homes, which had failed as a living milieu because of this insensitivity [Meehan 1979].

Second, valued environments spawn political action. The strength of these attachments usually becomes evident only when they are threatened, as with a major redevelopment project or a highway bisecting a neighborhood.

> Large-scale environmental change, not instigated by the inhabitants themselves and outside their control, often seems disturbing, disruptive, and divisive. Increased demands for active involvement in environmental decision making, the burgeoning growth of pressure groups, and widespread suspicion of policy-making bodies together reflect a belief that political decisonmakers cannot and will not do enough to protect our environmental interests [Gold & Burgess 1982, p. 2].

We have observed that politically active groups contested the original plans for Times Square, sought to slow the urbanization of San Diego, and sued to prevent local authorities from "taking" their land. Though their conditions were quite different, each had a sense of "turf" which called for its protection or enhancement and sparked joint action by persons who would otherwise have little in common. Thus, one must keep in mind these meanings to understand both the cooperation and the conflicts that mark planning choices.

2.2 ESTHETIC VALUES IN URBAN PLANNING

Four basic groups of values have traditionally influenced planning decisions in the market and political system. Their impacts were not equal in every situation and certainly varied over time, but the contribution of each endures today. These values have been closely tied to other political and cultural movements of their times, such as the Progressive Era (1900–1915), the "business culture" of the 1920s, the New Deal of the 1930s, and the civil rights movement of the 1960s and 1970s.

First, a cluster of *esthetic* values relate to the visual and sensual properties of the built environment. Civic leaders in the 19th century widely believed that the quality of a city's design had a profound impact on the morals, life styles, and ideals of its inhabitants. This concept of environmental determinism was believed to be particularly applicable to the "lower classes," who lived in squalid conditions and held the most menial jobs. The immigrant from a muddy Russian village who passed through Ellis Island into a filthy tenement and a job in a dark sweatshop was not expected to fit into "normal" American culture without such visual aids.

The answer advocated by many planners, but particularly by those in the "City Beautiful" movement just before and after the turn of the 20th century, was to recast public spaces according to the genteel values of beauty, dignity, and order that the upper classes already enjoyed at their own expense. In one interpretation,

> the municipal art, city beautiful, and civic improvement crusades grew as piecemeal efforts that aimed to convert a city built primarily for utility into an ideal form through artistic street signs, well-designed municipal bridges, using color in architectural elements, and improving public squares and buildings. . . . . . These crusades were aimed to express the fullness of the human spirit. . . . . so that the better impulses of the most elevated men would soon become common to all. [Boyer 1983, pp. 45–46]

These values had largely been neglected in the explosive growth of 19th century American cities. The ambitions of a laissez-faire industrial civilization had been in control, and the resulting ugliness and disorder made those cities depressing places to live in, particularly for those who lacked means to furnish their homes and workplaces in pleasing ways. Indeed, it was those upper-class members who became the advocates of esthetic values on behalf of the people who were apparently the least sensitive to them.

One expression of this drive for esthetic values was the "back to nature" cry that sought more land for parks and open spaces. The city improvers, as Boyer [1983, p. 33] relates, offered urban parks as a means of healing the social ills caused by congestion, a way to regain some of the lost balance between city and country. Frederick L. Olmsted, who designed New York City's Central Park, and other reformers held that "a civilization of cities would not survive if it was cut off from nature" and so "a synthesis had to be forged out of the rural landscape and the commercial and industrial order" [Boyer 1983, pp. 33–34].

One event that portrayed these esthetic values in tangible form was the World's Columbian Exposition in Chicago in 1893. Its creators believed it "would stand as a promise and pledge that the fullness of the human spirit could come to fruition in this new art of city making" [Boyer 1983, p. 46]. The Great White City that transformed the swamps of Jackson Park demonstrated to many visitors the purity and nobility that could be embodied in cities built according to the highest esthetic standards of Western civilization.

Later generations did not forget these values even though they were supplemented by others. Grand civic centers, public libraries, and railroad stations displayed them. Even the terminal building at Denver's International Airport of the 1990s was designed to reflect the majesty of the nearby Rocky Mountains.

2.3 FUNCTIONAL VALUES IN URBAN PLANNING

The second group of values guiding planning are *functional*. In contrast to esthetic values, functional values focus on the practical uses to which land is put and on the means necessary to carry on productive enterprises and accumulate wealth. They replace *beauty* with *efficiency* as the watchword.

One functional maxim is that land should be devoted to its "highest and best use." Every parcel should be allowed the most intensive (and profitable) use appropriate to its site and surroundings. By this standard, central business districts are proper locations for stores and offices, not for single-family homes, and industry is best located next to railroads and freeway interchanges. This optimal use is determined by the market, supplemented by such government regulations as are needed to protect the public interest. Since the preferences of the marketplace shift over time, what is "highest and best" may also change; thus planners and investors must remain flexible.

A second principle is that property values should be preserved to the maximum extent possible. A home is the largest investment that a typical household makes, and to protect its value is a prime economic and political goal. If an incompatible use such as a noisy factory were located next to a residential neighborhood, the adjacent homes would become less pleasant for residents and so sell for reduced prices. Many early efforts at zoning city land were to keep commercial and industrial uses away from residential areas, including the controversy in Euclid, Ohio that led to the U.S. Supreme Court's 1926 ruling, *Euclid v. Ambler Realty Co.*

Related to the above principle (but at times in opposition to it) is the landowners' right to use their land for their greatest benefit. The Ambler Realty Company sued Euclid because the city zoned for exclusively residential purposes a parcel of land it had previously bought for commercial development. It claimed that the zoning reduced its value and this, in its view, amounted to taking private property without just compensation, in violation of the Fifth and Fourteenth Amendments to the U.S. Constitution. The case reached the U.S. Supreme Court, which ruled by a 5–4 margin that zoning was a proper exercise of the city's police power to secure orderly development. However, courts since then have placed limits on government's powers to reduce land values where no clear public benefit is produced, as the Oregon case in Chapter 1 demonstrates. Local governments are also sensitive to the need to preserve land values because of the property tax revenue they derive from it.

Yet another functional value is accessibility: ease and speed of the movement of people and goods. Early in the 20th century, immobility replaced ugliness as the dominant evil in the eyes of many. Narrow streets were clogged with pedestrians, wagons and increasingly the noisy new horseless carriages. Employees were delayed in reaching workplaces from their homes, and freight movement to and from docks and depots slowed. The crusaders for esthetic values had advocated wide boulevards for their grandeur, but functionalists favored them as more efficient for moving large volumes of traffic.

By 1910, writers on planning asserted that city government's prime duty was to provide streets wide and direct enough to carry the volumes of traffic that would permit continued business and industrial expansion. While street railways and rapid transit lines were privately owned, cities were expected to coordinate their service to make sure all areas were adequately linked. Reduction of transfer time by the consolidation of railroad passenger and freight terminals was another high priority.

As the century went on, functional values incorporated the construction of urban freeways, government assumption of mass transit services, and public construction of airports, harbor facilities, bus terminals, and parking garages. Minnesota's wrestling with the future of its airport fits this aim. Few oppose this role of government because of the size of the investments required and the private sector's dependence on these means of public transportation.

Functional values were also evidenced in the concern for human needs. It has long been recognized that poor living conditions weaken the contributions that persons can make as members of the work force. Some turn-of-the-century reformers advocated tenement regulation, better sanitation, and recreation opportunities, not so much for the enjoyment of the individuals as for the well-being of the local economy. They viewed slum areas as cancers that would spread their ills to adjoining healthy neighborhoods. The resulting expenses would then have to be borne by the more prosperous taxpayers. Urban blight was thus bad business.

2.4 SOCIAL VALUES IN URBAN PLANNING

The social values are even broader than the esthetic and functional, rooted as they are in the interactions that citizens have with one another and the questions of fairness and justice that cling to them. Planners have used such terms as character, solidarity, identity, and mutual responsibility, which are deeply rooted in American culture. Early communities were laid out around common meeting spaces in which citizens could intertwine their lives. As villages grew into large cities, the challenge was to retain those virtues in

the face of pressures to become anonymous and unsocial.

Parallel with such social concerns ran a streak of moralism that stemmed from the nation's Judeo-Christian heritage. One nineteenth century expression of this moralism was a reform movement that sought to better the living conditions of "deserving unfortunates," to give children a better start toward becoming decent citizens, and to strengthen the moral fiber and character of immigrants from rural areas and Europe. The Social Gospel movement had emerged in urban Protestant groups by the 1890s and taught that such charitable programs were at the core of Christian faith and practice.

Social and moral crusaders first sought housing reform. This led in 1867 to the first laws regulating tenements in New York and in 1879 to a requirement that each room have an outside window. Further regulations were enacted in response to findings of the extent of disease and crime in neighborhoods inhabited by the poor.

At the same time, settlement houses began to provide health, educational, and recreational services in lower-class areas, and just as important, to supply focal points for social interaction. Learning from this experience, the Civic League of St. Louis proposed in 1907 that each neighborhood in the city be provided with a common center that contained a school, library branch, and playground in addition to the settlement house. This would ideally center the residents' interests in their neighborhood and stimulate them to participate in its governance [Scott 1969, pp. 72–73].

Accompanying the pressures on governments to intervene in community development, private philanthropists entered the scene to promote civic betterment. In 1895, Elgin Gould, a municipal government specialist, published a study of the housing efforts of European cooperative societies. He advocated that wealthy American investors construct "model tenements" for the urban working class, and formed a company to begin that enterprise. Unfortunately, those homes were not within the incomes of the average tenement dweller and there were far too many slums to be remedied by the limited resources that the private market could muster.

Reformers at the turn of the century also fought the corruption that plagued city governments. Businessmen and public officials jointly maintained the political machines that kept them in power and dealt out favors. Their collusion affected land use; the little power city government could exercise over it was "bought" with bribes and financial pressures. One remedy to this was to give voters power to legislate directly through the ballot box by initiative and referendum, the tool used now by San Diegans to limit their city's growth. Reformers also increased citizen participation in land use choices through the creation of lay planning commissions to advocate and advise on municipal plans and designs. Voluntary groups appeared first, coming from the same social stratum that produced the urban reformers. They saw themselves as politically independent and objective, attuned to broad community interests. Hartford, Connecticut, established the first official planning commission in 1907; 20 years later, 390 cities had such bodies.

Neighborhoods continued to be the focus of socially conscious planners. In the 1920s, Clarence Perry developed the *neighborhood unit* concept as a means to enhance social values. Concerned that the automobile was destroying community life in the traditional neighborhood blocks, he proposed an ideal neighborhood for 1,000 residents with its own park, local shops, and school, and a com-

plete separation of pedestrian from vehicle traffic. It had an identifiable boundary to separate it from adjoining areas to give it a character that residents would want to preserve. He argued that this would work as well for lower-income as for middle-class populations [Perry 1924].

By the 1960s, the federal Model Cities program, and others which stressed citizen participation in making and implementing local renewal plans, added a more explicitly political dimension to these social values. Residents' identity with the area and their neighbors was seen as essential to mobilizing for political action to secure aid and resist outside forces that would reduce liveability. "Community control" became a popular slogan, though such control was never fully realized. This was not a prescription for any particular plan, since Perry's norm for community size was no longer accepted. But it did stimulate later and more successful efforts at resident-centered planning and locally generated priorities for improvement programs.

The Civil Rights Movement that began in the 1950s added a new category of social values to the planning enterprise. Concern for the civil rights of African-Americans and other minorities had been muted as the nation struggled with urban blight, depression, and war. But with the swelling of post-World War II affluence, it became apparent that prosperity and social dignity ought not be limited to whites. When the U.S. Supreme Court ruled in *Brown v. Board of Education of Topeka* (1954) that segregated schools were inherently unequal and thus unconstitutional, some practices of land-use regulation as well as education policy were about to be overturned.

What the reformers of a half-century earlier advocated out of compassion, Dr. Martin Luther King, Jr. and his supporters sought as a basic human right, guaranteed by the Constitution. A landmark ruling on urban planning was secured in *Hawkins v. Town of Shaw* (1971) when the Fifth Federal Circuit Court of Appeals ruled that a city may not discriminate by race in providing such essential facilities as street paving, sewers, and drainage. Congress added protections for disabled persons in several steps from 1970 on, culminating in the Americans With Disabilities Act of 1990. Planners must now provide accessibility to buildings, facilities, and public transportation for the wheelchair-bound and those with other physical challenges.

As cities and their suburbs face mounting alienation and reduced solidarity in the 1990s, the agenda of social values remains relevant to planning choices. Neighborhoods that concentrate poverty and lack jobs perpetuate a culture of despair. At the same time, Americans at all income levels appear to be losing the sense of "civic engagement" that promotes mutual responsibility, absorbed as they are in their careers, amusements, and private lives [Putnam 1995]. Better urban design is not a sole remedy for this alienation, but as later chapters will show, modern planners see certain urban forms as potential contributors to renewing social values.

2.5 ECOLOGICAL VALUES IN URBAN PLANNING

The systematic concern for the natural environment of cities was the last of these values to emerge, becoming a broad public policy issue only in the late 1960s. It is partly descended from the esthetic values discussed earlier, but includes other elements as well. Advocates of the City Beautiful movement viewed parks and gardens as human constructs that could contribute to the enjoyment of life and the uplifting of the human spirit.

More recent environmental thinking, however, focuses on *ecosystem integrity*, recognizing its inherent values while also conscious of its many impacts on human life. It further adds attention to functional and social values with its concern for air and water quality and restoring polluted lands to productive uses.

The ecological view of the world, as explained by the landscape architect Ian McHarg [1971, p. 29], sees the farmer as the prototype of humanity.

> He prospers only insofar as he understands the land and by his management maintains its bounty. So too with the man who builds. If he is perceptive to the processes of nature, to materials and to forms, his creations will be appropriate to the place; they will satisfy the needs of social process and shelter, be expressive and endure.

McHarg offers a nature-based concept of planning that gives due attention to soils, watersheds, shores, forests, and habitats. This attention encourages planners to design clustered housing developments that protect open space and guard river corridors from building encroachments. This is one rationale for the regulation that the Dolans of Tigard, Oregon protested, described in chapter 1.

An early evidence of this concern lay in the efforts of Pittsburgh and Los Angeles to deal with their air pollution after World War II. Previously, industrial smoke was regarded as a sign of prosperity; people were working and companies making money. But a shift in thinking occurred, and people began to believe that quarter-mile visibility was an evil that could be remedied without weakening the local economy. Gradually, researchers also learned how wetlands and vegetation purify water and minimize flooding, as well as add oxygen to the air, and argued that these benefits had to be carefully protected.

By 1969, this consciousness had produced the National Environmental Policy Act, a legal landmark for planning. Based on the concern that population growth, high-density urbanization, industrial expansion, and the exploitation of natural resources were wasting land and excessively polluting air and water, the act mandated that all federal agencies assess the ecological impacts of their actions. The primary means for doing this was the environmental impact statement, embodying research into the specific effects of proposed actions. (The current results of this mandate for urban areas will be surveyed in chapter 9.) Most states adopted similar mandates, applying to privately sponsored developments as well as their own and those of their local governments. Teamed with later federal acts to combat water, air, and ground pollution, its mandates became the concern of every urban planner.

2.6 LANDMARKS IN THE AMERICAN PLANNING MEMORY

Earlier, we saw that the planning memory survives in laws, procedures, personal values, and the built environment itself. It has grown incrementally rather than by any grand design, as the participants responded to the needs and opportunities before them. These landmarks in time deserve our attention because of their later impact on planning thought and practice, whether as ideals to preserve, models to emulate, or mistakes to avoid.

Early city plans

The earliest city plans of colonial days offer insights into the dynamics of frontier community development. One of the first systematic plans was sponsored by William Penn for Philadelphia in 1682. It featured a gridiron street pattern with rectangular blocks be-

Figure 2.1   Pierre L'Enfant's original design of Washington, D.C., has been faithfully reproduced in the city's modern street plan.

tween the Delaware River on the east and the Schuylkill River on the west. A public square marked the center and four other blocks were devoted to parks. This type of configuration was ideal for subdivision and sale of small parcels of land. Thus it was widely copied as the frontier moved westward. Even San Francisco was laid out in this fashion, despite its steep hills that were very unlike Philadelphia's flat terrain.

When Congress decided to place the nation's capital on the swampy banks of the Potomac River, it commissioned a French designer, Pierre L'Enfant, to integrate European concepts into an appropriately grand and dignified design (see Figure 2.1). He superimposed on a gridiron street plan a network of diagonal boulevards radiating from major squares to provide distant views of government buildings. This included open malls from the river's banks to the "President's House" and the "Congress House." Although some parts of his plan were ignored in the city's later development, the malls exist largely as he designed them, and those squares and diagonal streets remain to channel the flow of the motorized traffic that he could not foresee. His work strongly influenced the later City Beautiful movement which sought to capture that grandeur for other cities.

Pullman and the planned industrial town

Some industrialists took up the challenge of planning in fine detail; the "company town" of Pullman on the south edge of Chicago is the best known, and its buildings remain today in a protected historic district. George Pullman wanted a clean and wholesome living environment for the workers in his railroad sleeping car plant to maximize their productivity. In 1880, work began simultaneously on his new factory and the employees' community adjacent to it. Within five years, Pullman included homes for 8,500 people, a grand arcade that served as a community center, a market house, a church, and a school. All horses in the town even had to be kept in one stable. Each building was architecturally innovative with ornamentation. All homes and business spaces were rented, enabling the company to supervise the community closely.

Pullman himself was a conscientious, methodical person, and these traits permeated his concept of the community. He later stated,

> The working people are the most important element which enters into the successful operation of any manufacturing enterprise. We decided to build, in close proximity to the shops, homes for workingmen of such character and surrounding as would prove so attractive as to cause the best class of mechanics to seek that place for employment in preference to others. We also desired to establish the place on such a basis as would exclude all baneful influences, believing

that such a policy would result in the greatest measure of success from a commercial point of view. [Buder 1967, pp. 42–43]

Pullman's philosophy thus enlisted esthetic and social values in the service of his functional values, a common impulse of American capitalism.

The community's philosophy of organization was ultimately discredited by labor unrest that led to a violent strike in 1894, caused in part by the company-as-landlord's refusal to reduce rents when it cut wages. By 1910, all of the property had been sold and Pullman was just another industrial neighborhood within the Chicago city limits. Many other company towns, often built by mining companies in remote locations, have gone into history as well. The U.S. government also sponsored such cities—from the nuclear research communities at Oak Ridge, Tennessee, and Los Alamos, New Mexico to the Navy's civilian-manned weapons center at China Lake, California.

Burnham's Plan of Chicago

With the turn of the 20th century, the making of large-scale city plans came back into fashion. The architect Daniel Burnham pioneered at this with a comprehensive update of L'Enfant's design for Washington, D. C., in 1902. He followed that with a plan for the reconstruction of San Francisco after its earthquake and fire of 1906.

But his apogee of accomplishment was the Comprehensive Plan of Chicago, commissioned not by the city government but by the Commercial Club, a leading business organization. Published on July 4, 1909, it upheld the City Beautiful tradition by envisioning an elaborate park and boulevard system throughout the larger metropolitan area and wide avenues converging on a grand civic center, as Figure 2.2 illustrates. The lakefront was to be reclaimed from the railroads and transformed into a complex of parks and lagoons [Burnham & Bennett 1970].

However, the plan also recognized the emerging functional values discussed earlier. Enough motor vehicles were then on the streets, with more expected, to require serious attention to traffic circulation. The plan included schemes for elevated and subway routes in the central business district, consolidation of railroad passenger and freight facilities, and expanded harbors at the mouths of the Chicago and Calumet Rivers. As he described it, "The plan frankly takes into consideration the fact that the American city, and Chicago preeminently, is a center of industry and traffic" [Burnham & Bennett 1970, p. 4]. Burnham hoped to marry happily these functional ideals with esthetic ones.

It is important that this plan was for the entire Chicago metropolitan area, not just for within the city limits. Burnham recommended that the city forecast uses of undeveloped lands that were certain to be added to its territory in the near future. Even more, he urged that the region be placed under a single metropolitan administration, with powers to implement his plan for parks and highways in the fringe areas [Scott 1969, pp. 106–107].

Much of the Plan of Chicago was never implemented. However, renewal of the lakefront took place beginning in the 1920s, producing the city's "front yard," Grant Park and Michigan Boulevard. Yet, it posed an agenda for planning that outlived its creators. The city's Board of Education required every eighth-grade student to read a version of it, *Wacker's Manual of the Plan of Chicago*. One of those students was young Richard J. Daley, later a mayor who carried out his own

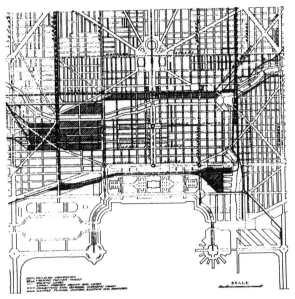

Figure 2.2 Daniel Burnham's plan for the rebuilding of Chicago displays a new lakefront, which one can view today, and a grand plaza and diagonal streets that never came about. Reprinted with permission of the Commercial Club of Chicago.

dreams of remaking the city [Miller 1996, pp. 12–13].

This plan made no provision, however, for housing or other facilities for the everyday life of Chicago's growing working class. It was drafted for the downtown business community and leading industrialists and reflected their interests. Even though the novelist Upton Sinclair had just portrayed the distressed living and working conditions of the mass of Chicagoans in *The Jungle* and social reformers like Jane Addams had been active there for decades, Burnham's plan was somehow above those mundane concerns. His only reference to slum conditions was a recommendation for "remorseless enforcement of sanitary regulations" [Burnham & Bennett 1970, p. 108]. A famous aphorism of his was "Make no little plans." The Plan of Chicago was grand indeed, but his successors came to realize that "little plans" also have a necessary place in benefitting the daily life of ordinary citizens.

The Garden City movement

While Burnham and his school of planners were fascinated by the great European cities, more holistic planning influences were also crossing the Atlantic. In 1898 Ebenezer Howard [1965], an English social reformer, published a city design that combined the benefits of town and country living for a population of no more than 32,000. It was to be self supporting, with its own industries and farms, and separated by a greenbelt from others like it. He sought to synthesize the market-based ideals of enterprise and production with the social values of a fair division of wealth and holistic community well being. All land was to be owned by the municipality and leased to residents, businesses, and farmers, whose rents would pay all of the city's expenses.

Howard formed a corporation which obtained 3,800 acres north of London, and in 1903 began to build the town of Letchworth according to his principles. It stands today, not a full embodiment of the Garden City ideal, but a viable and attractive community nonetheless. One element of its construction was a design competition for "cheap cottages" for working-class families, showing sensitivity for affordable housing as well as the esthetic and functional values.

Some American developers adopted this concept for residential developments. One expression was Forest Hills Gardens, a middle-class home development in New York City's borough of Queens. Clarence Perry's neighborhood unit principle was linked with the Garden City concept in the design of

Radburn, New Jersey. A suburban community without industry, its architects reserved much of the land for gardens and parks, and separated automobile traffic from the living area, which enabled residents to walk through most of the area without crossing a street. Although it too failed to address the housing needs of those who remained locked in slums, its features appeared in many later community plans [Scott 1969, pp. 59–60].

The Garden City ideal is alive once again in the 1990s, as "neotraditional" planners and architects envision cities that seek harmony in both their social and natural environments. Calthorpe [1993, p. 25] expressed it well.

> Understanding the qualities of nature in each place, expressing it in the design of communities, integrating it within our towns, and respecting its balance are essential ingredients of making the human place sustainable and spiritually nourishing.

A culture that is concerned with the loss of countryside, clean air, and social connectedness has found Howard's visions to be more relevant than they perhaps seemed in mid-century. Chapter 7 examines the neotraditional planning principles more closely.

Le Corbusier and the Contemporary City

A very different version of the Garden City was the vision of Charles-Edouard Jeanneret, a French architect who practiced under the name of Le Corbusier. During the 1920s he published his dramatic city plans featuring high-rise buildings and wide spaces between them. His *Ville Contemporaine* (Contemporary City) was to house three million people in apartment towers and garden homes. They would commute by subways to jobs in 60-story office buildings, yet be able to enjoy recreation in the ample open space between them. Residents would collectively own their homes, allocated according to their status in the hierarchy of production and administration. This design expressed his passion for order; the straight line and right angle were symbols of ultimate rationality. City design had to incorporate that geometry if it were to be truly human [Le Corbusier 1971].

Behind Le Corbusier's plans lay a unique blend of esthetic, functional, and social values. He rejected the chaotic 19th century city, dominated by unrestrained greed and exploitation of both humans and nature. Rather, rational design would seize control from these economic forces and embody the common good in every detail. Ideally, this would build a society from which interclass conflict is absent because all benefits are fairly distributed. It is therefore also a society without politics. Cities would be administered by an elite of industrialists, scientists, and artists whose technical expertise would supply order, prosperity, and beauty. The ordinary citizens need not be concerned with public affairs, but simply with the productivity of their jobs and enjoyment of their amenities. To him, towns were tools and houses were "machines for living" just as skyscrapers were machines for communication and trade [Fishman 1977].

Le Corbusier's designs, apart from his philosophy, have been widely adopted. High-rise structures, accessible to jobs and transit facilities, dominate most major city centers and the suburban rings served by freeways. Chicago's John Hancock Center blends high-cost homes, offices, and shops in one of the world's tallest buildings. But the Robert Taylor Homes that house Chicago's poor are also concrete expressions of Le Corbusier's designs, although they fail to follow his social philosophy. Contrary to his expectations, political and social conflict have not been banished from these sites because they only in-

creased the inequality in the distribution of society's benefits and costs.

The Urban Renewal movement

By the 1930s, many major cities' population growth virtually ceased. Most of their buildings were a half-century or more old, in more or less deteriorated condition, and often unsuited to their sites and the land uses that had evolved around them. In these cities, planning had a new task: to address the reuse of space and the rehabilitation or replacement of structures and public facilities. Thus, *urban renewal* rose to the top of the agendas of the city leaders and of Congress.

The problem of center-city decay and slum growth has both economic and social dimensions. Renewal can take place under private auspices, but only in conditions set by the market. A decaying tenement building or an abandoned factory does not present an attractive investment opportunity. The site may be inappropriate for new dwellings or shopping facilities, or its cost too high compared with the expected return.

Planners also recognized the larger social and economic costs of blight and the failure to renew an area. As the 19th century reformers learned, poor health, crime, and social disorder make depressed neighborhoods a sink for public funds and services. It was estimated that the city of Cleveland spent $2 million in 1934 on services in a slum that produced only one-eighth that amount in tax revenue [Boyer 1983, p. 244].

This condition also pointed to a deficiency in the planning process. Harland Bartholomew, a leading planner, confessed in 1931 that too much effort had been devoted to the business centers and fast-growing suburbs, to the neglect of those districts that were suffering the greatest population loss and physical decay. To rehabilitate the latter areas became the greatest planning challenge of that decade [Boyer 1983, p. 214].

The depression of the 1930s, while aggravating these problems with a decline in private construction and an increase in human misery, also stimulated new action by government. In 1937, Congress passed the comprehensive Wagner-Steagall Housing Act to grant funds to cities to clear and replace slums. However, the needs were far greater than the money available, and cities lacked experience with urban renewal. New York City's Housing Authority reported in 1934 that it had 17 square miles of slums, of which 10 were so unfit for habitation as to require immediate evacuation [Boyer 1983, p. 252]. Thus, nothing less than an areawide strategy would be sufficient, for a partial renewal effort would be futile if the blighted blocks around it remained.

By the end of the 1930s, three leading methods had emerged: public housing, in which local governments built, owned, and managed the dwellings; government incentives to private corporations to redevelop; and joint public-private action to renew areas that did not warrant total clearance [Scott 1969, p. 379]. Public housing had already been begun on a modest scale. The second method first received legal sanction in 1941 when New York State permitted corporations to acquire property through condemnation if they had already obtained 51% of the designated project area. The incentive for this investment was a ten-year freeze on the assessed value of the land for property tax purposes, in effect a subsidy from city revenues. The joint approach showed some success with a neighborhood improvement district in the Waverly area of Baltimore in 1939 [Boyer 1983, pp. 252–253].

Private renewal on a large scale appeared in New York City in the early 1940s with Stuyvesant Town, a project of the Metropolitan Life Insurance Company. It encompassed 61 acres and housed 24,000 persons in 13-story towers. The city's subsidy included not only the tax exemption but also the contribution of street and school lands and some new public facilities nearby. Controversy arose over what some observers deemed an excessive population density and the fact that no African-Americans were initially accepted as tenants [Scott 1969, pp. 421–423].

Urban renewal programs expanded vigorously after World War II, thanks to growing federal grants to states and cities. The question of its constitutionality had to be settled, however. It had long been legally permissible for governments to acquire private land (with due compensation) to serve public purposes for streets, schools, hospitals, and housing. But typical urban renewal programs were undertaken by private developers, and judges in some states struck down condemnations on this ground. In 1954, the U.S. Supreme Court ruled in *Berman v. Parker* that properties in blighted areas may be taken for rebuilding by private companies if they are part of a general municipal plan. The justices thus gave city councils the broad leeway for urban renewal choices that they already enjoyed for planning and zoning generally. Discussion of more recent experiences with urban renewal follows in chapters 6 and 7.

Levittown and the suburban boom

The end of World War II signaled a new building boom for urban America, making up for the construction slump that began with the Wall Street crash of 1929. As war veterans married and started families, they created a huge demand for homes that far exceeded the existing supply. Levitt and Sons produced a new idea: a mass housing development on the potato fields of Nassau County, just east of New York City. The first Levittown consisted of 17,400 homes, built on an efficient mass production schedule, along with schools, shops, and playgrounds. The first of its 82,000 residents occupied their homes in 1947, paying between $7,000 and $9,000 for the Cape Cod and ranch style designs. The Levitts followed that with similar communities in New Jersey and Pennsylvania. These planned suburbs were socially homogeneous by design, since no initial sales were made to noncaucasians [Jackson 1985, pp. 234–237]. Imitators soon created Park Forest, Illinois, Lakewood, California, and a host of other megasuburbs on big-city fringes.

Levittown was not the beginning of suburbia. In 1868, Frederick L. Olmsted began to lay out an upscale "garden suburb" to the southwest of Chicago; Riverside remains an attractive community, but its residents are far above working-class status. But what made mass suburbia possible more than anything else was Congress's creation of a means of financing home mortgages with relatively low interest rates and down payments. The Federal Housing Authority, together with even more generous programs for military veterans, opened the door to families of modest means, and developers promptly met their demand. Federally financed highways made it possible to commute quickly to big-city jobs, adding impetus to fringe-area growth. While "suburbia" today ranges from the most affluent and exclusive communities to poor and deteriorated enclaves, the image that the Levitt brothers gave it remains in the minds of many.

2.7 PLANNING TOWARD A NEW CENTURY

The urban planning enterprise stands at a major crossroad at the end of the 1990s, comparable to that which it faced at the beginning of this century. Then, the City Beautiful movement had to account for the technological innovations and social pluralization that transformed cities. Now, the dilemmas are not so much technical (despite the advent of the Knowledge Economy) as they are political and ideological. Planners and those who influence them must answer three interlocked questions.

First, what should city life really be like? Traditional planning, whether by L'Enfant, Burnham, or Le Corbusier, assumed a public interest consisting of unitary visions of good city life. The most widely accepted designs sought to transcend the disorder that individual selfish choices produced with beauty, coherence, and rationality. Although schools of planning disagreed with one another, they took for granted their competence at their mission. After all, what other reason did planners have for their existence?

But such unitary visions fragmented into many as the century progressed, the partisans of each competing for their share of public resources. A stridently individualistic society finds little that it can call a "public interest," whether the choice is to locate an airport, build modest-cost homes, or renew an abandoned industrial tract. Planning has often become no more than the effort to mediate between these competitors, counting any kind of agreement reached as success.

A second dilemma is more specific, but grows out of the first. Planning that aimed to serve public interests often had to restrict the choices of landowners to use their property. Regulatory actions like zoning reduced potential profits, and major projects that built highways and renewed downtowns affected wide areas for better or worse. But citizens are more defensive now, increasingly adept at lawsuits and political organization, and the intrusive plans are not succeeding as often.

Planners for governments at all levels are pressed to adopt a more laissez-faire stance in order to retain their positions.

The third problem stems from the changing role in our society of government, which has long provided many planners with their authority and power to act. The public distrusts what it sees as big government (and, admittedly, big institutions of all sorts), viewing its plans as serving the values of "someone else." This attitude is central to the property rights advocates who cheered the *Dolan* decision.

In the past, the federal and many state governments provided strong impetus for urban development, particularly in housing, mass transit, and infrastructures. But that contribution is steadily diminishing because of competing demands for more investment in medical care, education, and job placement for aid recipients, not to mention balancing the federal budget. Future initiatives for raising the quality of city life will come mostly from private sources, the amounts and impacts of which will vary considerably from one place to another.

The values that guide urban planning are personal, held and acted out by influential individuals and groups. Values do not make choices; people do. We can distinguish many roles that these people play, and two major categories are determined by the places they occupy, either in government or the private sector. The governmental participants in planning occupy the stage next in chapter 3.

FOR REVIEW AND DISCUSSION

1. How do "spaces" and "places" differ from one another in popular perceptions? How must planners think of them in the choices they make?

2. Define esthetic, functional, social, and ecological values and give examples of their expression in modern built environments. In what ways are they likely to conflict in actual planning choices today?

3. What purposes were most important to such city planners as L'Enfant, Burnham, and Le Corbusier? How different are their purposes from those of the planners who build and rebuild cities today?

3

Governments as Planners

3.1 PLANNING BY "A CAST OF THOUSANDS"

Cities' built environments display not only the values that chapter 2 described, but also the accumulated actions of the persons who pursued them. To identify the participants in urban planning might not seem much harder than listing the cast of a play: a finite number of actors arranged in order of appearance in a sequence of scenes. And one can certainly provide such a cast of the significant players in any of the planning contests described in chapter 1, for example.

But planning as conceived here is very much unlike a stage production. Any single decision is but one link in a long chain of related events from the distant past into the uncertain future, so there are no opening and closing curtains. There is not one play but many—several on one stage going on simultaneously with actors jumping between them. Too, there is no clear distinction between the cast and the audience, since the latter are free to assume spontaneous roles. A "planning critic" thus has a more challenging job than a drama critic.

Planning politics lacks predictable patterns of cooperation and conflict—either in the key issues that emerge or in who participates in deciding them. Schattschneider [1960, p. 18], explained how politics differs from a football game.

> Many conflicts are narrowly confined by a variety of devices, but the distinctive quality of political conflicts is that the relations between the players and the audience have not been well defined and there is usually nothing to keep the audience from getting into the game.

The circle of planners for Times Square was quite small in the beginning and readily agreed on a design for renewal. But the audience of area residents and business operators in the area climbed down from the spectators' seats and began to press for alternatives, which no one foresaw at the outset.

Thus the size of a conflict can be enlarged to the point of defeating the intentions of the original participants. Schattschneider [1960, p. 4] observed that "conflicts are frequently won or lost by the success that the contestants have in getting the audience involved in the fight or in excluding it." Thus one side in a planning controversy may well seek to keep the matter private and localized while the opposition, sensing defeat, tries to publicize it and enlist allies. Those who spearheaded the San Diego referendums realized that only mass voter power would protect the city's natural environment as they saw it.

The purpose of this chapter and the next is to provide a generalized "cast" of customary participants in planning decisions and identify the conditions in which they are likely to become involved. This chapter describes persons with a formal role in government and the agencies that confer their authority. Chapter 4 turns to the individuals and organizations in the private sector that make and influence planning choices. The boundary between these is not always clear, as the discussion of public-private partnerships will reveal.

We can identify three categories of planning participants within the realms of national, state, and local government. First, there are *professional planners* who have specialized education and credentials in this field and are employed by a unit of government to practice it full time. Some of these are generalists, responsible for a wide range of planning issues in a municipality or county. Others are specialists: highway planners in a state or county department of transportation, housing planners in a city agency, and economic development planners in a state commerce department, to give just three examples. They focus their attention only on the planning considerations that are in their official charge.

In the second group are the *public officials* who ratify planning choices with legal action and public funds: legislators, executives, and judges, along with their policy advisers. All of the legislators and many of the mayors and judges are elected to their posts. They are naturally the most sensitive to popular pressures, particularly in years when they run for reelection. City and county managers and heads of local, state, and federal departments and agencies are appointed by the elected officials. As generalists, they must balance many interests that compete for their time and funds, and thus have to take in a wider range of concerns than the planners do.

Less visible but not to be ignored is the third group, the *citizen planners* who sit on local planning commissions and official advisory boards and generally influence the choices of the first two groups by their actions and inaction. The roles they play can differ widely, depending on the type of issue that arises, the sequence of decisions about those issues, and their breadth of involvement. Their presence is intended to make the professionals and politicians more responsive to citizen interests and add a wide spectrum of advice. Most serve at the local level, but some citizen boards assist state and federal agencies also.

3.2 GOVERNMENTS AS POWER CENTERS

Planning is a government-centered process in many ways. Since it attempts to control the futures of urban communities, it must draw upon legal resources to mandate certain outcomes. Recall the five types of planning choices presented in chapter 1: all of them assume some role for the public sector, whether in taking the initiative for plans, ratifying a private proposal, or joining in a partnership for development. The amount of discretion allowed to public officials varies widely: street and sewer routings are routine actions, while location of an airport or a neighborhood renewal scheme permits much leeway.

Government is also at the center in that all land-use choices by the private sector require positive approval by some authority before they can be put into effect, from an electric power plant to a homeowner's addition of a porch. This role of government lies within its traditional *police power*, the broad responsibility to guard the health, safety, morals, and general welfare of the public. Courts have consistently upheld governments' positions in disputes of zoning and other land use regulation as long as they exercised this power fairly and reasonably.

This chapter divides the governmental planning participants into six groups, according to the level of government to which they belong. In many cases, however, they are interdependent; major planning choices such as the Minnesota airport involve officials (and conflicting interests) from two or more levels. This fact signals the decentralization and often fragmentation that prevails in making and executing urban plans. American urban governance allocates many decisions to the smallest local units practicable, and citizens tend to resist intrusion of higher authorities into local land use choices.

There were 86,743 units of local government in the United States as of 1992, and most play some role in planning as defined here (all local government totals in this chapter are from the 1992 Census of Governments, conducted by the U.S. Bureau of the Census). Many such jurisdictions are small in area and population, which greatly complicates planning choices, particularly on problems that cross municipal boundary lines and require voluntary cooperation by two or more units to solve. No other industrialized nation has so complex a network for local governance and its planning. Whether this produces better cities is a judgment call, but the system is doubtless harder for average citizens to understand and may be less accountable to them as a result.

It is important that we not see these governmental units as mere neutral arbiters between competing interests. Each jurisdiction represents one or more constituent interests, and so may clash with other players in the game. Governments are automatic participants in the games that Schattschneider described, but they can choose whose side to play on and switch sides at will. New York City officials favored the high-rise development in Times Square for the increased tax revenue it promised, although they came to support the more modest redevelopment when they recognized that it alone was feasible.

A government's participation can be complicated by internal division, however. A mayor might seek one outcome, while the city council opts for another. More often, perhaps, a planning department supports a development scheme but elected officials refuse to approve it. If internal deadlock arises, the city may not be able to play a clear role, and the decision falls to others by default. Delay is a common fallback; putting a proposal in limbo for a time may render a decision easier to make (if only because the proposal is withdrawn or revised to meet the objections).

3.3 GENERAL PURPOSE LOCAL GOVERNMENTS AS PLANNERS

The front line of urban planning by government runs through the wide range of local governments of the nation. Table 3.1 summarizes these units and their roles in planning.

The counties, cities, villages, and urban towns and townships are *general-purpose governments*, responsible for a wide range of services and regulations, from police and fire protection to streets, parks, and sewers. Land-use controls support many of these other functions within the police powers noted above. Each state's laws specify the powers of its local units and the procedures by which they exercise them, although there is much similarity from one state to another.

Table 3.1   86,000 local governments play various roles in planning decisions

Unit	Planning Role and Powers
City (village, borough)	Primary land-use decision maker for incorporated urban areas; extensive power to initiate and regulate development.
County	Same as city in many unincorporated areas; variable otherwise. Undertakes development of highways and other major facilities.
Town/township	Similar to city's powers in unincorporated areas in some states; in other states, minimal powers or none.
School district	Controls and develops its own properties with local government approval.
Special district/ authority (nonschool)	Varies with function; those which control essential urban services and facilities (e.g. transportation, natural resources, parks, sanitation) have extensive powers therein and a high degree of autonomy.
Metropolitan planning agency	Advisory and coordinating role in transportation, land use, and other regional services and facilities. No direct authority over land use.

The nation's 19,296 cities, boroughs (except in Alaska), and villages are legally termed *municipalities*. They are generally urban in nature (aside from the smallest ones) and were created at the will of their residents to provide the services and regulations that a more rural authority does not. Much of the literature on planning focuses on their situations and policies.

Most of the 3,043 counties are rural, but county governments in metropolitan areas have increasingly taken on urban functions, often with planning powers for areas not included in a municipality. Los Angeles County, California, acts as a municipal government for several hundred thousand residents in unincorporated areas. Often, county authorities are also responsible for regional roads and parks that require joint planning with municipalities. Counties on the fringes of metropolitan areas or in high-amenity growth areas face especially serious planning challenges but may lack the professional capacity or legal powers to cope with them.

There are 16,666 townships and towns in 21 northern states and most are rural units with few powers. In New England and a few other states, however, they exercise important planning functions like municipalities. Some townships on the fringes of growing metropolitan areas strictly limit residential and commercial development to preserve their semirural ambiance [Stephens 1989].

Planning policies in such governments tend to be shared by four groups of officials. In larger cities and some counties, elected mayors play a chief executive role and often take the initiative on major public and private developments. Chicago's mayors have typically been politically strong. Richard M. Daley, first elected in 1989, has been prominent in seeking a location for a new regional airport, while one of his predecessors, Harold Washington, sought to involve neighborhood residents, especially those of color, in the planning process. Also in this first group are the professional managers who oversee the entire administration and are responsible to the council or board that appointed them. In such units, the office of mayor does not have administrative powers, although such mayors may still exert important policy leadership.

Second, municipal councils and county and town boards enact land-use regulations and finance public improvements. Representing a variety of interests, they are often internally divided and may oppose the stance of their mayor and planning professionals. At times their debates reflect and publicize the divisions in the community at large over the choices, and so serve as a catalyst for expanding the scope of conflicts.

In the third cluster of influentials are the planning specialists described at the opening of this chapter. They consist of the full-time professionals with credentials in planning, engineering, urban design, and related fields, and the "citizen planners" who sit on official advisory boards and commissions on such matters as planning and zoning, parks and recreation, environmental quality, housing, building design, and redevelopment.

The most common structure in medium sized and larger municipalities and counties endows a department of planning and/or community development with authority for all five types of decisions described in chapter 1. It processes applications from private parties for land-use changes and new construction, prepares proposals for public projects ranging from streets to airports, and enforces the zoning and building regulations. The larger the department, the more specialists it will have in such fields as transportation, housing, economic development, and neighborhood relations.

The department is typically headed by a director, who is appointed by the mayor, council, or manager. The office has considerable potential for leadership on development issues (see section 5.6 for its alternative roles). The director must not only oversee the department's operations but also provide initiative to the city or county on planning policies. Two-way communication with the citizens and groups with development-related interests is equally important. Ultimately, success depends on the ability of department and director to induce higher officials, operating agencies, and private sector participants to complete the planning cycle and put the

plans into effect. Smaller municipalities and many counties lack a professional planning staff. They usually rely on clerks to handle routine land-use business and contract with private firms for such consultant services as they need.

The citizen boards, most visibly the planning commission, advise the department on all aspects of its work. Typically appointed to their posts by chief executives or legislators, they serve with little or no compensation. Membership ranges from 5 to 21, as the city chooses. The better-educated and higher-income homeowners, male and female, predominate in their membership, although in larger cities they are chosen to broadly represent the leading ethnic groups and geographic areas. Although these commissioners are ideally independent of partisan influences and thus able to represent the spectrum of community values, they often carry with them personal business and real estate connections which make them vulnerable to conflicts of interest. Their powers are usually limited to studying issues and proposals and recommending final action to the council. Even so, to the extent that they represent popular values and preferences and work conscientiously, they exert strong influence on the final choices.

New York City decentralized its citizen planning process to the neighborhood level in 1963, establishing 59 community boards. Members are volunteers appointed by their borough presidents and city council members and are assisted in their deliberations by staff and professional planners. All land-use applications must pass a review by the board in the affected community, which can recommend action to the city council. The boards can also veto plans of city agencies that apply within their borders. They have varied widely in their technical and political competence and strength of leadership and are most effective when they reach consensus about their objectives and means of achieving them, a quality that certainly applies to all planning authorities

In 1990, the New York community boards were empowered to initiate "197-a" plans for adoption by higher authority. A neighborhood in the South Bronx was the first to secure approval of its plan. Another one, pending in mid-1996, comes from the Red Hook enclave of Brooklyn, a declining waterfront area that has long been neglected by outside investors. In 1995, its board produced an ambitious and detailed renewal plan that could "reinvent" the neighborhood if enough resources could be mobilized to implement it [Angotti 1996].

Administrators in other departments, such as public works, constitute the fourth group of planning influentials. These persons are responsible for sanitation, drainage, water supply, transportation, building inspection, parks, and environmental quality. Their cooperation is essential to the fulfillment of any plan. Larger cities also have separate departments of housing and/or redevelopment which directly operate programs in these areas and so make crucial land use choices. Because they are delegated power to receive federal and state grants, borrow money, and acquire land, they can operate quite autonomously from other municipal agencies.

To keep these separate agencies working compatibly is no easy task in a large city or county with myriad demands and constraints. Competing political or bureaucratic interests often cause long-range plans to be distorted or ignored. For example, a public works department, by its action or inaction on a neighborhood drainage problem, can determine the future of development there, re-

gardless of any plan statements. Much depends on the power of the administrative mayor or manager to direct such agencies.

3.4 PLANNING BY SPECIAL-PURPOSE GOVERNMENTS

Urban regions are also overlaid by jurisdictions that are responsible for only one or a few related functions and are independent of the general-purpose units. Many of them participate in land-use planning related to their specific function. Their labels vary: district, board, commission, and authority are most common. They can be assigned any function of government, but most commonly they deal with education, water supply, housing, waste management, drainage, parks, hospitals, transit, and transportation terminals. The 1992 Census of Governments counted 14,556 school districts and 33,131 of all other types. The latter number has increased steadily over the years, a testimony to their usefulness.

Separate school districts exist in most states and are the most visible of these special governments. While their function is to provide educational services from early childhood through the vocational and community college level, they are also major owners and developers of urban real estate. Their choices to build new schools and close others present policy choices to municipalities and counties. An unused school building is an opportunity to create a community center, housing complex, or business facility.

Special districts of other types exist on several scales. Most are distinctly local, performing functions that the general purpose units that overlap them could take responsibility for, but for financial or political reasons were allocated to these instead. For example, watershed governments have boundaries that follow their drainage basins and may overlap many counties and municipalities. They often have power to veto building projects that would alter wetlands or increase the potential for floods. Strictly defined, these districts are governed by a board that is directly elected or chosen by other local officials, and have the power to tax their residents directly.

One of the largest special districts is the South Coast Air Quality Management District, which covers 13,000 square miles and more than ten million residents in southern California. It is responsible for imposing controls on moving and stationary pollution sources to bring the region into conformance with federal and state standards. This task calls for regulating traffic movements and certain kinds of land uses, among other policies, although its power to impose them on municipal and county governments is subject to political maneuvering.

Another type of special-purpose government is the *authority* or government corporation. While some are small, the most notable ones operate on a regional or a statewide scale, and some cross state boundaries as well. These resemble private corporations in that their boards are chosen by public officials rather than directly by the voters, and they are financially self-supporting. Often they were created to finance and operate such public infrastructures as sewers and airports. Since cities and counties are often limited by law in the debt they may incur, these districts make it possible to borrow and build as needed [Axelrod 1993].

The largest of these self-governing authorities is the Port Authority of New York and New Jersey, a many-function district operating within a 25-mile radius of the Statue of Liberty. In its holdings are airports, bridges, tunnels, bus and ship terminals, a subway line, and the World Trade Center towers.

Since it controls much of the transportation infrastructure, its planning choices are basic to the land use policies of the many municipalities which it overlaps.

Two problems stand out in the roles that the large authorities play in urban planning. First, they are relatively independent from the citizenry and their accountability is thus tenuous. The 12-member board of the Port Authority of New York and New Jersey has divided accountability: six each are appointed by the governors of the two states. Axelrod [1993] asserts that some districts have been less than responsible in borrowing and constructing and that the temptation of empire-building exists in all such units.

The second problem is that they do not necessarily mesh their plans with those of the general purpose governments which they overlap. For example, the unincorporated area around Houston is served by a number of utility and water districts. They sell household water to their constituents and apply the fees to repayment of the bonds that financed the systems. But their extensive pumping of ground water has contributed to land subsidence in the region, increasing the dangers of flooding and salt intrusion into the wells. These districts have generally refused to cooperate on any remedial plan, and the general purpose governments cannot compel them to do so [Perrenod 1986].

A unique type of authority that has mushroomed in the past decade is the *residential community association*. Technically, it is a "private government" which exerts legal control over the owners of condominiums, townhouses, and cooperatives which hold some or all of their property in common; more than 150,000 exist today [Barton & Silverman 1994]. The association maintains exteriors and surrounding grounds, provides for insurance and repairs, and sets rules for everything from exterior colors to pet ownership. Every resident must pay a fee to the association and can have a voice in its decisions. Some services it provides overlap those of the local government, such as maintenance of streets within the project, snow and waste removal, and nuisance control. Its policies focus on the quality of the residential environment and so tends to be more restrictive on members than in a "free" community. These very rules transform it into a surrogate local authority and partially supplant the public planning function. It also intervenes in planning politics concerning areas adjacent to its space in order to protect its residents' property values and preferred way of life.

3.5 METROPOLITAN AND REGIONAL PLANNING AGENCIES

Although metropolitan areas constitute geographic, economic, and social wholes, their governance is universally fragmented among one or more counties, many municipalities, townships in some states, and special districts. Many are interstate as well. Although some civic leaders in Boston recognized as early as 1910 the need for a comprehensive metropolitan authority there, political forces have prevented any establishments of such units. Since the 1960s, there have been a few consolidations of a central city and county government (Indianapolis, Jacksonville, and Nashville, for example) but suburban authorities were not included. Metropolitan service districts such as the Port Authority of New York and New Jersey only added to the fragmentation. Central city and suburban leaders alike feared that such reform would transfer power from them to a body whose purposes and actions they could not foresee or control.

Yet the need for serious integrated planning grew with the metropolitan areas and

could not be totally ignored. The first official agency was the Los Angeles County Regional Planning Commission, created in 1922. Although active and professionally competent, it was unable to plan far enough ahead to keep up with that region's booming growth in that decade and lacked the authority to enforce its plans [Scott 1969, pp. 206–209]. More public and private agencies appeared in other areas subsequently, but likewise lacked the legal and political standing to control the key decisions that shaped both the central cities and their suburbs.

In 1962, the initiative for regional planning shifted to Congress. It realized that the six-year-old interstate highway program had begun billions of dollars worth of urban freeway construction without any systematic planning for its relationship to land use, urban renewal, or mass transit. Thus it mandated that after 1965, highway grants would go only to those metropolitan areas that had a comprehensive transportation planning process. In response, the local governments, transit agencies, and state highway departments quickly conformed.

Congress further required, in the Demonstration Cities (later Model Cities) and Metropolitan Development Act of 1966, that applications by local units for federal funds be reviewed by an areawide planning agency. The latter was to comment on whether each project was consistent with the plans of the surrounding communities and with any comprehensive metropolitan plans that existed. Such projects included hospitals, airports, water and sanitation facilities, transit, highways, and open space acquisition. The comments were not binding on the federal office providing the funds, but enabled the latter to judge the merits of the application within an areawide pespective. Popularly known as the A-95 review, it had only minimal success in inducing comprehensive metropolitan planning and was terminated early in the 1980s.

In further response to the federal stimuli, voluntary interlocal cooperation took the form of councils of government (COGs). Typical is the Association of Bay Area Governments (ABAG) which surrounds San Francisco Bay, covering an area with 602 local authorities. Such councils are usually composed of representatives from those local governments, who are free to decide whether and how intensively they will participate. COGs often prepare plans for land use, housing, transportation, open space, and related issues but lack the power to compel members to comply with them. Such successes as they have had were due to reaching consensus among the crucial implementors. ABAG has been assisted by several private-sector organizations that generated their own plans, in effect forming a public-private partnership for regional management [Rothblatt 1992].

Also growing in popularity are voluntary intergovernmental planning efforts comprising parts of metropolitan areas. The 37 local governments in the Monongahela ("Mon") river valley, a segment of metropolitan Pittsburgh, struggle with industrial decline and deteriorating housing. Many of them joined a consortium of community development corporations, the Mon Valley Initiative, to rehabilitate homes and promote jobs in small companies with aid from several major foundations. A council of governments in that valley has negotiated some cost-saving sharing of public services. However, the area's historic political fragmentation hinders further needed progress [Ehrenhalt 1995].

Two metropolitan areas have stronger planning agencies. The Metropolitan Council of the Minneapolis-St. Paul region was created by the legislature in 1967 to coordinate the area's physical infrastructure development.

Its 16 members and chair are appointed by the governor from districts in the region. At this time, it maintains an urban growth boundary, beyond which it will not approve sewer extensions and intense urban development. It is also implementing a program to extend affordable housing into the suburbs, with financial incentives to cooperating communities.

Perhaps the most advanced is that of Portland, Oregon, with a directly elected regional council that is responsible for growth management, transportation, and land-use planning. Together with the area's counties and municipalities, it seeks an orderly expansion of the urbanized area and its service networks. Its staff is designing a Regional Framework Plan for future adoption that will incorporate all the elements of the local plans into a coherent whole [P. Lewis 1996, chs. 4 & 6]. Tigard, the scene of the Dolans' dispute, is in this region, and Fanno Creek flows through one of its envisioned "green corridors."

In the mid-1990s, the major thrust of metropolitan planning is through the metropolitan planning organizations (MPOs) mandated by Congress in the Intermodal Surface Transportation Efficiency Act of 1991. Primarily focused on transportation and funded by the US Department of Transportation, the MPOs are charged with a broader focus for planning than before, to include environmental and other issues impacted by highway and transit spending. These are further discussed in section 8.1.

3.6 STATE GOVERNMENTS IN URBAN PLANNING

State legislatures and administrators take part in urban planning in four basic ways. First, they are property owners in their own right and can undertake such developments as they choose in any locality. Departments of transportation locate highways and airports. Other agencies do locally specific planning when they place a prison, office building, hospital, or university in a community. While they are sensitive to local concerns and regulations for political reasons, their plans cannot ordinarily be rejected by city and county officials.

Second, they grant the legal power that localities have to plan, and they mandate certain policy goals and procedures. Many states require that cities and counties prepare and follow comprehensive plans. California, for example, stipulates that local plans deal with open space protection, seismic safety, and coastline protection in addition to the familiar land use and housing regulation. They also ensure fairness and consistency by specifying the procedures that local units must follow in their planning actions.

Third, states establish specific land-use regulations that localities must follow. A state department of natural resources, for example, limits development along urban shorelines, controls drainage of wetlands, and sets rules for waste disposal and maintenance of fuel tanks. Minnesota, for example, requires that new building lots adjacent to many of its 10,000-plus lakes be of a minimum size, typically 15,000–20,000 square feet. Likewise, most states have enacted building codes for health and safety protection which local units must adopt and are not allowed to vary.

Some state governments are increasingly assertive in urban growth management and protection of the environment and in some cases override local choices. As of 1992, 13 states had enacted comprehensive legislation that centralized to some degree planning decisions that had been up to city and county officials. Their major purposes were to pro-

vide for balanced economic and housing development in the most cost-effective and ecologically sensitive manner [Bollens 1993]. Section 9.5 further develops their role in urban growth management.

States can choose between two basic models of intervention into local choices. In the *regulatory* model, a state agency can directly modify or veto a local action. This has ordinarily been applied only to sensitive locations, such as a high-density development along a scenic shoreline. The *planning* model, by contrast, allows localities to draw their own comprehensive plans within state land use standards and objectives—and the state may call for changes when they do not conform. The latter has become the approach of choice in recent years as the most workable compromise between the two levels of authority [Bollens 1993].

Florida, for example, followed the planning model in enacting the Growth Managment Act in 1985, having learned from previous efforts that most local officials were unable or unwilling to do comprehensive planning without major stimuli from the state. The Act has three key concepts. First, local plans must be consistent with all relevant state policies and with the plans of neighboring localities. Second, development may occur in an area only if the infrastructures of roads and utilities are in place or arranged for. Third, the local plans must consciously minimize urban sprawl, protect rural areas, and promote infill development within urbanized areas. Florida's Department of Community Affairs reviews each local plan and may reject or require modifications as necessary to meet these requirements [Turner 1990].

Oregon pursues similar objectives in its land use program, first enacted in 1973. It too requires cities and counties to comply with a series of goals in their plans, such as protecting agricultural land, and the state Land Conservation and Development Commission oversees their compliance. One feature is the Urban Growth Boundary, a line around metropolitan Portland and other cities beyond which no urban development is to be allowed by the local governments. This restriction provides the authority wielded by Portland's metropolitan council described above. While these controls have been accepted by a majority of the public and shown success toward achieving the goals, the growth pressures that much of Oregon currently experiences could weaken commitment to them [Abbott et al. 1994].

All states have economic development programs to create jobs and tax revenue. Following either an entrepreneurial strategy of direct investment or a recruitment strategy to provide tax and financial incentives, they induce existing businesses to expand or new ones to locate on local sites. In doing so, they work with local planners on site selection, building design, and provision of roads, utilities, and other support systems, and often share the financing with them. By one count, there were 2,222 separate state economic development programs in 1990, which supplemented many more offered by individual cities and counties [Leicht & Jenkins 1994].

Finally, many states have broader programs that assist local communities in their economic, physical, environmental, and social development. North Carolina, for example, supports community projects through the state's allocation of federal Community Development Block Grants, supplemented by its own funds. It has particularly targeted economically distressed counties to create jobs and improve their infrastructures. In so doing, it seeks to create partnerships that link local governments with each other and with businesses and nonprofit organizations, and to build the self-help capacity of local residents [North Carolina 1995].

3.7 THE FEDERAL GOVERNMENT IN URBAN PLANNING

Washington, D.C., was long remote from the activities of urban planning. The federal government's influence began to rise through its aid to public housing in the 1930s and the urban renewal and interstate highway programs of the 1950s. The decade of the 1960s was the turning point, however. The federal government's impact on metropolitan planning, reviewed in section 3.4, is but part of the larger response by Congress and several federal agencies to the demands of urban-based interest groups, which included mandates reforming socioeconomic policies and the land use choices deriving from them.

Federal participation has taken three major forms. First, as with the states, the everyday operations of federal agencies impinge on the planning choices of cities and counties. In many metropolitan areas those agencies are major landowners, and where their military bases, office buildings, hospitals, and post offices have impact on their surroundings, local planners must attend to these relationships. Many localities have found abandoned military facilities both a challenge and opportunity for redevelopment. The federal officials involved may fail to cooperate, however, and even take initiatives contrary to local wishes.

Second, federal regulatory policies affect local land use choices. Section 404 of the Clean Water Act requires anyone who proposes to deposit materials into open waters or wetlands to obtain a permit from the Army Corps of Engineers. The Environmental Protection Agency (EPA) also may veto such a permit if it judges that filling would endanger water quality or wildlife and if there is a reasonable alternative to it. Local planners must consult detailed maps to discern whether a proposed development would encroach upon a waterway or corps-designated wetland, and must anticipate a federal denial with one of their own.

Federal regulations under the Americans With Disabilities Act of 1990 are also relevant to planners. Public buildings, parks, and other facilities must be accessible to persons in wheelchairs, and many parts of building codes have been rewritten to conform. When the Maryland Stadium Authority planned the Camden Yards baseball park in Baltimore, it consulted with disabled people and made the entire facility and concessions area accessible. Likewise, public transit operators must provide some kind of handicap-usable service within a half mile of their regular bus routes, at least until enough wheelchair-accessible buses are running [Minton 1992].

Third, the greatest impact of Washington has come by means of its hundreds of grant programs to state and local governments. Housing was an early target: the 1937 Housing Act was both a political response to the unemployment of the Depression and a humanitarian remedy to wretched slum living conditions. But it also bestowed financial power on planners and reformers who had sought housing reform since the turn of the century. The act required that local authorities using the grants tear down at least one substandard dwelling for each new unit of public housing constructed, clear testimony to Congress' concern for slum clearance.

The Housing Act of 1949 went further to declare that housing quality was to be a matter of national, not simply local, policy. Congress declared that the general welfare required a remedy for the serious housing shortage by replacing deteriorated dwellings with new and wholesome homes. Together with later amendments, it expanded grants for urban renewal, enabling cities to purchase blighted land, clear it, and sell it to private developers at below-market prices. But it stipulated that grants could be awarded only to cities with a comprehensive redevelopment plan. Because the early renewal efforts had actually reduced the number of modest-cost homes, Congress intended that more careful research and coordination would upgrade the capacities of local planners to meet pressing needs.

Federal highway aid has also exerted great influence on urban planning, in the location of the roads themselves and their many social and economic effects. The National Defense Highway Act of 1956 was the landmark, laying out the interstate highways for which Washington contributed 90% of the construction cost. What resulted was the the network of urban freeways that greatly accelerated suburban growth, destroyed or transformed many inner-city neighborhoods and central business districts, and cut the patronage of mass transit. Although the states actually designed and built the roads, they followed federal standards.

The 1960s witnessed the maturing of the civil rights movement as well as the inner-city violence spawned by the rising but frustrated expectations of African-Americans. In 1965 Congress established the Department of Housing and Urban Development after years of lobbying by urban interests, recognizing the pressing claims that cities had on federal policy and financial aid. The Demonstration Cities (soon renamed Model Cities) and Metropolitan Development Act of 1966 targeted federal funds for social services as well as physical redevelopment to specific neighborhoods judged to be in greatest need. One provision of this act was that residents of the areas served must be included in the planning for projects carried out there. This participation was not at first effective in most cities, but had longer-term consequences to be noted in chapter 4.

Congress shifted the emphasis again in 1974 with the Housing and Community Development Act. To promote "community development," broadly defined, it consolidated seven categorical grant programs into a block grant, giving local officials broader leeway to allocate funds to meet unique needs. These included urban renewal, housing rehabilitation, water and sewer facilities, parks, and human service projects. The act preserved requirements for locally generated plans and citizen participation in formulating them. A 1977 amendment added the Urban Development Action Grants, which aided economically depressed cities to support private developments that would otherwise not be undertaken.

The 1980s marked a gradual retreat from federal intervention in urban planning. Presidents Reagan and Bush asserted that businesses and nonprofit institutions were the dynamic forces of urban progress and should be relied upon to finance it as well. Federal funds for housing and community development were reduced, reflecting a more conservative and financially pressed mood in Congress as well. Private investment has filled the gap in some cities, particularly in the more prosperous Sunbelt, but not in such declining industrial centers as Detroit. The cutbacks continued into the mid-1990s under intense pressures to balance the federal budget.

To identify the net result of 60 years of federal endeavors for urban planning is difficult.

The effects have varied from one locality to another, depending on local economic conditions. The Watts neighborhood of Los Angeles and New York City's South Bronx are far different from Orlando and Phoenix, even though federal aid has benefited them all. Yet, we can discern certain impacts, if limited to the programs for physical development and land use.

First and most obvious, local planning activity increased greatly after 1954, and metropolitan planning was stepped up in the mid-1960s. These efforts encompassed a wide range of urban economic, social, and environmental problems. Planning teams were often composed of persons from a variety of specialties: social work, public health, economics, and ecology as well as the traditional planning-related disciplines. The flow of federal funds supporting research, citizen participation, and plan making directed the attention of urban political systems toward the many prospects for inner-city renewal, suburban growth control, infrastructure development, and human services that remain on their agendas today.

A second and more important effect was that the planning process became much more a matter of intergovernmental bargaining. As chapter 2 showed, early city planners held the ideal that their decisions should reflect a rational understanding of what was best for the community as a whole. They conceded that compromises would be necessary for action, but only among the political and social forces within each city. But now the planning bargains have national scope. This is partly due to the legislative origins of the programs. City officials and their private-sector allies joined to lobby Congress, and compromises had to be made and remade in writing the bills. Once passed, the laws were open to various interpretations, and individual cities and states sought to adapt the regulations to their local conditions. Often, local officials used political leverage to bend rules on spending grant funds.

On some issues, particularly highway locations, bitter struggles entangled federal and state highway officials, mayors and local planners, and civic and neighborhood organizations. For example, popular protests in New Orleans defeated a proposal for an interstate freeway that would have cut off the historic French Quarter from the Mississippi River [Baumbach & Borah 1981].

In a bargaining situation, being rational or virtuous is not enough. An official or agency must have sufficient power resources to prevail. The federal government did have the money to grant or loan as well as the authority to stipulate how the funds were to be used, but it was also under pressure from a network of financial, construction, and social interests to spend it to strengthen job- and wealth-producing enterprises. Local forces organized in the 1930s to influence Washington through the National League of Cities, United States Conference of Mayors, and associations of specialized offficials in such fields as planning, housing, redevelopment, transit, parks, and sewage treatment. These forces remain active today.

The bargains that these contestants struck were always open to revision. They returned to the table annually to review the outcomes of the previous agreements and make adjustments to reflect changed conditions and power alignments. The varied fortunes of the federal housing and highway programs summarized above typify this process. Each decision shaped a new situation to which subsequent agreements had to respond.

This is not to say that federal priorities necessarily conflicted with local objectives. In-deed, the urban political and economic interests' lobbying shaped those priorities to a great extent. Even so, the pathway of funds and rules to the city halls was complex and lined with innumerable forms and regulatory details. For the cities in greatest distress, the aid enabled them to do what they could not have done otherwise, but it made them more dependent on those dollars. As aid shrank in the 1980s and 1990s, even greater distress threatened where it could not be replaced.

The third impact is obvious in the physical shape and arrangement of metropolitan areas, although the federal programs usually reinforced trends that would have prevailed anyway. Mortgage guarantees enabled millions of households to buy homes, and most vacant land suitable for housing was on the urban fringes. The Federal Housing Authority and private lenders showed preference for suburban locations and white borrowers over central cities and persons of color. Washington financed freeways on which the new suburban residents could travel to their central-city jobs, and also aided residents of the entire metropolitan area to commute to fast-growing suburban factories and offices. Federal water-quality funds enabled the new municipalities and special districts to lay sewer pipes and build treatment plants to serve the newcomers.

Many city centers have also benefited from federal programs as well. The urban renewal schemes subsidized many homes, office buildings, and public facilities. Use of community development grants and tax-exempt bonds stimulated downtown rebuilding at an unprecedented rate in the 1960s and 1970s. The same urban freeways that enabled the suburbs to expand and disrupted many downtown areas also permit drivers to reach the central business districts of most cities in reasonable travel times. The centers of San

Francisco, Atlanta, Washington, and Chicago are also more accessible by new and expanded rapid transit systems that were largely financed with federal funds. Residential development has even come to some downtowns: more than 13,000 dwelling units were built in and close to Chicago's Loop from 1979 to 1986, many partially financed by federal aid.

Probably the least benefited (or most harmed) by national programs have been inner-city neighborhoods inhabited by the poor and persons of color. Large public housing projects and smaller scale rehabilitation programs have supplied mixed benefits, but for many cities the pace of deterioration has overwhelmed their limited public and private resources. In fact, the projects have concentrated the very poorest households in certain neighborhoods in an atmosphere of despair and crime, isolated from the job opportunities and good schools that better-off areas enjoy. Too, the exodus of employers to the suburbs, also enabled by federal programs, has deprived the poor of the jobs that were once within their reach.

A final impact of federal programs, though somewhat delayed, has been the rise of citizen and neighborhood organizations in many cities. The mandated participation in the Model Cities, Community Development Block Grant, and other programs disappointed many hopeful observers. In some cities the political leaders resisted any threat to their own supremacy, and in many places the disadvantaged residents lacked the skills and experience needed to take charge of their own planning. A study of such programs in Milwaukee and Baltimore found that they primarily served the goal of economic development and through that the political purposes of their mayors and other elected officials. Very little directly went to benefit low-income residents, who were not able to exert sufficient power [Wong & Peterson 1986]. But as time went on, the descendants of many of these committees came to grasp their opportunities and became effective participants in the planning process. Indeed, the federal mandates served to raise their awareness of their lack of power and of the tools they needed to remedy that lack. Their present activity is surveyed in chapter 4.

3.8 FEDERAL AND STATE COURTS AS PLANNING ARBITERS

The courts have been major actors in urban planning due to their role in settling disputes over the meaning and application of laws. Because land use regulation involves government interaction with private parties on a one-to-one basis, conflicts naturally arise over interpretations. If they cannot be settled by negotiation, the courts are the obvious recourse.

Most cases related to planning originate in state courts, because it is typically an interpretation of a state law, constitution, or local ordinance that is in contention. Each state has a network of city, county, or district courts that first try such cases, and most are settled there.

Occasionally, major policy questions are also resolved in the settling of individual cases. When the Southern Burlington County chapter of the National Association for the Advancement of Colored People sued Mount Laurel Township, New Jersey, for its zoning that discriminated against low-income households, it went first to the local trial court. After appeals, the final ruling was made by the New Jersey Supreme Court in 1975 and reinforced by a further decision in 1983 (*Southern Burlington County N.A.A.C.P. et al v. Township of Mount Laurel* and *Mount Laurel II*). (Section 7.4 further discusses this case and its surrounding issues.) While rulings by state supreme courts are not binding in other states, some have influenced legal arguments and decisions nationwide.

Some cases from state courts are appealed to the federal system and a select few are chosen by the U.S. Supreme Court for decision. This was the experience of the Dolan family of Tigard, Oregon, in the dispute in the fourth case in chapter 1. The Court does so only when there is a substantial federal question at stake; in this instance it was the "takings clause" of the Fifth and Fourteenth Amendments. When the high court refuses to consider an appeal, the last previous decision made stands as final.

A few disputes go directly to the federal courts on grounds that relate to federal law or the U.S. Constitution. When Renton, Washington required in 1981 that theaters showing sexually explicit films be located at least 1,000 feet from any home, church, park, or school, a theater owner sued the city in the federal district court in Seattle. He claimed that the ordinance violated his First Amendment right to freedom of speech and press. The U.S. Supreme Court took the appeal and the justices decided by a 7–2 vote that local governments may use their zoning laws to restrict location of adult-clientele theaters (*City of Renton v. Playtime Theatres*, 1986).

During the 20th century, substantial case law on planning has accumulated by means of federal and state court rulings. In general, local authorities have substantial powers to legislate land use controls within all relevant constitutional guarantees. Courts normally uphold municipal planning actions as long as they are consistent with their own laws and are not "arbitrary and capricious" when applied to individual situations. Attorneys who are skilled in land use law can have great impact on the outcome of such controversies,

and judges vary widely in the mindset with which they approach new issues.

This chapter has shown that governments' planning-related actions are always within a complex web of mutual influences. One reason for this is to keep each actor accountable; thus state authorities watch local, federal agencies keep an eye on states and localities, citizen groups watch all three, and the courts must settle suits against any of the parties. Whether the resulting complexity and delay that so often surrounds choices is a fair price for the accountability is open to debate.

This web of intergovernmental relations in planning is enveloped by the private sector, which add many more influences and means of access. It is often difficult to separate the choices of a unit of government from those of the private participants, so closely are they related. That sector, in the marketplace and "civil society," is the subject of the next chapter.

FOR REVIEW AND DISCUSSION

1. What factors affect the scope of conflict in planning issues? What criteria would you use to judge whether it is too wide or narrow in a given case?

2. In what ways is American local government fragmented among many decision makers? How does this fragmentation affect typical urban planning decisions?

3. What role do metropolitan agencies play in urban planning today? For what reasons is it so limited in most regions?

4. How do state and national governments participate in or influence local planning choices? Is this involvement excessive or insufficient, in your judgment?

5. For what reasons are judges and courts increasingly involved in planning decisions? How has that affected the overall power of planners and local officials?

4

The Web of Planning Participants

4.1 THE SPECTRUM OF STAKEHOLDERS

The planning enterprise belongs to every citizen, according to the logic of democracy. Thus the boundaries of government's authority are highly permeable when it makes decisions affecting people's lives, property, and sense of wellbeing. Schattschneider's observations on the scope of conflict cited at the opening of chapter 3 apply most of all to the nongovernmental participants whom this chapter surveys: who takes part, for what reasons, by what means, and with what effects.

A key question for identifying these contestants is, "Who are the *stakeholders* in a given planning choice?" This term implies ownership, but it is broader. Stakeholders are those affected by the choice in some identifiable way and so have a presumed right to be consulted on it, to petition for a certain outcome, and in general to have their concerns treated seriously. Those who build or rebuild, design, or finance that building are obvious stakeholders. Too, homeowners in a neighborhood scheduled for major rehabilitation have the right to be informed and heard, as do renters of homes in the area and operators of businesses. Those rights may extend to the residents of other parts of the city who shop or work there, or whose taxes and services may be affected by that program.

The circle of active stakeholders has a vague perimeter which can change over time. The larger the number of recognized stakeholders in a choice, the greater is the probability that conflict could occur over it and the smaller the amount of influence that an average person could exert. In many cases, stakeholders are self-selected. Some are habitually involved in issues that interest them, while others who have as much or more at stake pay little or no attention to them. Regardless of legal or ethical criteria for certifying stakeholders, the benefits of that status really flow to those who intervene deliberately in the choices that make the city what it becomes.

4.2 THE ECONOMIC DOMINANTS AND PROFIT SEEKERS

The use of land has high stakes. While the values described in chapter 2 have both tangible and intangible dimensions, their lowest common denominator often is money. The sheer volume of urban land values, current and potential, is one facet of this. Battery Park City, a 92-acre project on New York City's Hudson River shore, had a price tag exceeding $1.5 billion. Newark. New Jersey has the prospect of a $270 million educational, technological, and residential University Heights Science Park, planned by a public/private partnership. The stakes in such projects include not only the direct private and governmental expenditures, but also the dollars that change hands in the spillover business they generate in years to follow.

The most visible private participants are the land development professionals, including architects, construction firms, and real estate brokers. *Developer* is a broad term for the persons and companies who package a given project, from design and financing to government approvals and construction. Even a medium-sized commercial or residential undertaking requires land assembly and preparation, utility access, a funding package from one or more sources, and a host of regulatory approvals from several governments. The developer has a strong incentive to pass each waypoint as quickly as possible as the amount of investment grows. Since major firms operate nationwide or globally, much of a city's growth depends on choices by outsiders. Japanese, British, and Canadian companies are active in many American cities, which disturbs some observers, but they certainly supplement the resources that Americans can generate domestically.

Among the largest developers has been the Levitt Company, which produced its Levittowns in New York, New Jersey, and Pennsylvania in the 1940s and 1950s, as described in chapter 2. At the other end of the nation, the city of Irvine, California, embodies the dream of the Irvine Company. Its 120,000 residents occupy part of the ranch that the family has held in Orange County since 1876. Over the years it grew to include several planned residential clusters, commercial and industrial space, shopping malls, and a campus of the University of California. The company's current owner, Donald Bren, enjoys close contacts with public officials and contributes generously to Republican candidates [Sterngold 1995].

Perhaps the largest corporate developer in the nation is Opus U.S., based in Minnesota but with six regional operating subsidiaries that have considerable autonomy. In 1995, it had more than 8.3 million square feet under construction, concentrating on industrial, office, and retail facilities [Apgar 1996]. Like most such companies, it prefers to operate quietly, seeking public approvals with a minimum of popular attention—which could become opposition. Its success is due to its accurate perceptions of what the market demands and will pay for, yet its own choices do much to guide market trends and thus determine the success of local efforts at economic development.

Better known personally is the late James Rouse, whose firm, Enterprise Development Company, renewed such historic structures as Boston's Faneuil Hall and the Baltimore Harborplace and undertook smaller inner-city commercial projects around the country. Most of these have been public-private partnerships, demonstrating Rouse's skill in forming these linkages. The planned city of Columbia, Maryland, was also his creation. Collectively, these large developers take the initiatives that most strongly influence the shape of central cities and their suburbs, because they have the entrepreneurial skills and resources to make the partnerships work.

Thousands of medium-sized and small developers also make vital choices that shape the built environment. They may convert a potato farm in New Jersey into a 50-home subdivision or a California orange grove into a convenience shopping center. A single project may not be controversial or have great impact on the environment, but taken together, many such actions transform a suburban or rural community. While most developers oppose public regulations that limit urban sprawl, as the San Diego conflict demonstrated, others support them, perceiving lucrative opportunities in the limited space that is designated for development in fast-growing regions.

Attorneys who advise clients on land use issues and conduct litigation over them are essential participants. In complex developments, many governmental approvals are necessary, and much time may be required to assemble land parcels, clear titles, and settle lawsuits by opponents. In fact, developers now assume that litigation will be an integral part of the process, and prepare as thoroughly for it as for the actual construction. Many of these attorneys argue cases in which they have no personal stake other than their fee. But others are employed by developers and as such are members of their teams. Government agencies have their attorneys as well, who may be directly employed or in private practice on retainer. Yet another type of attorney is committed to certain planning values, perhaps environmental preservation or homes for low-income persons, and so plays an advocacy role in planning conflicts. The outcomes of lawsuits may hinge as much on the quality of the attorneys' preparation and argument as on the theoretical merits of the case, and a class of land-use law specialists has emerged to dominate this field [Dunlap 1996a & b].

Those who finance urban development constitute another pivotal class of participants. They include commercial banks, mortgage firms, insurance companies, private and governmental pension funds, and other institutions that make and manage real estate investments. For example, the Teachers Insurance and Annuity Association, a pension fund for persons in education and research, had $72 billion in assets at the end of 1994, most of it invested in some form of real estate. Directors of these institutions, by deciding whether and to what extent to finance a proposed project, can speed or slow developers' activity. In many cases, these financial institutions are direct partners in major projects, shaping their location and design. Seeking the best possible return on their investments, they judge proposals in the cold light of their prospects in a very competitive marketplace.

A sensitive social as well as economic issue is that lenders have historically refused to invest in neighborhoods they deemed to be of high risk—a practice called *redlining*. This has had the effect of preventing areas in danger of decline, often inhabited by low-income persons and those of color, from reversing that trend. It has been reduced in the past decade due to the federal Community Reinvestment Act of 1977 and political pressures behind it, although banks' concerns to keep a "healthy" loan portfolio remains a hindrance. By contrast, a lender may *greenline* an area, targeting it for loans to stimulate renewal. The South Shore Bank of Chicago and its parent Shorebank Corporation had, by 1996, financed renovation of 17,000 homes in the city, mostly for low-income working households, plus neighborhood shopping facilities (an ex-

Figure 4.1 Jeffery Plaza, a shopping center in Chicago's South Shore neighborhood that was financed by the South Shore Bank. Photo by Sylvia Lewis.

ample is Jeffery Plaza in Figure 4.1). With its assets of $270 million, it has been a model for similar efforts in Cleveland, Detroit, and other cities to finance developments that would not otherwise attract lenders. The pace of greenlining has accelerated in many cities; in 1996, several major banks invested in the National Association of Community Development Loan Funds, a nonprofit lender to small enterprises that draws capital from foundations as well.

Land speculators, who may also be any of the above persons, are another source of plan-ning influence. Foreseeing abundant profits as suburban areas expand, they purchase land in the path of growth and hold it until demand rises to a desired level. At that point, they request a rezoning to the use they expect to yield the highest price. They also exert pressure for the routing of roads, sewers, and other services that will enhance the value of the parcels. In some places, they have spurred development of land that would probably best have been left open or used in another manner.

Beyond these are businesses of all kinds that participate as current or prospective landowners, tenants, and users of related facilities. If they are large (relative to the size of the community), the sheer size of their buildings, employment, and tax payments give them major influence. They can thus se-cure the zoning changes, utilities, street im-provements, and other benefits that enhance their investments. The Dolan hardware busi-ness expected to have no trouble winning ap-proval of its expansion in Tigard until local officials raised the environmental require-ments that sparked the lawsuit.

A large corporation can also block projects it finds detrimental to its interests: Northwest Airlines consistently opposed construction of a new Minneapolis-St. Paul airport. As the present facility's largest user by far, it would bear most of the cost of a new one. Since large corporations operate facilities in many cities, their headquarters, located perhaps in New York, London, or Tokyo, makes decisions af-fecting the success and failure of plans in other cities. The political processes of those cities have little or no influence in the corpo-rations' boardrooms.

By choices to maintain their existing prop-erties or allow them to deteriorate, such busi-nesses shape and limit the planning options of a community. A major retailer on a shopping street can strengthen an entire district by investing in improvements. But by neglecting or even abandoning the property, it can turn away customers and affect neighboring merchants. Landlords of modest-rent apartments in areas with high land costs have a strong incentive to replace those buildings with more profitable structures and so compound the loss of homes for lower income persons in central cities.

Planning politics also attracts trade and professional associations that represent collective business interests. Their policy concerns are usually broader than specific site choices. Chambers of commerce (and similar groups by other names) are located in nearly every city, along with separate groupings of downtown and neighborhood businesses. Just about every skill and specialty related to the planning process, from architects to parking ramp operators, has an association that speaks for it. For example, the first impetus for the construction of the Bay Area Rapid Transit System that links San Francisco with its eastern neighbors came from the Bay Area Council, an alliance of leading corporations based in that city's downtown. Its key aim was to maintain property values in that district by improving its access by suburban commuters [Whitt 1982, pp. 42–44].

Finally, the news and information media play several roles in planning choices. First, by choosing to publicize (or not) a given issue, a local newspaper or television station can define it in the public mind and influence the size of the conflict over it. Nationally, the television networks and newsmagazines decide which events and conditions in one city to publicize elsewhere. With their propensity to portray distress, crime, and violence, they can lead the public to view all large cities as dens of iniquity and unworthy of public spending.

Playing another role, home-owned media enterprises that depend on local advertising and thus on the economic health of their area usually back the development initiatives of the business community. Indeed, a media company may be an entrepreneur itself. The Minneapolis Star and Tribune Company was a vigorous advocate for the Hubert H. Humphrey Metrodome on its present site in that city's downtown. It was also the largest investor in a consortium which secured exclusive development rights in a 50-block area surrounding the stadium site [Klobuchar 1982].

4.3 THE INSTITUTIONAL PARTICIPANTS

A cluster of groups that do not provide direct profits to their members also participate in planning choices. First, labor unions may choose to back or oppose certain projects. In such cities as New York, Chicago, and Detroit, labor leaders are active in many public decisions. In most cases, their prime interest is job creation for members, and a megaproject like that first proposed for Times Square would have kept building-trades workers busy for years. Thus they have an affinity with developers and business interests for new construction and rehabilitation. Unions also have good reason to present a united front with business to convince prospective employers that their city has an attractive labor market. Nevertheless, unions' influence on these matters is probably weakening in proportion to their steady membership decline.

On the other hand, charitable foundations and not-for-profit social service organizations have a growing role in planning. Since some kinds of construction, particularly modest-cost housing, small business stimulation, and restoration of historic structures, offer little if any profit, their sponsors cannot rely on most sources of financing. The Ford Foundation has bankrolled countless local developments over the years, either directly or though intermediary channels. Sometimes a profitmaking developer spins off a foundation to support socially worthy goals. James Rouse created the Enterprise Foundation in 1981 to provide loans and grants to neighborhood housing improvement groups in many cities. Its treasury, nourished by his company's profits and gifts from other sources, has dispensed loans and grants to neighborhood housing groups in many cities. The foundation's impact on planning lies in its ability to help cities fulfill renewal plans for which public funds are lacking. Locally-based foundations have also proliferated to support civic projects.

Church congregations and other religious groups are also present in planning politics, although less consistently. They may lobby on social and moral issues that touch land use choices. One congregation may advocate that the city close down an adults-only theater in its vicinity, while another protests lack of action to house homeless persons. Churches have long had the power in many communities, formally or informally, to veto the grant of liquor licenses within a certain distance of their property. As major owners of land free of property taxation, their choices of how to use it also enter into local plans. A growing congregation that seeks to buy adjacent homes for building expansion can run into opposition from neighbors who view it as a threat to their residential environment.

Some members of the clergy have mobilized their churches as developers. The Allen African Methodist Episcopal Church is a vigorous entrepreneur in its neighborhood in New York City's borough of Queens. It has sponsored a school, a shopping center, and housing for families and seniors, claiming to have provided some $25 million in develop-

ment all told. The church has a unique political resource, to be sure: its pastor, Rev. Floyd Flake, also represents that district in the U.S. House of Representatives, and it thus enjoys a direct pipeline from federal aid channels [Sengupta 1995].

Church alliances have also been instrumental in both pressuring for planning decisions and sponsoring developments themselves. South Bronx Churches brought together Catholic, Lutheran, and other congregations to spearhead renewal projects in that highly depressed area and exert influence on city plans and proposals by other developers. A substantial stock of affordable housing is one result of their efforts [Rooney 1995]. Its leaders were able to gain influence with city officials beyond what individual clergy and parishioners would have attained.

4.4 CITIZEN PARTICIPATION IN PLANNING

This large and varied category encompasses those who do not fit into the two preceding categories. We can define a *citizen* as a person, not holding an official public role, whose aims are rooted in relatively individualistic interests or those of the social community with which he or she identifies. The interest may be financial, as when a resident seeks to protect the value of a home from the degrading effect of a nearby waste disposal site. It could also be ideological (e.g. to prevent government control of a person's land use choice), esthetic (to protect a woodland or historic structure) or social (exclusion of a housing project likely to place "different" people next door). Certainly they need not be altruistic; vigilant homeowners can be as selfish as huge developers in their own realms. The difference is thus more a matter of scale and power than commitment.

Citizen involvement also may be more

emotionally intense than that by corporate participants. Imagine a city council meeting in which a developer seeks approval of a supermarket next to a neighborhood of single family homes. The attorney, architect, and engineer representing the developer present competent but dispassionate evidence for the project, displaying professionally drawn maps and sketches. Then the adjacent residents stand up, one after another, to claim that the store will reduce their property values, flood their backyards, increase their traffic, and endanger their children. Unless they are unusually well prepared, they will present few hard facts. Yet, they argue with a passion that draws the sympathies, if not always the support, of council members who realize that the protestors are also voters. Planning politics can thus be more volatile when emotions are engaged in the choices that have to be made and the scope of conflict is easily expandable.

Local governments have paid increasing attention to enabling and stimulating citizen participation in planning choices. After the federally mandated committees and processes of the 1960s and 1970s (traced briefly in chapter 3), self-generated citizen activism grew in many cities. Local officials responded with a variety of legal mechanisms to draw their views into the decisions. Scavo [1993] identifies four categories of participative mechanisms: (a) making government proceedings more accessible to citizens, (b) obtaining the views of residents on city policies and services, (c) empowering neighborhood groups to contribute to decision making, and (d) involving citizens in producing public services as volunteers. A quantitative assessment of the use of these means ranked the cities of St. Paul, Honolulu, and Columbus, Ohio, at the top.

An example of neighborhood empowerment is found in Scavo's highest-ranked city. In 1975, the St. Paul city council established a network of 17 district councils, with members elected periodically by residents. Each was assigned a city employee to provide planning and administrative expertise. The councils receive notification of all development applications for their respective areas and have the opportunity to support or oppose them before the planning commission and city council. They can also generate proposals for capital spending in the neighborhood [Berry, Portney & Thompson 1993, ch. 3]. Over the years, some councils have been highly active while others are largely dormant, depending on their leadership at the time and the nature of pending issues. Yet, most officials believe the network to be useful and pay attention to well-founded district positions.

Voluntary citizen organizations are diverse as the interests that are affected by planning. First, there are many broad-based associations at the city or metropolitan level concerned with the overall quality of governance. Some were instrumental in putting planning on the city's agenda more than a hundred years ago. Societies supporting parks, beautification, and urban order in general appeared in Philadelphia, Baltimore, and San Francisco among many others. Often made up of influential citizens, they saw many of their aims realized [Scott 1969, ch. 2]. Later groups advocated metropolitan-area planning in New York, Los Angeles, and Minneapolis-St. Paul, though with less success. A recent example is the San Diego chapter of the Sierra Club, which spurred the growth-control efforts in the 1970s described in chapter 1. Ordinarily concerned with wilderness protection, this group adapted well to its urban setting.

Other organizations have more specific constituencies, such as an ethnic group. For example, Communities Organized for Public Service (COPS) was formed in San Antonio in 1974 to speak for the many Mexican-American residents. Its first objective was to demand better public services for its members' neighborhoods and to mobilize their voting strength on the city council. In the process, it also worked to halt a major development on the "Anglo" north side, fearing both pollution of the municipal water supply and a further diversion of the city's resources toward that more affluent area [Babcock & Siemon 1985, ch. 5].

Civic associations are influential in many communities and regions. Leagues of Women Voters are found across the country and frequently address planning-related issues. While they are nonpartisan and avoid endorsing candidates for office, they provide information on controversies that members can use in their personal activity. Another typical organization is the "citizens league" that draws in business, professional, and other influential persons to study and recommend public policies. Minneapolis-St. Paul's Citizens League has functioned for three decades to shape choices in such matters of transit, downtown renewal, highways, development finance, and housing; its example has inspired many copies.

New citizen organizations may appear with stimuli from local government agencies. VISION 2020 in metropolitan Atlanta mobilizes a broad base of citizens for renewal on a wide front. Many citizens became involved in ten Initiating Committees and the Community Collaboratives charged with creating action plans. As of 1995, it had apparently produced a major change in that region's decision-making style. A similar effort was organized in the Oklahoma City urban region, responding to popular desires to expand community networks and enable

people to discuss common issues before they become active [West & Taylor 1995].

Because planning choices always have very localized impacts, we must also understand the role of neighborhood organizations and influences. The term *neighborhood* has many definitions, depending on how people recognize boundaries to their valued environments. For some, it is the immediate block or street on which they live. For others, it is their relationship with a particular institution, perhaps a public school, church parish, or park. Still others are designated by local government as service areas or planning regions as in St. Paul.

Much organization at the neighborhood level responds to a perceived threat, whether physical deterioration, crime, or an event such as a redevelopment proposal or highway routing. It is not unusual for even small-scale planning decisions to mobilize neighbors if it is publicized sufficiently. A large developer began to level and rebuild an old residential area next to the University of Minnesota campus in Minneapolis with the city officials' blessing, envisioning a "new town in town." But residents of the remainder of the area, many of them students, organized in its defense and successfully used several legal tools to halt further demolition. The Cedar-Riverside neighborhood remains today, partially rehabilitated, as a monument to their efforts [Stoecker 1994]. Many other groups, however, have had only a negative agenda, opposing a potential change without any positive counterproposal.

Urban territorial units are natural bases for political organization, judging from research on neighborhood associations in Baltimore. "If physical force is regarded as the hidden engine that drives political systems, physical space is seen as the traditional and singular medium in which this energy source achieves tangible expression." [Crenson 1983, p. 15] That people have to live and do business in close proximity creates political concerns that set up both cooperation and conflict. These concerns may be either internal to the area or linked with citywide, state, and national issues. Thus, Crenson asserted [1983, p. 17], "the residents of a neighborhood do not constitute a private group at all, but a miniature 'public'—more like citizens than like members of a private association."

One highly active citizen organization is the Dudley Street Neighborhood Initiative in the Roxbury area of Boston. It originated in 1984 with the help of a local foundation, and gradually drew in residents who were angry at the city's failure to maintain public services and attend to abandoned buildings and lots. About a third of its 24,000 residents, mostly of color, live below the poverty line. It was unusually successful in developing indigenous leaders and creative thinkers, and produced extensive plans for new homes, recreational facilities, schools, and job development, which have largely been adopted by city officials. Leaders aggressively secured grants from other sources, including the Ford Foundation and city and state agencies [Medoff & Sklar 1994]. Such resourcefulness is essential for the success of any ambitious community group.

A neighborhood organization is often most effective in the long run when formalized as a community development corporation (CDC). A CDC is a nonprofit entity that can receive grants and loans from various sources and invest them in housing, business, job training, and other community improvement projects. It may also mobilize community members' labors as "sweat equity." Some CDCs have profit-making subsidiaries that function as entrepreneurs in their own right. Many of these

are descendants of neighborhood associations or protest groups of the 1960s that determined that empowerment is better obtained through control of the economic resources within their communities rather than through advocacy tactics. . . . . . Community-based development enables the deprived to control material assets and allows the poor to gain respect and dignity as players in the economic and housing field." [Rubin 1995, p. 129]

As of 1995, there were some 2,200 such organizations in all 50 states. They had developed nearly 450,000 dwellings and 23 million square feet of commercial and industrial facilities and created 67,000 permanent jobs [Stanfield 1995]. A vital funding source for many of them is the Local Initiatives Support Corporation, a nonprofit private agency that taps corporations, foundations, and public agencies. The commission chooses local projects for partial support and advises the CDCs on how to raise the remainder and spend it effectively. As of 1994, it had distributed more than $1.3 billion to CDCs. [Holmstrom 1994].

CDCs can take many faces, depending on their leaders and the needs of the neighborhood. One of the largest is the New Community Corporation, organized in 1968 in Newark, New Jersey by Msgr. William Linder, whose parish served the city's poorest area (see Figure 4.2). By 1994, it owned and managed 2,500 low-income housing units, a nursing home, a credit union, a community newspaper, and a shopping center. To be sure, such growth has not been without problems, such as disagreements over specific developments and prickly relations with city officials. Even so, it has been a model for many similar efforts [S. Lewis 1993].

This category of citizen participation also includes the political parties, candidates for office, and campaign organizations that pro-

Figure 4.2 Msgr. William Linder in front of a converted church that houses the offices of Newark's New Community Corporation. Photo by Sylvia Lewis.

duce elected officials for all levels of government. Elections for most local posts are legally nonpartisan, but groups of all sorts are free to take part with endorsements and campaign help. They can influence planning choices when such a controversy becomes an issue in a given election. For example, pro- and anti-development movements may contend for election of local officials, particularly in cities and counties that face rapid growth.

The San Diego case in chapter 1 illustrates another type of voter involvement: direct policy making through the initiative and the referendum. The initiative is a process of enacting new law by ballot: it takes place in two stages in those states and localities which permit it. The first step requires circulation of a petition that contains the text of the proposed law. If the petition obtains the signatures of a set percentage of the state's or city's registered voters (typically 5 to10 percent), it is formally presented to the legislative body. Should the latter not act in a certain period of time, the question goes on the ballot at the next general election and a simple majority of those voting can enact it. Such an initiative may be used to rezone a specific parcel of land or to amend the city charter or state constitution with a general provision. San Diegans made a major long-range planning choice in their first initiative vote in 1985 [Caves 1992].

The referendum is a different sort of action

and comes in two forms. One is a repeal of a law already enacted by a legislature or council. This takes place in much the same manner as the initiative, beginning with a petition, and it too is permitted in only a minority of states and localities. The second form of referendum, a requirement that voters approve borrowing of funds through general obligation bonds, is much more widely used. A city council or school board, for example, may plan street improvements, a park, or a new school building and choose to finance it through long-term bonds. While the voters by law pass judgment on the increase in the public debt, they also rule on the particular project, and its apparent justification or lack of it usually drives their vote.

In these displays of voter power, any of the groups already discussed in this chapter can play vital roles. They might take the lead in defining the issues to be brought before the public and draft a legally valid statute in the case of an initiative. Further, they can circulate the petitions and publicize them. If an election is called, they mount a campaign pro or con, and in larger cities may spend major sums of money on media advertising, mailings, and billboards. The San Diego growth vote campaigns pitted the ample resources of the development professionals against the environmentalists' numbers and organization.

Individual citizens, not organized in the ways already described, play more sporadic roles in planning politics. They can speak at hearings, sign petitions, write letters, and discuss issues with neighbors, but unless they cross the line into leadership or add to the numbers of a group, they seldom have effect. To file a lawsuit takes only one person, of course, and can be a route to victory, but even these are typically shared efforts. Yet, because these individual citizens are always potential political actors, even just as voters, prudent

decision makers are sensitive to their concerns.

Citizen participation in all of the above forms has been repeatedly defended as a counterweight to the biases of the business interests, a democratic expression of "the people" as opposed to the rich and the self-seeking. But in speaking of government by the people, one must always ask, "Which people?" Several questions are wrapped in this one.

First, one must ask how representative the particular citizen group is of those for whom it claims to speak. Many studies have shown that those who take part in planning efforts are typically of middle to upper income, above-average education, and in business or professional occupations, along with home owners and long-time residents. There are proportionally fewer women, members of minority racial and ethnic groups, and persons under the age of 30 or over 65. The willingness to participate and the capacity to do it effectively depend on personal skills that are cultivated by, and lead to success in, higher education and higher-status occupations. Citizens who lack these qualities tend to believe they can have no influence and so do not even try. Knowing this, officials who seek the sense of the public on planning choices must be alert to the views of those who are absent.

A second problem contrasts with the first: many and conflicting citizen voices on an issue. This can happen when several organizations represent one neighborhood, as in the Uptown district on Chicago's North Side. As of 1979, four larger groups plus a host of block clubs sought to influence city policy in that diverse and rapidly changing area [Warren 1979]. That can be an advantage if they actually represent all of the perspectives that such a neighborhood contains. However, when citizen opinion is deeply divided, city officials may have a freer hand to make decisions by criteria of their own choosing.

Questions also arise over the long-term effects of citizen participation. The short-range and self-serving demands of community groups and individual landowners may conflict with the needs of the larger community. When the choice is to locate a needed facility such as a waste management operation or a halfway house for criminal offenders, the NIMBY (Not In My Back Yard) response will block any action if citizen opinion is the only determinant. Planners and others who try to provide for collective benefits farther into the future will be frustrated by this. Some cities and private foundations have sought to raise the level of citizen expertise with education programs and through close liaison between neighborhood groups and planning staffs, as St. Paul has done.

These concerns are not limited to citizen activism, of course. Participation by developers and other businesses is also self serving. When the conflict over a particular issue widens, often the best that one can hope for is a balanced debate in which every possible viewpoint is pressed by someone. The public decision makers thus gain the information they need for a responsible choice.

4.5 COALITIONS AND REGIMES IN PLANNING

An undertone running through chapters 3 and 4 has been *power*. This is the key currency of politics and the means to secure one's goals in a contested situation. Each governmental and private participant deserves attention to the extent that he, she, or it has influence over planning choices (or perhaps *should* have influence). Thus, to exert power is to secure an action or outcome in a contest that would not otherwise result.

But planning politics is not a simple two-person game, as should already be obvious. It takes place amid both cooperation and conflict, as allies and opponents enter and leave the contest and change sides. For this reason, it is necessary to examine power *structures,* which are the consistent relationships among persons and institutions that determine outcomes. Jones [1983, p. 176] defined a power structure as "the regularized exercise of power within a social system [which] takes place repeatedly over time. . . . . and involves a set of regularly interacting individuals." So informed, one might explain why major developers regularly secure approval for their projects in most cities, and yet why the original Times Square design had to be modified. A grasp of the "power map" of an urban area is necessary to foresee with any confidence how the area will develop in future years.

There are at least four distinct ways to measure how much power a given participant has and why. First, power can exist in the ability to define a problem and determine whether it merits public attention. The reformers in turn-of-the century American cities perceived the wretched conditions in which the poor lived, as did the conservative wealthy, when they cared to look. But was it a problem? and for whom? Those who defined slums as a natural and inevitable fact of city life, not to be tampered with by government, used their power to exclude housing quality from public policy debates. When the reformers were elected to office and gained popular attention, they obtained the power to redefine slums as a public problem, a necessary step toward action on them. Thus, to be able to add issues to, or exclude them from, the public agenda, is an exercise of power [Bachrach & Baratz 1963].

A second way of viewing power is as the ability to act in a future conflict. This "potential power" exists behind the day-to-day control of money, credit, jobs, land, and information. It is like a lake behind a hydroelectric dam: the water is there but not presently used to generate current. Hunter [1953] concluded from his research in Atlanta that a "law of anticipated reactions" is at work in public decisions. For example, because a person in the community has a great deal of money or is a major employer, others will seek to fit their plans and actions to his because they expect him to use his resources to turn a conflict to his favor. Similarly, a mayor with a veto power over ordinances and budgets has potential power that she can use in an upcoming battle over downtown renewal. Since planning is inherently a future-focused process, these anticipations often determine reality.

A third kind of power becomes obvious in open conflict situations. There, it is the quality of relationships that confers power. Bachrach & Baratz [1963, p. 635] state that it exists when "(a) there is a conflict over values or a course of action between A and B; (b) B complies with A's wishes; and (c) he does so because he is fearful that A will deprive him of a value or values which he, B, regards more highly than those which would have been achieved by noncompliance." This can happen when a city council balks at subsidizing a new plant for a local industry. But when the company announces that if it does not get the aid it will close the plant and move out of state, it poses an unacceptable deprivation to the city—loss of jobs and tax base. The council yields to this show of power.

The fourth view of power looks to the outcomes of political conflicts over time, to see who "won." Planning distributes home and business locations, means of mobility, access to parks, employment opportunities, and many other benefits. The "powerful" are those who consistently gain advantages at the expense of others. Employers of office and manufacturing workers increasingly prefer suburban locations near airports, freeways, and high-amenity residential areas. But the employees themselves often cannot afford to live nearby and are confined to less desirable central-city locations and a long trip with no public transportation. Such a long-term distribution reveals who really has power, according to this perspective.

After identifying the individuals and groups that have power in planning choices, one must examine the consistent ways in which they interact. The power structures one finds in a given city, county, or metropolitan area can vary in size and diversity. However, two features are common to nearly all of them. First, decisions are normally made by a few persons. Even when many groups and public opinion exert strong influence, or the voters have spoken by their ballots, the situation has previously been defined and the alternatives framed by those active up to that point. This does not, in itself, specify who were involved or which interests they represented.

Second, the circle of players who are cooperating and contending expands and contracts with time. The scope of conflict can shrink as well as grow and it makes much difference who remains in the arena when crucial choices are made. The alignments of power often change as a decision moves through the stages of proposal, enactment, and implementation. Time is a crucial element of power wielding, creating opportunities for those who realize the right moment to intervene. Few circles are entirely closed, but those who want to be powerful resist sharing power with those who would question or disrupt their intentions.

For these reasons, power in complex planning situations is best understood in a *coalitional* perspective. Wirt [1974, pp. 5–6], introducing his research on San Francisco, defined the city as a complex set of transactions between persons and groups for both material and symbolic goods that they value. They can include homes, jobs, development opportunities, or a pleasant mountain view. The boundaries of this "market" extend far beyond the city limits; transactions made by governments and private parties in Washington, New York, and Tokyo determine who gets how much of which goods. To make these exchanges, coalitions are constantly formed and re-formed, creating new allies and adversaries.

Coalitional politics interweaves cooperation and conflict. People may join in agreement on a downtown renewal program but oppose one another on a highway project. Some groups, such as downtown business interests and bankers, are frequent allies, while neighborhood associations seldom make common cause with them. The fragmentation in both private interests and governmental authorities that this chapter and the previous one describe makes these coalitions necessary, since no one participant has the means to undertake a major development by itself. But this condition renders these coalitions unstable from one issue to the next. The politics of planning centers on the task of creating and maintaining agreements among groups and leaders who may stand to gain from cooperation.

Wirt [1974, pp. 47–48] offered a typology of power structures based on diverse coalition forms. At one end of a spectrum (from those with the most concentrated power to the least) is the *stable dominant group* that consistently decides all issues of importance to it. This approximates the elitist power structure that Hunter [1953] perceived in Atlanta. One step over is the *dominant constellation*, composed of two or more clusters of interest that

tend to prevail over all others in a context. The alliance of major business and labor organizations that seek economic development in a depressed area is a structure of this type and has prevailed in industrial cities like Detroit.

A much looser form is the *occasional coalition:* an alliance that prevails in policy choices more often than not, but does not win often enough to dominate the process. At the far end of the spectrum is the *temporary coalition* which lacks the cohesion to exert power on more than one issue. These coalitions may well specialize by issue; one that takes interest in highways will probably not have time to address housing problems also.

Coalitions have no specific geographic or political boundaries. Minnesota's airport controversy has spilled across the state, due to the users who live outside of the metropolitan area. The property rights coalition is nationwide, since situations like the Dolans' arise in many communities and the arenas of action include Congress and the federal courts. Much depends on the breadth of the given choice, as suggested in chapter 1. Comprehensive goal setting, when it engenders conflict, may call in one or more broad coalitions that clash over basic values, as in the San Diego growth choices.

The *urban regime* concept helps characterize how the major participants relate to one another. Stone [1989, pp. 6–9] began his study of Atlanta politics and development choices by seeking out "who cooperates and how their cooperation is achieved across institutional sectors of community life." He defined such a regime as "the informal arrangements by which public bodies and private interests function together in order to be able to make and carry out governing decisions." Regimes have power in that they can focus the community's resources on achieving change, since they have the power to attain future objectives. The relationships within each regime are generally informal but over a period of time become habitual due to shared stakes and regular communication. The redevelopment plans for Times Square evolved from the negotiations within New York City's regime, as each participant discerned what was desirable and feasible.

The private-sector regime members whom Stone identified were most often of Atlanta's business and professional elite, and this is typical of communities of all sizes. However, a second concept is useful to denote a broader pattern of popular participation: the *civic infrastructure*. This comprises the networks of "formal and informal lines of communication among stakeholders from different sectors," [Wallis 1993, p. 132] the means by which citizens at all levels of power can participate. It is less distinct than the regime since the range of interests tends to be broader and the stakeholders do not communicate among each other as regularly. Yet, the growth control movement in San Diego owes much of its power to a coalition of concerned citizens.

These participants in the regimes and the civic infrastructures draw on a repertoire of eight major tactics for exerting influence [Sayre & Kaufman 1965, pp. 482–496]. Most visibly, they express their views on planning decisions in *public hearings* before city councils and other lawmaking bodies, planning commissions and similar advisory groups, state legislatures, and administrative agencies such as natural resources departments. This tactic is most relied upon by persons who lack access by other means. If these expressions are not augmented by other forms of political action, they probably have little effect.

Second, extensive *informal consultation* with public officials is the special province of "in-siders," those who enjoy close and influential connections. An understanding between a land developer and a planner reached over coffee may not become a final decision, but at least sets the context for it. Because it takes place away from public view, it is more conducive to complex negotiations that can turn confrontation into agreement.

Third, organized *interest groups* provide advice and views to policy makers from their particular vantage points. This can take place when an ethnic group makes a formal response to a neighborhood improvement plan or a city's chamber of commerce proposes a plan for industrial redevelopment. Large cities have a network of groups representing environmentalists, people with disabilities, transit riders, and homeless persons, among many others. Such organizations may also do research and propose solutions to problems, augmenting the limited resources of most governmental planners.

A fourth tactic is to intervene in *electoral politics*. Pro- or anti-development interests have occasionally promoted the election of mayors and legislators sympathetic to them. Individuals and groups can endorse candidates and contribute campaign funds, though they must be careful that voters do not perceive them as buying favors thereby. As the San Diego case showed, planning interests can have a direct impact on policy by petitioning for ballot initiatives and campaigning for them where state laws permit [Caves 1992].

Filing a lawsuit on a planning conflict is the fifth tactic. This is increasingly common and used not only by businesses (as in the Dolan case surveyed in chapter 1) but also by a variety of interest groups and concerned residents. The aim is often to establish or overturn a general legal principle as well as to win a favorable judgment on the immediate case.

Interest groups often give legal and financial aid to the litigators when the outcome will affect their broader concerns.

The sixth method, *arousal of public opinion*, fits a situation when a decision with potentially broad public effect is about to be made quietly. An opposition group, fearing defeat, takes seriously Schattschneider's observations on the scope of conflict and calls to the sidelines for new contestants to enter the game. It can use the news media, mass demonstrations, boycotts, petitions, and door-to-door canvassing to recruit support. The San Diego growth control interests used these means quite effectively for a time, though they found that the public may not stay aroused indefinitely.

The seventh tactic, *forming coalitions* among interest groups for mutual support, also broadens the conflict. Several neighborhood organizations may ally by agreeing to back each other's causes and thus multiply their influence. In the Minnesota airport case, business-related groups presented a joint argument that the region's economic future depended on a larger facility (though they ultimately failed to convince the government policy makers of this). Most such alliances are temporary, lasting only as long as the threat or opportunity exists.

The final form of involvement is *active implementation*, which occurs as plans are taken off the drawing board and put into effect. Developers and their associates accomplish this in their financing and construction actions, while homeowners who choose to participate in a rehabilitation program are crucial to its success. The plans for Times Square depend on the investment choices of several large corporations, including Walt Disney.

These intricate patterns of power and participation reappear in chapters 6 through 10 that focus on specific issues and politics—economic development, housing, transportation, environmental protection, and the cultural landscape. At this point, the foundation has been laid for examination of the planning process itself. Its practitioners have evolved many tools and procedures for making their choices, which are the focus of Chapter 5.

FOR REVIEW AND DISCUSSION

1. What stakeholders could you identify in the four cases cited in chapter 1? Why is it often difficult to draw a clear boundary line around them?

2. What professional specialties must developers draw on to plan and execute major projects? Why have these projects often been costly and time-consuming, and sometimes unsuccessful?

3. How do you distinguish "citizen" participants in planning from the other groups? What factors often hinder or discourage them from taking part in planning choices affecting their homes, neighborhoods, and livelihoods?

4. What are the bases of success of many community development corporations? What political and technical skills and resources do these CDCs need to accomplish their goals?

5. In what formal ways can voters affect planning politics through the ballot box? How effective is this voting as a means of influence?

6. Why is so much of urban politics carried on through coalitions? What skills and resources does a coalition need to be effective?

7. What is an urban regime? Which persons and organizations are likely to compose it in a community with which you are familiar?

5

Planners at Work

5.1 PROFESSIONAL STANDARDS AND TRADITIONS

Urban planning as a profession came of age early in the 20th century. To be sure, its pioneers such as L'Enfant had grand visions, but the everyday choices that shaped cities displayed little of what we today regard as rational and orderly. To gain this professional status, planners sought a body of facts on how the city was arranged, accepted goals for its future, and methods of selecting the most efficient and effective means to build that future. Indeed, a generic definition of planning is "the use of reason and understanding to reduce collective uncertainty about the future." [Hoch, 1994, p. 15] And by most standards, it has come a long way in that direction. While lacking the "hard" science of engineering and medicine, its practitioners do employ accepted techniques that give them considerable influence in many situations.

This profession has a moral as well as technical dimension. "Most professional planners undertake their work as a moral journey—a vocation rather than an occupation." Just as practitioners of medicine must often try to remedy the effects of unwise living, planners

target "the social and public problems generated by the pursuit of private plans." [Hoch 1994, pp. 13–14] But this goal can put them in conflict with many of those private plans, as when a developer wants to replace a suburban woodland with a "big box" discount store. Planners with an inner commitment to protect open space could easily take an emotional as well as rational stance on such issues.

Other observers of planning emphasize the professional duty to persons who have little or no representation in a land use controversy. *Advocacy planning* is taking the interests and needs of the disadvantaged as the planners' own. For example, when a redevelopment proposal would remove many units of low-cost housing from the edge of a downtown area, such an advocate will work to protect those units or replace them elsewhere. Wherever possible, they would encourage the disadvantaged to speak for themselves and seek to amplify their voices. This concern may be difficult to practice when the long-range interests of disadvantaged groups are not clear, or when one such group directly opposes the claims of another.

The planners referred to in this chapter

consist of two groups. First, many are employed by units of government. They consist of the professionals described in chapter 3 with credentials in planning, engineering, urban design, environmental quality, redevelopment, and related fields. They work not only in local government but in state and federal agencies for transportation, housing, natural resources, and others that impact the uses of urban land. Their mandate is to serve the public interest as defined by the laws and regulations of their agency and unit of government.

Planners also work in the private sector. Some are with development and construction firms and so serve the specific purposes of the employer. Others are with consulting firms that are retained either by governments or private companies for limited services, similar to attorneys who serve various clients. Still others are in nonprofit organizations such as Nature Conservancy that make autonomous land use choices. Faculty members and researchers in academic institutions contribute to the profession through teaching and analysis. It is common for persons to move between these in developing their professional careers.

Diverse competencies in planning spread across all types of employers. Generalists, usually serving local governments, address the broad issues in comprehensive planning, zoning, and land use controls. A day's duties may range from reviewing a shopping center proposal to a variance request for an extra large garage to drafting an ordinance on the size of dog kennels. Working with them are professionals who specialize in one segment of planning: multifamily housing developments, traffic control and road design, industrial parks, waste management, or urban forestry, for example. Major plans are team efforts that blend the efforts of the specialists and generalists.

In all of these employment situations, planners face conflicts of loyalty. They must decide whose interests are primary for them in a conflict: their employing agency, their immediate supervisors, the citizens of the community, or their sense of professional duty and personal values. They can limit their practice to the "technical" side of planning and the analysis of hard data, or concern themselves with broader social, political, and ethical questions that their work raises. These dilemmas also confront professionals in law, public health, and other fields, and planners arrive at just as many different responses.

However planners exercise professional competence, the networks of political power as portrayed in the two preceding chapters continually limit or channel it. When a major development choice has many participants, its journey from conception to approval and implementation is apt to be lengthy and twisting. Politics, understood particularly as the struggle for power, injects into planning a high degree of uncertainty as to its outcome and the path that it follows. Whether it is locating an airport or rebuilding Times Square, planners must be no less professional while they ride the waves of controversy.

This chapter focuses on processes for making *comprehensive* plans. They call for a grasp of the "big pictures" that incorporate the separate efforts of planners in housing, transportation, and other specialized fields, and which lead to the many specific choices in zoning, redevelopment, and infrastructures. This discussion also concentrates on local governments' efforts, since they must make a coherent whole of the many streams of planning that affect an area. The generalists' skills are paramount in this realm, in contrast to the specialized areas of planning described in the following five chapters.

5.2 PLANNING RESEARCH AND INTELLIGENCE

Comprehensive planning has four necessary stages: intelligence, goal-setting, plan preparation, and plan implementation. These have a logical sequence, although real-life planning often has reversals and fast-forwards. Planners for government agencies and private employers alike must work through these stages, whatever their specialties and duties.

Intelligence is used here in the military sense of *information that serves a strategic purpose.* Planners who seek to direct change in a community require information about current conditions, the forces for change that may or may not be under their control, and the alternative courses of action with their likely consequences. To gather it consistently, they establish information systems that cover, for their city or county,

(a) demographic data and population trends,

(b) the ownership and current use of each parcel of land, and which parcels are suitable for development or renewal,

(c) the economic base—employment, production, retail and wholesale businesses, and their land values,

(d) the extent and quality of the housing stock,

(e) the infrastructure of sewers, water supply, other utilities and related urban support facilities,

(f) environmental features—topography, waters and shores, air quality, soils, vegetation, and pollution sources,

(g) means of transportation and levels of traffic, transit ridership, and vehicle access,

(h) social problems that warrant public intervention, such as crime, homelessness, and inadequate child care facilities,

(i) other community facilities such as schools, parks, cultural centers, places of worship, and sports facilities,

(j) and any other features that are valuable to the area's common life and which merit development, protection and/or enhancement.

Such information has many sources: census data, land ownership and tax records, topographic maps, building permits and site approvals, to name a few. Some data, such as housing quality, may be obtainable only through on-site surveys. Since available data may be so out-of-date as to be unusable, planners must find ways to update them and track the changes as they occur. That there are many public and private agencies that collect and store (and may refuse to share) relevant data further complicates the task.

Many planning departments conduct research on their city, county, or region; others hire private firms or academic specialists to collect data in the above categories. The research should also identify trends and reasons for them. National and regional changes in the economy and in personal life styles can be forecast with reasonable confidence for the short term. Where confidence levels are lower, as with projections of traffic in a certain corridor, one can still identify a range of possibilities. High technology and service enterprises are growing everywhere, and planners must foresee their land and service requirements and prepare to meet them. Data also show that the average age of the population in most communities is increasing and household sizes declining, mandating dwellings and services needed by single parents, persons living alone, and the active and invalid elderly.

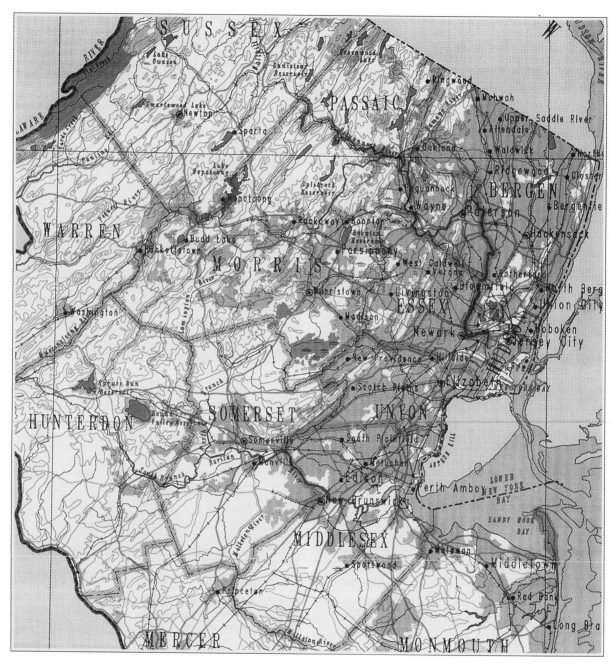

Figure 5.1 Map of northern New Jersey, including its most urbanized area, generated by a geographic information system. Source: U.S. Department of the Interior, U.S. Geological Survey, *Geographic Information Systems.*

Armed with such information, planners can consider adding or altering goals that define directions for the future.

A common method of research is the resident survey. Designed to give citizens a sense of participation in the planning process as well as to elicit their views, surveys can supply useful data if questions and respondents are properly chosen. This was a major factor in the adoption of a well-publicized growth pacing program in Petaluma, California, in the 1970s. Once the city council had declared population pressure a serious issue, it sent more than 10,000 questionnaires in an effort to define the acceptable limits of expansion. The 24 percent of residents who responded favored stringent controls, and the city proceeded to design them [Rosenbaum 1978]. Survey designers must guard against biases in responses, however. Generally, those who have little education, low income, and high transience respond at a low rate to mailed questionnaires, and their preferences must be obtained in person.

Once collected, these data must be integrated into a comprehensive information system in a form that the public as well as professionals can understand. Planners now make extensive use of *geographic information systems*, which assemble information and display it graphically—in effect, linking data with their locations. They make it possible to overlay a basic land-use map with transportation and utility networks, watersheds, employment centers, and vegetation types. This capability enables planners to weigh quickly the impact of a new shopping center on traffic loads on surrounding streets, identify flood danger areas, or inform an industrial prospect of all the sites over five acres suitable for manufacturing. Figure 5.1 is a map of northeastern New Jersey printed from data that indicate urbanized areas. On a much smaller scale, Figure 5.2 displays land uses in one suburb of St. Paul and enables planners to identify vacant spaces readily, among many uses.

Such geographic data systems are being expanded to cover metropolitan areas, watersheds, and sensitive environmental areas, to support more comprehensive decision making about them. They will soon be further enhanced with unprecedentedly sharp photos from commercial satellite imaging. New technology will produce pictures that display objects as small as one meter in size, an obvious boon to monitoring open space and waters, tracking pollution, and examining building sites.

5.3 GOAL SETTING AND PLAN MAKING

All planning presumes goals to be achieved in the future. As stated in chapter 1, this task is to respond adequately to common needs, fit the financial and technical capacities, and have (or gain) public support. Such goals expand and apply the values portrayed in chapter 2. For example, a city attuned to social values will be sensitive to the lack of modest-cost homes for its lower-income population and seek to increase that supply in locations close to workplaces. A goal indicates the direction and magnitude of change that is desired but not the details of where, when, and how to bring it about.

While goal setting is a positive activity, it requires analyses of the problems besetting the community. Declining heavy industry, a military base about to close, deteriorating housing stock, or loss of retail business all demand attention from planners and officials. A widespread recognition emerged in Charlotte, North Carolina, in 1990 that its inner city area fell far short of the quality of life enjoyed by the rest of that booming metropoli-

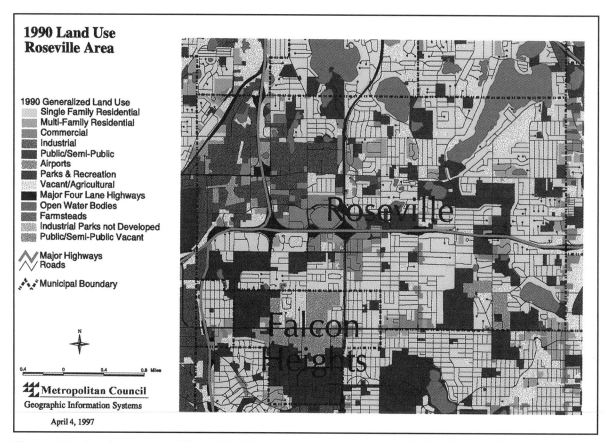

Figure 5.2 Land-use map of Roseville, Minnesota, incorporating individual parcel data. The original map, much larger and in color, provides a highly readable guide to the city's planners. Reprinted with permission of the Metropolitan Council.

tan area. City officials enlisted the business community and citizen organizations to form City Within a City (CWAC) to raise living standards in the inner city, aiming for economic development, housing and infrastructure improvement, and improved safety. A typical goal was to use public dollars strategically to stimulate private investments in homes and businesses. CWAC participants found that cooperative goal-setting was a crucial step in building the teamwork necessary to later action [Borgsdorf 1995].

In many communities, goals are based on the expectations that citizens have of their government and economic enterprises. The study by Williams and Adrian [1963] of four Michigan cities showed sharply different preferences. In one, authorities were expected to promote vigorous economic growth, while in another, residents demanded protection and enhancement of the residential environment. This would likely make a difference in the way the two cities responded to a proposal for a new industry adjacent to a residential area, for example.

The nature of the city's or county's existing

land uses, availability of space for development, and social and economic status tend to prescribe goals. Affluent suburbs, whose residents draw their income from workplaces elsewhere in the region, need only aim to preserve the status quo. But for a distressed Detroit, rebuilding of its economic and physical resources is the first priority. When a city has extensive open land within its limits, as does San Diego, more options are available to it than to San Francisco, which can only alter sites that are already developed.

Goal setting in many communities has been a matter for organized citizen participation. The regional goals formulated by Portland's Metro authority (embodied in *Region 2040*) emerged from numerous public hearings and workshops and over 17,000 citizen comments and suggestions since 1989. These goals include restraining urban growth in the agricultural and forested areas, encouraging means of travel other than the automobile, and increasing density in selected urban neighborhoods with good transit service. The region is under steady pressure from population growth, and the goal of restraint is being challenged by developers seeking lower-cost land for housing and industrial sites [P. Lewis 1996, chs. 4 & 6].

Comprehensive goal setting is difficult where there are diverse and clashing interests. Large cities and metropolitan areas must accommodate so many economic and life style sectors as to hinder agreement on most goals. Further, many citizens and politicians oppose such efforts by governments, believing that planners and other "bureaucrats" have too much power already. To them, a truly democratic regime is sensitive to public wishes expressed over the short range but refuses to commit to long-range schemes that the average person does not comprehend. In many places the decision making process is too fragmented for the government to make specific or extended commitments; the participants consider the future too unpredictable to foreclose any options [Rider 1982].

The step from goals to plans is crucial. Plans state how the specific aims are to be accomplished and include a high level of detail. In a changing residential market, for example, a city may decide to "maintain and enhance housing quality." But this requires answering such questions as "residences for whom? single- or multi-family? at what price levels? what should be rehabilitated? where should new dwellings be built?" A community with 95 percent of its housing stock in single-family homes must consider whether to allow duplexes, townhouses, and rental units to accommodate those who cannot afford or do not need a $200,000 home on a half-acre lot.

The primary means for integrating the goals and applying them is the *comprehensive plan*. Such a plan is normally adopted at once with the intention to control all future development. However, it is necessary to update the plan regularly in response to new conditions and opportunities and to changing settlements of disputes. Table 5.1 displays its typical elements: goals, current situation analysis, projections for the future, detailed program components, and means of implementation.

The comprehensive plan is attached to one or more maps that give locations for anticipated land uses, highways, and areas of special concern such as flood plains. These maps differ from the official zoning map (to be discussed below) in that they have less regulatory detail and are forward looking in their estimates of land requirements. Maps like these are also prepared for smaller areas, such as the central business district or a redevelopment zone. Their main uses are to edu-

Table 5.1   Sample table of contents of a typical municipal comprehensive plan

I.   Planning goals and objectives: statements on the nature and characteristics of the community that are sought.

II.   Analysis and forecasts of community conditions; data and general statements on:
   A.   Land uses and condition of structures, particularly in areas subject to change.
   B.   Economic base: employment, trade, land values, tax base, revenue sources.
   C.   Demography: social characteristics, growth/decline rate, population distribution, social needs.
   D.   Physical environment and natural resources: topography, hydrology, vegetation, soils, minerals.
   E.   Circulation systems: streets and highways, traffic levels, mass transit, airports, rail service, water transportation.
   F.   Infrastructures: water and sewage facilities, parks, schools, public safety, energy supply.

III.   Elements of the plan
   A.   General land use: location and density of each type.
   B.   Housing preservation and renewal.
   C.   Transportation facilities and services.
   D.   Public utilities and sanitation.
   E.   Environmental protection and pollution control.
   F.   Economic development.
   G.   Social services (including education, health, and provision for special needs).
   H.   Parks and recreation.
   I.   Aesthetics and historic preservation.
   J.   Special plans for subareas and neighborhoods embodying any or all of above in greater detail.

IV.   Means of plan implementation
   A.   Zoning and development ordinances.
   B.   Official map indicating planned land uses and zones.
   C.   Incentives and programs for securing the desired development and cooperation of private sector.
   D.   Capital programs for public investment.
   E.   Cooperation with other units of government—federal, state, county, school and special district.
   F.   Political processes and institutions for plan adoption, review, and revision, including public information programs and means of citizen participation.

cate the public on planning choices and to provide context to the zoning and other detailed maps.

Comprehensive plans vary widely from one locale to another. Some are limited to preserving what is already on the ground and remedying any imminent deterioration in it. This is most likely in a fully built city that does not see itself in a crisis mode. A second model looks to a future of renewal, anticipating the outside forces that provide both threats and opportunities. Large parts of Chicago, Detroit, and Cleveland require reuse of their industrial land, rebuilding of housing stock, and preservation of blight-endangered areas. Planners there recognize that the private market lacks sufficient resources to fulfill many of their ambitions in the short run, and so seek to direct most efficiently what resources are available.

Yet another facet of comprehensive planning focuses on growth. This is at the center of the San Diego controversies highlighted in chapter 1 (in addition to that city's concerns for redevelopment of its older areas). Comprehensive planning is the effort to project uses to which the currently undeveloped land will be put and in what sequence. That also calls for long-range plans to extend the street and utility networks, build schools and parks, and provide all other supporting facilities.

A growth plan can also be useful for a whole metropolitan area, even though no one agency has power to enforce it. Portland's Metro, as already mentioned, works closely with the cities and counties to control urban sprawl and offers its guidelines for the most efficient sites for expansion. In 1996 the Metropolitan Council of Minneapolis-Saint Paul presented to its constituency a set of growth options for the region. These included, first, a continuation of current trends toward decentralization into rural areas, second, higher density growth in the already developed cities with no expansion into rural zones, and third, focused urban development in certain center-city and suburban "growth centers." The actual choice of strategy remains with each city and the council has direct control only on sewer expansion, but this plan lays out overall consequences of the combined local choices [Metropolitan Council 1996].

Planners are finding computer-assisted design (CAD) and simulation increasingly helpful in comprehensive land use designs. Not only can computers draw maps in great detail, but they can also portray potential environments in scenes that enable a viewer to gain a "feel" for a street scene, office building complex, or stadium in its setting. This can enable the general public, particularly persons who cannot grasp map-based data easily, to respond intelligently to plans. This technology calls for even more skill on the part of planners, not only to undertake the mechanics of design but also to formulate the fine details that such sophisticated systems are able to portray.

5.4 IMPLEMENTATION OF PLANS: REGULATIONS AND DEVELOPMENT PROGRAMS

Planners' greatest challenge is often to apply their choices to specific locations in a legally binding way. Over the years, many urban plans have not shaped the built environment as intended because no one applied the legal means that actually control land use. Planners often label the various means of implementation as *tools*. One type of tool is regulatory, by which government controls the choices of private landowners and developers; that is the focus of this chapter. Public agencies can also be proactive with programs of their own and of the partnerships to which they belong in such matters as housing and transportation; those issues occupy much of chapters 6 through 10.

The best known of the regulatory tools is *zoning*. Legally, it is rooted in the traditional police power of government to protect the public health, welfare, and safety. Politically, it is a multipurpose device to achieve several social and economic purposes of the community's leaders. In simplest form, it is the division of land into distinct categories of uses, permitting some and excluding others. The intent is to minimize or prevent evils resulting from "wrong" uses of certain areas or from incompatible uses of adjoining land. Before zoning, cities had little or no control over what was built and had to tolerate whatever land-use pattern the private market gradually developed.

New York City adopted the first comprehensive zoning regulation in 1916. It established three land use districts (residential, commercial, and unrestricted) and five building-height districts. Among other provisions, it forbade future factory locations in Manhattan north of Twenty-Third Street. Streets which were currently residential were limited to that use, with businesses restricted to the ends of blocks and to main through-fares. Significantly, this ordinance was sponsored by owners of high-class shops along Fifth Avenue who were alarmed by the garment factories being erected next to them that were introducing hordes of immigrant workers whom they deemed incompatible with their clientele. Planners and other influential persons also sought to limit population density in Manhattan, the growth of which posed enormous traffic congestion and public service demands [Scott 1969, 153–158].

Zoning was quickly embraced by many cities that faced rapid growth in population and in motor vehicle use during the 1920s. After the U.S. Supreme Court upheld the constitutionality of zoning in *Euclid v. Ambler Realty Co.* (1926), city officials were less fearful of lawsuits over their restrictions. Yet, zoning was not, in New York City or most other places, linked with any long-range plans to deal with those growth challenges. It was typically the reaction to current problems as viewed by the business community and subject to piecemeal adjustment as land markets changed.

Zoning was also used to foster economic and racial segregation. Social custom dictated the lot sizes and building standards that tended to stratify residents by income. Middle-class neighborhoods benefited from the zoning walls that excluded not only shops and factories but also the kinds of homes inhabited by low income persons. Atlanta established racial zoning in its 1922 code: African-Americans were excluded from white-zoned areas and vice-versa, writing into law the apartheid long sanctioned in both northern and southern cities.

Zoning is today almost universal. Of large cities, only Houston holds out; its voters have thrice rejected proposals to institute it, most recently in 1993. While that city controls drainage, parking, and building setbacks from streets, it does not specify land uses in the detail common to zoning ordinances. In addition, many property deeds there include restrictive covenants which limit the uses to which the owner may put the land, and since the covenants are legally enforceable, they provide some of the controls that zoning does elsewhere.

The typical zoning policy consists of a *zoning ordinance* and an *official map*. The ordinance defines the land-use categories; residential, commercial, and industrial are most common, and may be supplemented with zones for public facilities, agriculture, open space, and other uses. Many zones are futher subdivided: R-1 for single-family residences, R-2 for two-family attached dwellings, and R-3 for multifamily buildings, for example. A large city may have a dozen or more residential zones to provide for structures of different sizes, heights, and densities. Specific codes vary from one locality to another.

The zoning ordinance states the permitted uses in each zone. A commercial zone (perhaps C-1) located next to homes may be limited to convenience grocery stores and similar enterprises that serve a small area. A C-2 zone would permit a moderate-sized shopping center with supermarkets, banks, and the like. Other commercial zones accommodate large shopping malls and service stations, motels, and restaurants. Business that are regarded as nuisances, such as scrap yards and adult entertainment centers, may be further segregated. It is common to allow establishments serving liquor to exist in several zones but only by special permit, wherein the city sets limiting conditions such as hours of operation.

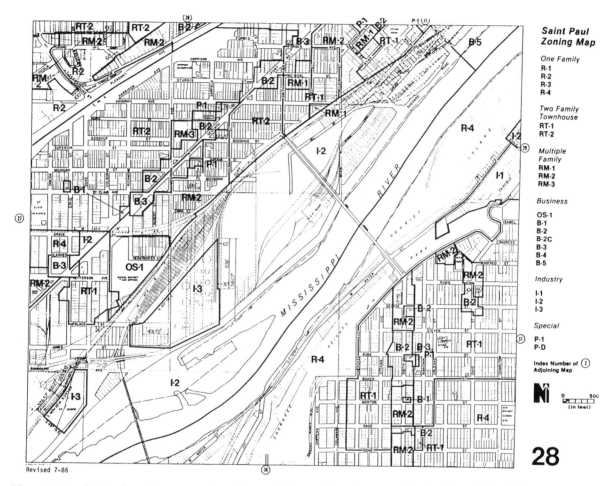

Figure 5.3 St. Paul zoning map, showing a mixture of land uses on both sides of the Mississippi River (1987). Source: City of St. Paul.

These zones may be either *cumulative* or *exclusive* relative to one another. If cumulative, all of the uses permitted in a "lower" or more restrictive zone are also allowed in a "higher" one. That is, single-family homes would be acceptable in a multifamily residential zone, although the reverse would not. But if the zones are exclusive, only those uses specified for each zone are permitted. The latter obviously achieves greater separation of land uses.

The *official map* portrays the zone designa-tion of each parcel of land in the city or county. It must be precise enough in its boundaries to leave no doubt as to how the ordinance applies. This is illustrated in the zoning maps in Figures 5.3 and 5.4. The first displays a mixture of land uses in St. Paul neighborhoods bordering the Mississippi River. The river corridor is historically indus-trial, but established commercial and residen-tial uses are close by. Most of the residences are old, yet some neighborhoods are well maintained, and the challenge is to prevent

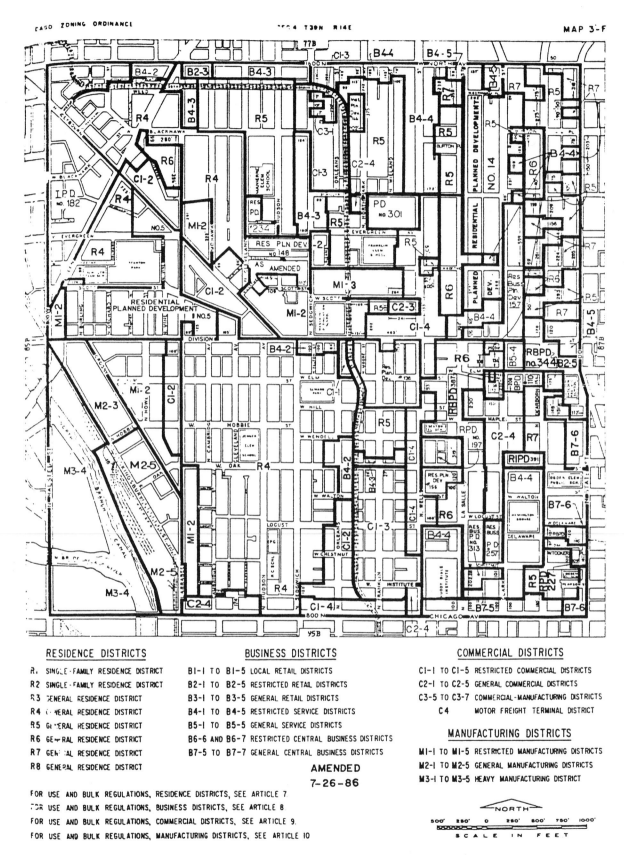

Figure 5.4 Chicago zoning map from Near North Side, with an intricate blend of small districts (1987). Source: City of Chicago.

blight from spreading from the industry-concentrated areas. Figure 5.4 depicts a segment of Chicago's intensely developed Near North Side and illustrates how zones can apply very fine distinctions to individual lots.

Other policy tools supplement zoning controls. *Subdivision regulations* govern the division of land parcels into smaller residential or commercial lots, basically determining how the community will reproduce itself. They presume that a large development must be guided by standards that ensure the harmony of all parts. A typical residential subdivision must meet rules on lot dimensions, size and location of houses, grading, landscaping, streets, utilities, and drainage. A builder's proposal must be sufficiently detailed to display all of these features so they can be individually approved. The developer normally bears the costs of all improvements and adds them to the price of the lots. A more affluent area will expect larger (and thus more expensive) lots and homes that attract new residents who are like the existing ones. A diverse city is likely to adopt more permissive regulations, with housing opportunities for the less well-to-do.

Plans for major public projects are systematically set forth in the *capital improvement plan*. It schedules construction of streets, parks, water and sewage facilities, libraries, and similar one-time additions over some future period. It also projects the means of paying for each, whether from general or special funds, property assessments, federal or state aid, or borrowing. Planners are responsible to see that the projects are compatible with one another and fit the long-range comprehensive plan. Thus, if they forecast large-scale residential building in a certain area, they must make sure that utilities and means of access will be extended at the same time. This usually requires coordination with the county,

school district, and other special districts that make capital investments within the city's limits.

Building codes add further demands to planners' work. Enacted either by states or individual cities, they set the standards to be followed for all structures and their plumbing and electrical facilities. While planners need not be concerned with the required maximum distance between electrical outlets in homes, they do have to pay attention to utility services and major design features. Code requirements have become more strict on such matters as fire safety, insulation, and water conservation, affecting the costs of the buildings that must conform to them.

Some cities also have design review processes that evaluate the esthetic qualities of new developments and renewal projects. This is usually done by a committee of local citizens (similar to those on a planning commission) and/or design professionals. New Orleans set up one of the first of these committees in 1936 to review changes in the historic Vieux Carre, popularly known as the French Quarter. Communities with expensive homes and high-amenity environments often require new dwellings to conform to architectural styles endorsed by such a body.

Zoning programs can be further refined with special *overlay districts*, additional controls imposed on areas with unique qualities. Often used in historic neighborhoods, there may be restrictions on signs, lights, building materials, and designs that are not required elsewhere in that zone. An area with sensitive wetlands and shorelines can be overlaid with protective restrictions on setbacks and waste treatment systems.

A more flexible type of large-area control is the *planned unit development (PUD)*. In this concept, a developer proposes a total plan which may include several types of homes, shops, offices, and/or public uses for an area of 10, 100, or more acres. The emphasis is on achieving a harmonious whole that benefits the community, and the zoning and other legal standards may be modified to achieve this. For example, an office building may be allowed on part of a parcel that was zoned residential. Further, a PUD may permit a higher residential density than the code allows on one portion of the site if the developer commits another part to open space. This requires negotiation between the developer and local officials, the latter having the latitude to bargain for the city's best advantage.

Another tool to add flexibility to regulation is the *conditional use permit.* Through it, a city will allow a certain use not ordinarily permitted but with restrictions to protect the public interest. For example, a locality that routinely excludes churches from residential zones can grant such a permit for a site deemed suitable for one. It attaches conditions, however, on its size, parking, and building access to avoid detrimental effects on nearby homeowners. Another type of conditional use permit may grant a temporary use of a property when such use is deemed beneficial to the public.

Incentive zoning offers flexibility of another kind to local governments and developers. It permits the latter to exceed a general zoning standard in exchange for providing a public benefit, such as open space. New York City allows additional floor area to high-rise structures that include public-use areas or low-income housing, which would not have been provided otherwise. There are outer limits to such agreements, and the burden is on local government negotiators to obtain benefits for the public that are proportional to what the developer obtains.

What makes zoning and related control tools a focus of political conflict is their appli-

cation to very specific locations. Since it often amounts to saying "no" to a landowner's intentions, politics springs from efforts to change it to a "yes" (or pressures for the opposite). Where diverse land uses are close to one another, the likelihood of conflict rises further. While power to rezone specific sites rests with the city or county council, they cannot ignore pressures for and against rezoning and must balance contrary interests. For example, many cities have used zoning to banish adult entertainment businesses to areas far from homes and schools. New York City now requires that the pornography shops and nude bars that once marked Times Square locate only in industrial areas. While most residents cheered this move, the American Civil Liberties Union contested the restriction, citing it as a violation of the First Amendment [Scherer 1995].

The intricate zoning patterns on the official maps represent numerous decisions that could have spawned conflict. They are vulnerable to political pressure because a change can be made at one small point without annulling the plan as a whole. An owner may press to have a quarter-acre site changed from residential to commercial zoning so he can open an video-rental shop in a private home. Such "spot zoning" often takes place and a person could make a plausible argument for any one such action. But when a council grants many of these, each for a "good reason," it gradually repudiates the plan that was designed to separate residential from commercial uses.

A person who seeks a zoning change usually applies first to the city or county planning department if there is one, or in a small community, directly to the legislative body. Many states' laws require holding a public hearing, of which owners of nearby property are notified and notice published in a newspaper. The first consideration is often by the planning commission or zoning board, which recommends action to the council. A two-thirds majority vote in the latter is commonly required for final approval. If the request is denied, the applicant may appeal to a court. This process allows zoning changes to be considered in several different arenas.

A landowner may, instead of a rezoning, request a *variance*. This is a legal deviation from one or more provisions of the code, allowed in defined "hardship" situations. It is not used to permit a different use in the land parcel, but rather a reduced setback from the lot boundary, smaller lot size, taller structure, or larger garage, to name a few examples. Some planning departments or commissions may grant these on their own, while in other cities and counties they are approved only by the council. Since these are one-by-one choices they offer temptations for favoritism.

Often, when a parcel is rezoned, a structure that already exists becomes "nonconforming." For example, a city may redesignate as residential an area which contains a small factory that had been legally operating there. In this case, the factory is permitted to continue, either indefinitely or for a set period of years. However, should the building be abandoned or seriously damaged by fire, it must be removed.

Because of the political conflicts that cling to it, zoning administration has long been a source of corruption. All local officials who own land have a potential conflict of interest. Family and partisan ties and the flow of campaign contributions can easily bias decisions. States and local governments try to minimize this with laws that require open meetings, impartial hearing examiners, and abstention from voting by a decision maker who has a personal stake, but creative persons have found many ways to evade these requirements.

With a comprehensive plan and the implementation tools in place, planners can assess proposals by large and small landowners and developers. They must examine an array of interdependent factors such as the following:

(1) Design of the project: what each part and the whole are to look like and how the parts relate to one another.

(2) Individual structures and facilities (i.e. factories, hotels, stores, office buildings) and their placement on the site.

(3) Means of access to the project for persons and goods, and the storage of vehicles.

(4) Utilities that serve the site.

(5) Impact of the project on the natural environment and surrounding property: air and water quality, noise, visual effects, congestion, ecosystem integrity, and land values.

(6) Social impacts of the project on employment, housing, schools, public health, and criminal behavior.

Planning review typically takes place in several stages. A proposal, say for a shopping center, subdivision of homes, or office structure, first goes to the planning staff of a city or county. They examine it for conformance to the relevant codes and may submit it to others for specialized review, perhaps a watershed district, fire chief, or highway department. If it passes their basic tests, it is often sent to various citizen review boards—planning commission, environmental protection board, and/or neighborhood bodies that are so empowered. They may provide any positive or negative response they choose, and most planning commissions have power to recommend specific changes that are reasonable and within the law.

The final authority to pass on the proposal rests with the elected officials of the city or county, subject to any constraints in federal or state law. An applicant who is rejected is free to sue in court with a claim that the decision was unfair (as the Dolans did in Tigard). Likewise, others who believe themselves harmed by that choice may sue. Thus the officials must take care to state their reasons in terms that they can defend in court. The more complex a proposal is, the more time and layers of review it requires, and any litigation can extend it further. Many controversial projects have been tied up for years in review and were often dropped when their sponsors ran out of will or money. Indeed, opponents can use this strategy to defeat an unwanted development without actually securing its rejection.

5.5 EVALUATION AND FEEDBACK

Most evaluations of the results of zoning and its related tools point to several factors [Abeles 1989]. First, it has often been used to draw class distinctions in residential environments, in the form of exclusionary zoning. Indeed, this was its original intent, for in separating different land uses, it also walled off social groups' homes and workplaces from one another. Second, because the zoning power belongs to individual municipalities and counties, it does not lead to coherent land use patterns across metropolitan areas. Communities have used it to enhance their own tax bases and social goals, understandably, but have no incentive to meet the larger region's land-use needs. A suburban city may secure more than its share of "clean" industry and commercial centers that yield high property tax payments, but it is free to refuse to zone for homes that modest-income employees of those enterprises can afford.

More broadly, these tools are not adequate to secure the positive developments that a city or region may need. The zoning described in this chapter, which is basically negative, is called *Euclidean*, after the U.S. Supreme Court's decision in *Euclid v. Ambler*

Realty Co. It is particularly vulnerable to legal contests, which then shifts to the courts the planning choices that belong to elected officials and their professional and citizen advisors. By contrast, we can label as *noneuclidean* the more flexible and positive approaches to land-use guidance described in the previous section, such as planned unit developments.

The older large cities (and aging neighborhoods in newer ones) cannot find in the traditional zoning regulations much help toward renewal, according to Abeles [1989]. Due to political and technical hindrances, they cannot change zone designations quickly enough to accommodate new opportunties for homes or workplaces. Indeed, one aspect of New York City's renewal has taken place because some zone regulations were ignored. In the 1970s, when the city sought to protect manufacturing areas and the jobs they provided, it restricted large tracts to that use alone. As time went on, however, entrepreneurs in video production, computer software, and graphic design found spaces in the old factories, along with such new retailers as Home Depot. City planners, realizing that the zones did not accommodate the changing economic opportunities, welcomed this productive activity by looking the other way. Now they seek to formalize this flexibility [Johnson 1996].

The following chapters catalog the many positive means of securing the desired outcomes in the fields of economic development, housing, transportation, environmental protection, and the social amenities. Land-use regulation cannot stand by itself as a policy, but must be applied and evaluated for how it serves those ends.

5.6 PLANNERS IN THE POWER STRUCTURE

Planners, whether in government or private employment, play political as well as technical roles. To win approval for any plan and its implementation requires not only a "quality" plan but also support from those who make and administer laws and spend money. Many planners have little grasp of bureaucratic structures and procedures [Baum 1983, pp. xiii–xvi]. They tend to see themselves not as power wielders but as specialized problem solvers. This model of the profession, in Baum's view, is entirely inappropriate to the roles that most planners actually have to play in affecting social and economic conditions. It is necessary to ask, then, how planners fit into the structures of power outlined in section 4.5.

Leading professional planners have played several different political roles, as suggested by Catanese [1984, p. 59]. The most traditional is the "apolitical-technical" role, in which one applies the formal techniques with no overt effort to to advocate particular political or social values. Yet this is a political role in a larger sense, for such a "technician" upholds the political choices of the dominant leaders and coalitions. This can occur when a planner in an upper-class suburb drafts a zoning ordinance that excludes lower-income households, knowing that the council would enact nothing else.

Catanese's second role depicts planners as "covert activists." They take on the outward stance of the apolitical-technical role but become involved behind the scenes with political action and politicians in order to influence the value choices that surround their plans. Norman Krumholz, planning director in Cleveland from 1969 to 1978, played this role under three very different mayors. He was a strong advocate for the poor and minorities but operated through private meetings with elected officials [Catanese 1984, pp. 49 & 76].

The role most explicitly injected into the power structures is the "overt-activist." Planners in this role openly "support politicians, political parties, and causes that they believe are most in keeping with their values" [Catanese 1984, p. 60]. They seek public visibility, assuming that their professional expertise adds credibility to their causes. Such activity, in their view, advances the progressive values for which the profession claims to stand.

Three types of the overt-activist stand out. One type takes a personal role as advocate for a group of citizens, particularly those who are politically and economically disadvantaged. He or she applies professional skill to enable them to move from apathy or futile protests to active and comprehensive planning. Tom Angiotti, who assisted the Red Hook community in Brooklyn as described in chapter 4, is in this category [Angiotti 1996].

Edward Kirschner is typical of the second type of overt-activist planners, who take part in elective politics and the formal decision making machinery. He led a 1970s citizens' movement in Berkeley, California, that advocated greater collective control over the community's land and economy. His coalition won most elective offices and dominated city politics until 1981 [Clavel 1986, ch. 4].

More dramatic is the third type, the power wielder who concentrates on major projects, of whom Robert Moses is the best example. For more than forty years, he initiated tens of billions of dollars in projects in New York State, particularly the New York City metropolitan area. Beginning with state parks in Long Island, he planned and secured funding for parkways and freeways, bridges and tunnels, urban renewal efforts, and finally the 1964 World's Fair. His relationships with elected officials and lending institutions were so close that no one was able to thwart his ambitions until Governor Nelson Rockefeller maneuvered him out of his power base in 1968. Moses was no friend of the poor, however; he did nothing to develop mass transit, for example. In fact, the parkways he designed leading to the Long Island parks and beaches were crossed by bridges too low for buses to pass under, and so could be used only by persons with their own automobiles [Caro 1974].

The power that planners have is always related to who employs them and who is powerful in that agency or company, and (especially for the citizen planners) to the allies and supporters they speak for and influence. Much depends on their skills in dampening the controversies rooted in emotional and adversarial politics and promoting instead rational consideration of the issues that concern the whole community. The San Diego and Times Square cases in chapter 1 illustrate particularly well the demands that planners, citizen as well as professional, in the private as well as public sector, promote a sober and inclusive political process that makes room for the many stakeholders' interests. Only limited power can (and should) reside in technical expertise. Rather, planners do best to leverage their insights into a larger understanding of the public interest. As Hoch concludes [1994, p. 345],

> Planners should identify, invent, and nurture political deliberations in which planning plays an important role. In such cooperative political settings, good professional practice comes less from the application and display of expertise and more through the clarity, efficacy, and popularity of planning visions and arguments shaped through political deliberation.

The following chapters examine the specialized goals of planning. Each portrays a central responsibility of government in our age, yet one which depends heavily on the market and individual choices for success. Successful planning is above all cooperative planning, the enterprise of building partnerships and harmonizing goals and decisions.

FOR REVIEW AND DISCUSSION

1. What choices and dilemmas do professional planners face in their varied job assignments? In how many different ways can they resolve them?

2. What *intelligence* must planners gather to do their jobs well? How can they best keep abreast of the rapid changes taking place in their communities and regions?

3. What factors shape the goals that a community sets for itself? Thinking of a particular community that you are familiar with, how much freedom does it have to set and change its development goals?

4. What are the major tools that planners have to control land use? What are the limitations and drawbacks of each one?

5. How important is it that a city or county have a comprehensive land use plan? What factors prevent it from preparing such a plan, and more importantly, from implementing it over time?

6. What resources for exercising political power can planners draw on? How much power should they exercise vis-a-vis elected officials and private interest and citizen groups?

CHAPTER

6

Planning for Jobs and Wealth

6.1 THE ECONOMICS AND POLITICS OF URBAN LAND

Land is worth money and can be used to make more money. Whatever else land means to a city, its current and potential dollar values dominate the political choices made about it. Planning politics gets its unique character from the marketplace for urban land, those who do business on it, and the paths in which money flows to and from those enterprises.

Economic development and employment generation ranked high among the goals of urban planning listed in section 1.5. Local authorities, like the national government, have long been expected by the public to pursue vigorously these economic ends. For localities, the major upsurge in the pursuit of jobs has come in the past twenty years and their planning process is being harnessed ever more closely to it.

Three basic economic goals guide policy makers at both the national and local levels. First, they aim for *affluence*, evidenced by ris-

ing levels of income, goods, and services. A second goal is *full employment*, all persons being able to find work at a living wage. Third, they pursue *equity*, the fair distribution of the fruits of affluence such that no group is consistently disadvantaged.

To progress toward these goals, a city's economy must make efficient use of the three major factors of production: land, labor, and capital. Of these, local governments have major control only over their land, since their regulatory and development choices shape the economic uses to which it is put. They provide such public assets as transportation, utilities, and social amenities that help fix its market value. Further, by the complex of choices they make for a larger area, such as renewal of an industrial district, they set the limits and possibilities for the use of each of its parts.

Decision makers thus are compelled to think holistically of their cities as economic enterprises. Peterson [1981, p. 4] asserts, "The place of the city within the larger political economy of the nation fundamentally affects

83

the policy choices that cities make. In making these decisions, cities select those policies which are in the interests of the city, taken as a whole." Those holistic interests are focused on their economy, particularly "a competitive edge in the production and distribution of desired commodities relative to other localities." [Peterson 1981, p. 22] This edge supplies the prosperity that fuels the government's ability to provide services and amenities that win political support from a satisfied citizenry.

Thus, a central purpose of urban planning, whether by a government or by its allies in private enterprise, is to seek the "highest and best" economic return from land. This return may consist of the maximum profit for a developer or landowner on one site, the creation of the greatest number of jobs on another, or simply the highest market value of a piece of property. Land that borders freeway interchanges is thus judged to be best used for shopping centers or truck terminals rather than single-family homes, whereas sites next to scenic waters are most lucratively marketed for high-priced residences.

Planners who work for developers and other entrepreneurs have an additional role in blending labor and capital with land to seek profits in specific projects. When they target Times Square for renewal instead of the South Bronx, for example, they direct the flow of economic resources and job opportunities to one set of beneficiaries rather than another.

This search for economic value can clash with the esthetic, social, and ecological values discussed in chapter 2, and the dissonance often sparks political conflict. Officials who grant legal approvals seek settlements that maximize the total value for a development. For example, they may link the demand for better housing for lower income persons with industrial growth, in the view that higher paid workers can better afford homes. Or a city council might argue that it cannot spend more on parks until its tax base is strengthened by commercial and industrial growth.

Land values and economic activity also depend on a particular city's role in the national and global economy, as Section 1.6 indicated. Some metropolitan areas have come to play strategic roles in the world's "commodity chains" that link raw materials with the sale and consumption of finished products. They have the concentrated human and technological resources needed to keep those chains in operation: financial and legal services, communications networks, educational and research facilities, and means of intercultural contact.

> Above all, they have established themselves as centers of authority, with a critical mass of persons-in-the-know about market conditions, trends, and innovations—people who can gain one another's trust through frequent face-to-face contact. . . . . [They] act as pivotal points in the reorganization of global space: control centers for the flows of information, cultural products, and finance that, collectively, sustain the economic and cultural globalization of the world. [Knox 1997, pp. 21–22]

Knox [1997] identifies New York, London, and Tokyo as the three preeminent world cities by the criteria cited above. Ranking just beneath them in the United States are Chicago, San Francisco, Atlanta, Miami, Los Angeles, and Washington, D.C. These centers relate closely to one another: a decision in New York to build or close facilities can reverberate from Miami to Anchorage and alter the choices that local planners make. Decisions made in Seoul, Stuttgart, or Sao Paolo can have the same effects.

These global centers of authority and information thus materially influence the economic development of all other places.

Smaller metropolitan areas need strong linkages with these centers and with one another to obtain resources that sustain their economic activity and attractiveness to investors. Although Boston is not in Knox's first tier of cities, it prospers due to its broad base in education, finance, medicine, publishing, and high technology, enabling its governments and private enterprises to invest in housing and infrastructures. Charlotte, Houston, and Seattle have similar assets for growth. Detroit, by contrast, lacks such a base and has been less successful in diversifying beyond the heavy manufacturing that is its declining mainstay.

The economic tasks of planners thus vary according to the locational opportunities they have. However, each city, large and small, has assets which its regime can build and enhance. Orlando is booming as a tourism center in the heart of Florida, while Boise, Idaho, and Salt Lake City, Utah, draw Californians seeking a less-crowded environment and lower living costs. The nation's economy is sufficiently diversified to spread growth to many locales, and the most enterprising cities claim more than their share by providing the supporting systems of communication and human skill.

Within each metropolitan area, we can distinguish four types of locations in terms of their development potentials. First, the *growth center* draws the major commercial or industrial investments. Historically, this has been the downtowns and industrial corridors of central cities, but one must now add the "edge cities," which Garreau [1991] applies to the 200-plus major shopping centers, office parks, and multiuse complexes that cling to the suburban freeways of every metropolis. Figure 6.1 shows such a development in suburban Boston. Land costs there are high, but investors perceive equally high profit potential in them. These sites are ordinarily chosen by the market, but government incentives can make sites more attractive than they otherwise would be. New York City's Times Square, in the midtown Manhattan growth center, is targeted for redevelopment since adult theaters and pornography shops are judged not to be its highest and best use.

A second type of location is the *inner transition zone*. This is typically near the central city downtown and comprises the smaller businesses, industrial buildings, and residences that may be abandoned or underused, dubbed TOADS (Temporarily Obsolete Abandoned Derelict Sites) [Greenberg et al 1990]. Figure 6.2 illustrates this condition in Chicago. Some of the land is occupied by parking lots and outdoor storage. There may also be homes of lower-income persons in rooming houses, cheap hotels, public housing projects, and older single-family dwellings. This zone has potential either for major redevelopment or further deterioration, depending on the choices of investors and governments. Some cities have rehabilitated the older housing or placed new homes there, while others take advantage of lower land values to expand public institutions. Chicago chose this zone for new stadiums for the White Sox and Bulls and an abandoned railroad yard just south of the Loop for a medium-density residential community.

The third sector, the *relatively stable established area*, has lower change potential. Much of it is occupied by homes, neighborhood shops, and institutions and can be found either in central cities or mature suburbs. Its main challenge, as seen by its residents, is to maintain its quality and exclude the kind of development that would threaten their sense of security. When a part of it is disrupted, as with a freeway, it becomes more of a transition zone with varied prospects for change.

Figure 6.1   A modest-sized Edge City in Burlington, Massachusetts. Reprinted with permission of the Massachusetts Department of Public Works.

Finally, the *outer transition zone* is marked by low-density uses but, on the edge of the developed areas, is ripe for their expansion. Land values are relatively low, but parts of it have good access to transportation facilities. Since this zone contains future "edge cities," the challenge is to control the change from rural to urban uses in an orderly manner to minimize congestion and enviromental damage. This is the zone upon which the growth limitation politics in San Diego focuses, and

in which Minnesota might have placed its new airport.

Each parcel of land in these zones has a specific governmental unit planning for it and a cluster of private interests that have a stake in its future. These interact over time, responding to problems and proposals in turn. The growth centers probably draw the most powerful business players, attracted by the stakes in land values and profits. By contrast, the stable established areas are strongly de-

Figure 6.2 Even healthy downtowns like Chicago's can be surrounded by deteriorating buildings. Photo by Dennis McClendon.

fended by homeowner and small business groups. Planners must be sensitive to such stakeholders without losing sight of the larger region's interests in an area's development.

6.2 STRATEGIES FOR URBAN ECONOMIC DEVELOPMENT

Underlying the thrust for economic development has been the theme of *growth*, in population, wealth, knowledge, and mastery of natural forces that is deeply imbedded in Western culture. It has many expressions in urban planning, which seeks to promote and channel it in the most beneficial directions. Molotch [1993, p. 31] characterizes the city as a "growth machine," whose governmental and private power structures have a common interest in programs that intensify land use and profits from it. From the earliest dates of urban settlement in the United States, community leaders sought railroads, harbors, and industries to put their cities "on the map." Today's governing regimes are no different, despite the changes in the technological stimuli. The economic dominants described in chapter 4 are the most visible in this process, although many of the citizen participants support growth in their own way as well.

Growth can take many forms, however, and spread its benefits widely or narrowly. Planners and developers in the public and private sectors must adopt a basic strategy of economic development and have two divergent models to choose from. The traditional approach is often labeled *corporate* or *entrepreneurial*. Its advocates view the private sector as the primary "growth engine" in choosing specific projects and locations within a city or its suburbs. Government's role, to them, is to support those plans with legal approvals, adding financial subsidies when a given project is not fully competitive in the marketplace. This approach removes such choices from the political arena on the ground that they are managerial and technical rather than open to public debate [Leitner & Garner 1993]. It further assumes that government and business interests are in fundamental harmony and that all the city's residents gain when such corporate-sponsored development takes place.

A further assumption of the corporate approach is that a city's potentials for growth are largely determined by the global market and technological forces and its own location on the opportunity maps in investors' minds. A coastline site or an international airport thus confers advantages on a region that a town in a remote inland area cannot claim. This handicap also applies to depressed sites within a metropolitan region; Camden, New Jersey in the Philadelphia area appears to repel hopeful investors. Public planners are tempted to give up any hope of growth or renewal of such areas due to the market's lack of interest in them.

This corporate strategy has drawn critics (for example, Levine, 1989) who assert that development partnerships often have not benefited cities in proportion to the public funds spent on them. Many urban residents did not share in the benefits, and the development enhanced a few parts of the area (primarily the growth centers) while leaving the worst-off neighborhoods unaided. Indeed, the business interests that directly participated usually drew handsome profits at heavy cost to the taxpayers.

Thus the alternative *community-based* strategy seeks to distribute more widely both the wealth and political power, returning a larger share of the benefits to the city's least advantaged communities. Specific programs in that strategy would develop the city's own resources with smaller scale projects that train and employ residents, retain and expand local businesses, and return the profits to the community for further investment. Under the late mayor Harold Washington in the 1980s, Chicago sought broad neighborhood participation in industrial revitalization plans that targeted the many depressed neighborhoods rather than the highly developed Loop [Levine 1989].

This strategy most often guides the community development corporations mentioned in section 4.4. In many cities, they have aided small retailers, manufacturers, and construction and service enterprises. Where successful, this effort multiplies the number of entrepreneurs who are committed to the city and its neighborhoods; contrast this with large corporations that are likely based in another city and have no enduring loyalty to any one location [Betancur, Bennett & Wright 1991]. From this viewpoint, no community is condemned by its location to stagnation or decline. There is always some potential for growth, but the planning community must do some creative thinking to enhance the resources that are available.

In a few cases, city governments have embarked on either temporary or long-term ownership of selected economic enterprises, ranging from retail centers to minor league baseball teams. They seek thereby to retain a degree of control over future development and its impacts and to claim a share of the profits to reduce tax burdens [Imbroscio 1995]. Planners who choose this strategy must overcome major legal and financial obstacles, not to mention political objections to "municipal socialism."

While growth as an ideal has many noneconomic benefits and costs, it is usually operationalized in material terms: dollars invested, buildings constructed, jobs created or preserved, goods and services sold, taxes paid, and population retained or gained. These efforts depend largely on private investment from local and outside sources, but government's resources may be crucial as seed money. Local citizens may demand that tax dollars be invested in projects with broad payoffs; thus schools, parks, art museums, and sports stadiums are used to foster growth. In the 1980s, Seattle built a $157 million convention and trade center bridging Interstate 5. It not only supplied patrons for nearby hotels and restaurants but drew together the two sides of the commercial district that the freeway had divided years earlier. Hundreds of millions of dollars of private investment followed. Success is not assured, however; Detroit's $350 million public/private support of the Renaissance Center, a massive office, hotel, and convention facility built in the 1970s, drew economic activity out of the adjacent downtown area and furthered its physical decline [Garvin 1996, pp. 92–95].

Local leaders also have less tangible but equally urgent reasons to seek growth. Pagano and Bowman [1995, p. 3] found from their research on ten medium-sized U.S. cities that they "rely on a vision of their future cityscape. . . . . [and] reestablish, repackage, even reinvent themselves in an attempt to find their niche" in the hierarchy of places with which they compare themselves. Their logic is built on their history, but also on an image of what they could become if they tried to. So, for example, regimes in Huntsville, Alabama, and Orlando have aggressively pursued their many Sunbelt advantages for growth, while Lowell, Massachusetts, sought to build on its heritage as a pioneer in the 19th century industrial revolution.

To be sure, even communities and regions whose leaders have a strong commitment to growth will have conflict over implementing it. Central cities vie with suburbs for employers, and one suburb competes with another to land a lucrative business. On the other hand, groups seek to keep "disruptive" uses out of certain neighborhoods to protect their residential environment but very much want them within easy commuting distance. They can cooperate only when they perceive an opportunity to enhance all of their interests at the same time. Efforts by cities to recruit new employers generally draw broad public support as long as the benefits are likely to be spread widely.

Even growth-limitation efforts do not necessarily signal opposition to growth. The moratorium in San Diego (see the case in chapter 1), which bills itself as the "city on the move," was not meant to halt development. It only had the effect of temporarily channeling commercial and residential growth onto other vacant land. In general, suburban growth limitation efforts have aimed at either controlling the pace of growth to permit adequate servicing of it (as in Petaluma, California; see chapter 10) or to keep unwanted land uses and lower-income people away from affluent residential areas.

6.3 THE FLOW OF URBAN MONEY

Urban economic development is big business. Between 15,000 and 18,000 governmental, private, and partnership organizations in the nation promote it. One estimate is that their spending exceeds $10 billion a year, plus $4 billion added by the federal government in grants [Goldsteen & Elliott, 1994, p. 252).

Capital for urban development has several sources. They differ not only in the methods of raising it and the amounts they produce but also in the political choices they entail. One dollar is not the same as another; each comes with obligations and limits imposed by governmental funders or private financiers. Thus the flow of funds is extremely complex in its technical detail and varies over time. This survey is necessarily simplified, providing only a broad outline.

The first category of funds is local government revenue. General-purpose governments are financed by a combination of real estate levies, aid from the state and federal government, improvement assessments, and fees charged for the services they provide. The proportion of each in the total varies widely among states, and often within states as well. The *real estate levy* is used everywhere and is based on the assessed value of the taxable property in the city or county. Since commercial and industrial sites are more valuable for their size and yield a larger volume of revenue than dwellings, most authorities have a strong incentive to keep and attract them. And as a result, the successful cities gain an even greater advantage over communities that are less well endowed.

The *improvement assessment* is also a universal source of funds. A project such as street paving, sanitary sewer, or water supply raises the value of the affected property, and thus its owners are charged part or all of its cost. In new subdivisions, the developer pays these assessments in advance and passes them on to buyers. In some commercial areas, such as in New York City, *business improvement districts* impose charges for desired services that the city does not provide. Such choices can be highly controversial when there is lack of agreement on the need for the improvement, who shall be included in its boundaries, and the proportion of project costs to be assessed (versus the amount drawn from the general fund).

A newer form of local revenue has grown rapidly in importance: the *impact fee* or *exaction*. In high-growth areas, especially in the South and West, cities and counties charge commercial and residential builders not only for the cost of streets and sewers in the project but also for fire and police stations, parks, schools, and road and drainage improvements in the surrounding area. The rationale is that the development is of such a size that it imposes costs on the community as a whole and should share that burden. This too raises concerns among developers, who fear that financially pressed cities will impose fees on them that exceed the genuine public costs of their projects.

Cities and counties draw upon fees and taxes not related to property as well, with much variation between and within states. Some states permit them to levy general sales taxes on top of the statewide rate or remit to cities a portion of the sales taxes they collect within the city. Some special districts also draw funds from this source. Those with large retail enterprises within their boundaries benefit disproportionately, which is an incentive to secure even more such development.

Other revenues come from local income taxes (in about 3,800 cities, counties, and school districts), selective taxes on gasoline, liquor, and utilities, license fees on everything from businesses to bicycles, and user charges for sewage, trash collection, parks and recreation, parking, transit, and airports. Most local authorities recognize that the quality of public services is a major factor in economic development, but they face hard choices in selecting revenues to support them. If their burden on local businesses is seen as excessive, they can lose to competing communities, yet those businesses are the primary sources of funds for future development.

A further source of funds for urban development is debt, which can be beneficial if well managed. Local authorities frequently borrow for long-term projects by selling either *general obligation* or *revenue* bonds to investors. The former are guaranteed by the full revenue base, and so entail a relatively low risk for the lender. General obligation bonds are ordinarily used to finance projects that will not produce income, such as schools, roads, and parks. Most states require that such borrowing be approved by the voters in a referendum, a safeguard against excessive debt as well as an opportunity for the public to judge the project itself.

Revenue bonds finance projects that are expected to produce income sufficient to repay the lenders, such as utilities, modest-cost housing, hospitals, and sports stadiums. They are riskier investments since they are not guaranteed, and a lack of revenue could cause the borrower to default on them. They thus pay a higher rate of interest than general obligation bonds. In 1993, local governments issued approximately $93 billion in general obligation bonds and $198 billion more in revenue bonds. Their total bonded indebtedness in that year amounted to $1.257 trillion [Leonard 1996, pp. 319, 323].

An attractive feature of both kinds of bonds (which state governments use also) is that interest paid to the lenders is free from federal income taxation. They are also free of state taxes when held by residents of the state in which they are issued. This permits governments to borrow at a lower rate than corporations can. In 1997, the average municipal bond sold at an interest rate three to four points lower than the typical high-grade corporate bond. This exemption from taxes is effectively an indirect federal subsidy to state and local development efforts.

A further use of local funds is to repay loans used to finance more significant development projects that will have a life span of several decades. When these loans are backed by the total tax revenue of the city, county, or district, a portion of that revenue must be reserved each year for their repayment with interest. When the debt load has become heavy due to ambitious borrowing, this repayment obligation rises proportionately. These dollars are spread among many functions—patching streets, operating parks, and policing. They also use these funds for small capital investments that they undertake on their own. Special districts have varied methods of financing, but usually include those listed above. Choices of public physical improvements are set forth in a *capital budget,* often programmed for five years or more into the future.

Federal and state aid in several forms has been a major source of funding for urban development since the 1940s. Section 2.6 recounted the origin of the federal housing and urban renewal programs, which enabled many cities to take the initiative in their own economic development. Congress has periodically reconsidered them in the light of disappointing results, and such aid is now only a small fraction of its original level. In fiscal year 1991, for example, federal programs for community and regional development totaled less than $4.3 billion.

The dominant federal program since 1974 has been Community Development Block Grants, which had provided more than $60 billion by 1996. Since it gave substantial discretion to local officials, it funded projects ranging from glamorous downtown hotels to modest-cost dwellings. In the past ten years, the bulk of the funds has been required to benefit low- and moderate-income persons. At present, allocation of the grants has been coordinated between city and state governments.

A much-discussed concept for stimulating depressed urban economies is the *enterprise zone,* which has been reborn in federal policy as the *empowerment zone.* The former originated in Great Britain and was endorsed here by President Reagan. The central idea is that government offers incentives to private investors and employers to locate in areas of cities most needing development. These included selected tax reductions and credits and reduced interest rates on loans. Although Congress did create such a program in 1987, it failed to provide federal tax incentives and so the action had no effect. However, most states went ahead with their own enterprise zone programs that reduced state tax burdens in various ways. For example, a company that located in such a zone might qualify for a reduced property tax rate, a corporate income tax credit for each person hired, and an exemption from the sales tax for purchase of new equipment. The results of these by the early 1990s are mixed. Riposa [1996, pp. 543–544] found that while many of them created new jobs, they did not have the desired effects on the targeted neighborhoods since the persons hired often lived elsewhere. Louisville, Kentucky, and Passaic, New Jersey, claimed major benefits, while others had little success.

After reconsidering the experience with enterprise zones, Congress adopted empowerment zones in 1993. This program was designed to supplement the traditional tax incentives with government funding of training, children's services, neighborhood security, and other assistance to back up the job creation efforts. A larger purpose is to promote participation by residents in the communities through partnerships among the many organizations already active there. The Department of Housing and Urban Development designated six empowerment zones (in Atlanta, Baltimore, Chicago, Detroit, New York City, and Philadelphia/Camden) to receive $100 million each plus federal tax incentives, and 67 other areas targeted for lesser benefits. Since the program is scheduled to last ten years, results will appear only gradually [Riposa 1996].

The logic of empowerment zones is reminiscent of the community development programs of the 1960s and 1970s, and success will depend heavily on how the local partnerships define their opportunities and secure their funding from private as well as govern-

mental sources. Determining priorities and allocating funds has sparked political contests between city officials, neighborhood organizations, and business representatives. It is important to have realistic expectations and to recognize the persisting factors that caused these zones to be depressed in the first place [Berger 1997]. Early reports from Detroit's 18-acre zone, however, suggest that there is market demand for depressed-area locations. 29 companies had announced plans for facilities there, spending more than two billion dollars on them. The biggest of the investors is Chrysler, which builds its fast-selling Jeep Grand Cherokees in the zone, and many of the other companies have contracts to make parts for the major automakers [Meredith 1997].

Every state has a set of economic development agencies and programs which add to the federal and local resources. These efforts target both the supply and demand sides of the market. The former consist of programs to minimize costs of business relocation and expansion, to stay competitive with other states and communities seeking the same enterprises. Each of these has direct local impact, although some cities inevitably benefit more from these development choices than others. However, Eisinger [1988] argues that states have increasingly turned to demand stimulation by aiding formation of new businesses, expanding markets, and furnishing venture capital for even risky enterprises. Pennsylvania began its Ben Franklin Partnership in 1982 to support local technology development, and Ohio followed with the Thomas Edison Program in 1983; both involve nearby universities and colleges as well as local governments. Some of the state investments are drawn from their public employees' pension funds, which hold nearly one trillion dollars in assets. Very little state money goes directly to city governments for this, but their subsidy programs have major impact on local land use and employment.

A further joint state-local support for economic growth is *tax-increment financing,* by which cities and counties subsidize the costs of industrial and commercial development. Basically, the city dedicates the increased property taxes that will be collected on the new store or plant to pay for the public improvements that are made on that site. States participate in it by replacing the tax revenue that would otherwise go to school districts.

Money from all of the above public sources is often used to leverage private investments. Local businesses, lending institutions, trade associations, chambers of commerce, and foundations view their contributions to community building as enlightened self-interest. Several national organizations channel a blend of governmental and private funds to selected local projects. The nonprofit Local Initiatives Support Corporation has raised $1.7 billion since 1980 to assist community development corporations in job creation, housing, and similar enterprises.

Local communities have many types of organizations that oversee economic development. The largest number are directly part of a city or county government, sometimes in the same agency that does land use planning but more often separate from it. Thus they respond to the political imperatives of the local executives and lawmakers. Some are multi-governmental, linking a city and county, several adjacent cities, or an entire metropolitan area. Of increasing importance are public-private partnerships, in which one or more public agencies joins forces with a chamber of commerce or business association, each contributing funds and sharing the workload [Bartik 1996]. A highly active development enterprise can become the dominant planner,

one to which other agencies are willing to defer.

6.4 INDUSTRIAL DEVELOPMENT

The steel mill closes, the automobile plant downsizes, and the computer chip factory opens in the suburbs—these events portray the massive industrial changes the United States is experiencing. The global process of economic and technological restructuring both creates opportunities and destroys them, and only the agile survive.

All urban areas thus have a mix of upward and downward forces in their economies, trends toward both prosperity and decay. Phoenix, Arizona, and San Jose, California, for example, see few forces for decline as college graduates flock to their specialized service and high-technology jobs. By contrast, the older cities of Gary, Indiana, and Camden, New Jersey, suffer from the opposite trend. There, blue collar workers who earned $20 an hour now sweep floors or fry hamburgers for a small fraction of that wage. The demand on planners in all those places is to nurture the upward potentials and halt the downward, factors which are to a great extent beyond their control. Job creation is a political imperative for many elected officials, who spur their planners to ever greater efforts to retain and recruit employers.

These changes powerfully impact the built environment. An abandoned factory or polluted scrapyard is a blight on an inner-city neighborhood, while a new plant or warehouse pours heavy traffic onto two-lane suburban roads a few miles away. While these location choices yield financial advantages for individual companies, they create public burdens.

Planners in the public and private sector face three major challenges, depending on their location and employer: to expand the sources of economic livelihood, fit new enterprises most compatibly into their surroundings, and secure the most constructive redevelopment of derelict industrial and commercial land. In this highly competitive world, victory goes most often to the aggressive and resourceful.

In meeting the first challenge, the political and economic leaders must grasp their community's potential and not attempt the impossible. A global or regional "center of authority" [Knox 1997] like New York or San Francisco can lure a wider variety of enterprises than would be interested in Detroit or Hartford, Connecticut. Access to suppliers and markets, size and skills of the labor force, local taxes and operating costs, and executive preferences for attractive places to live confer advantages on some places over others. Phoenix is a magnet for tourists and retirees, Boston has rich educational offerings, and Seattle is on the front line of the Pacific Rim. Smaller cities that lack distinct economic identities but market themselves effectively may also find success: Spartanburg, South Carolina, and Vance, Alabama, respectively, host new BMW and Mercedes vehicle factories. The latter is expected to employ 1,500 workers when fully staffed, and approximately 15,000 related jobs in the area will follow. However, tax breaks and other subsidies for Mercedes from state and local treasuries will total some $300 million, a severe burden on a state with pressing social and educational needs [Myerson 1996].

Each urban area has competitors for growth. Tucson, Arizona, as well as Phoenix, draws tourists and pensioners, New Haven, Connecticut, is Boston's rival as an educational center in the Northeast, and Portland vies with Seattle for the Asia trade. Most investors survey several locations and if none has a clear advantage otherwise, the nod will go to the city with the highest bid. That bid can consist of the preferential financing described in the previous section: tax abatements, industrial parks, and other grants and loans. Additional incentives include aid in securing a site, cleaning up existing pollution on it, employee training programs, and personal attention to visiting executives.

A similar process is necessary to retain an employer who expresses interest in moving away. In 1980, General Motors decided to replace two obsolete plants in Detroit, and told officials that if sufficient land were not available in the city, it would find it elsewhere, and in the process move out 6,000 jobs. Mayor Coleman Young and the Community Economic Development Department acted quickly to acquire 460 acres in a neighborhood called Poletown and displaced its 3,438 residents and 143 businesses and institutions. The monetary cost included $200 million in federal and local public subsidies for land acquisition and site preparation. Today General Motors is building Buicks, Oldsmobiles, and Cadillacs in a factory on that site, which has about 5,000 employees and pays $12 million annually in local taxes [Jones & Bachelor 1986].

Cities and counties can promote their employment base through their zoning powers and development of industrial parks. Zoning, as chapter 5 showed, is primarily a regulatory tool, more useful for excluding unwanted land uses than for inducing desired ones. However, such restrictions can appeal to a developer looking for an attractive site for a corporate headquarters or high-technology laboratory. Many communities have special zones that are limited to such facilities and thus openly invite them. Controls prevent noise, smoke, outdoor materials storage, and heavy truck traffic, and require landscaping and architectural features that give the site a campus-like appearance.

The industrial park adds to the zoning restrictions government provision of roads, utilities, and other infrastructures that attract employers. These are common in suburban areas with their expanses of open land, but also appear in center city redevelopments. Charleston, South Carolina, established such a zone in 1995 on the 1,600 acres of a naval base and shipyard which the Defense Department closed. In the first year, this industrial park had attracted 21 companies and 4,100 jobs to the site [Spaid 1996].

Chicago designated several industrial corridors as Planned Manufacturing Districts and planned to upgrade such necessary infrastructures as highways and rail links. City officials also aid industrial redevelopment by helping to assemble land parcels divided among several owners for sale to a new investor.

A special type of industrial park is the business "incubator," which provides low-cost space and shared equipment for new firms seeking a foothold in their markets. Typically, they occupy older buildings that can be remodeled at minimal cost. As of 1992, there were over 470 of these around the nation. One of the first was the University City Science Center in Philadelphia, initiated by a public-private partnership and benefiting from its proximity to the University of Pennsylvania and Drexel University. In 1992 it was home to 105 organizations with more than 6,000 employees. Many firms that started there have moved out to find larger quarters. A high failure rate plagues new industrial firms, but those which start out in an "incubator" evidently have a better chance to succeed [Steffens 1992]. Local partnerships also aid "incu-

bation" by coordinating the flow of private venture capital to new firms, as does Anoka County, Minnesota.

A major hindrance to industrial development in older areas is the soil and water pollution that has been left by their former occupants. Regulations on disposal of wastes were uncommon in the past, and those that did exist were often ignored. Now, these abandoned sites, called *brownfields* (to distingush them from the *greenfields* in undeveloped suburban locations) have little appeal to developers. An owner is financially liable to clean up what pollution remains there, and on many sites no assessment of soil conditions has ever been done. Chicago and Illinois agencies have determined the costs of cleanup at several locations and arranged for financing it, and thus enabled the properties to be restored to the employment and tax rolls [Chicago, City of 1995].

Industrial development is also channeled and can be delayed or stymied, by political conflict. Residents near a site may oppose building a factory or warehouse on an open site near them, fearing increased traffic, intrusion on their views, and lowered property values. Economic development requires that chemical plants, truck freight terminals, waste processing facilities, and similar "bad neighbors" be located somewhere in a region. Such "LULUs" (Locally Unwanted Land Uses) often have large negative externalities, notably noise, odors, pollution, and ugliness, and could pose health and safety hazards if mismanaged. When opponents successfully mount a NIMBY (Not In My Back Yard) campaign, planners have to find less resistant locations. These locations may also be less desirable from an environmental or engineering standpoint.

Planners are also looking ahead to the

"civic hardware" needs of the information economy. For many companies, the prime infrastructure will be the fiber-optic cables that link them with the world's electronic networks, without which most economic development will stall. By early 1996, the public utilities department of Anaheim, California, had installed 50 miles of such cables through the busiest districts, and more than 60 data-intensive companies had bid for access to it. The city will get a percentage of the fees collected by the telecommunications firms operating the service. Another innovation is the remote worksite, from which employees can communicate with the "home" office. In the Los Angeles, New York, and Washington metropolitan areas with their long commuting distances, such suburban worksites can reduce travel and thus congestion and air pollution. No long-range local plan for industrial development can now ignore these new potentials for organizing work, whether the facilities are actually provided by public or private enterprise. Chapter 11 looks ahead to their future development.

6.5 DOWNTOWNS, UPTOWNS, AND EDGE CITIES

The most visible sector of a metropolitan area is its downtown: the cluster of major office buildings, retail stores, government edifices, hotels, and cultural centers. This visibility gives it a political dominance as well, as mayors and city legislators are often judged on how well this focal point of the urban economy flourishes. Many downtowns are not flourishing, to be sure. Their structures date back a century or more, and they have lost customers and employees, and consequently, investors. This is not true for the global authority centers and those which enjoy concentrated office and civic activity. And many oth-

ers with fewer resources are spending to spur a resurgence in their business districts. But where government investment must supplement or take the place of private funds, political conflict rises over how and where those limited resources are spent.

There are five kinds of business districts in metropolitan areas, in terms of the policy issues and choices that guide them. These districts are primarily retail and office centers, but they may contain other magnets that concentrate activity. The *traditional downtown* is one, of course. Even if reasonably prosperous, it is still likely to have declining retail activity and an increasing concentration of offices. Managerial, financial, legal, and governmental personnel must stay in the information stream to be effective, which requires personal contacts in the form of meetings and meals. In this respect, only Manhattan can be Manhattan; Newark is not in that stream. Electronic mail, fax transmissions, and video-conferencing, so useful for many purposes, cannot substitute either. What retail activity remains downtown generally serves the daytime office workers and perhaps the lower-income households living nearby. An important downtown adjunct is the convention center that draws visitors who spend money from ample expense accounts in hotels, restaurants, and places of entertainment.

The challenges that these downtowns present to planners vary with the factors that promote expansion or decay. In some, it may be necessary only to channel the growth the market initiates. San Francisco voters, in a 1984 referendum, limited the height of buildings and the rate of new construction and imposed strict design standards. Their city has a healthy downtown retail, information, tourist, and convention trade, nourished by a strong public transit network and a cultural ambiance unlike any other. Cities on the opposite end of the spectrum may be unable to retain even a minimal commercial health in downtown; Gary, Indiana has virtually no central business district.

Most places stand between these extremes, and must inject public funds and subsidies to stimulate private investment that would not take place otherwise. Frieden and Sagalyn [1989] document downtown renewals in such cities as San Diego, Baltimore, and Pasadena, California, which required a sensitive blending of not only funds from the public and private sector but also ideas and organizational talent. Holding to the traditional rather than the community-based strategy of development, they argue that "cities have shown great skill in making adjustments without sliding back into the old implementation deadlocks. Fast learning and shrewd management may not be able to solve every problem, but they can handle at least a few more at the margin" [Frieden & Sagalyn 1989, p. 316].

Much planning time has been devoted to redevelopment of downtowns, with mixed success. Robertson [1995] identifies five major strategies that various cities have pursued to "rescue" their central business districts from the negative trends of the past decades: (1) converting downtown streets into pedestrian malls to attract shoppers and visitors (although some malls have failed to prosper; see Steinhauer 1996), (2) constructing indoor shopping centers to sustain retail trade, (3) preserving historic structures and converting them to specialty shops and tourist attractions, (4) connecting them with waterfronts, which are redeveloped as parks and other public amenities, and (5) office construction, with the hotels, shops, and restaurants that serve their professional and clerical workers.

Depending on the city, these projects have been supplemented with convention centers and facilities for sports and the arts. Several concepts or images of downtowns have competed for planners' attention, and no one has become dominant. Indeed, a lack of focus on basic purposes has often wasted energy and resources [Abbott 1993].

A second type of business district serves the *neighborhoods* of central cities and their suburbs. Here one finds the grocery, hardware, and drug stores which serve the daily needs of residents. Medical and legal offices, bank branches, and restaurants occupy other spaces, along with small specialty businesses that find these locations to be the least expensive. Early in this century, business districts like these sprang up at the intersections of streetcar and bus lines, while now they locate where motorists have easy access and parking. Planning choices are related to the larger neighborhoods from which these centers draw their economic and physical vitality. If homes remain of constant quality and personal security is protected, these businesses thrive. Many cities have neighborhood renewal and preservation programs that aid small businesses to modernize and expand.

The third group consists of the *new downtowns*, the major suburban shopping centers that have drawn so much trade out of the first two types. As the affluent population moved to the suburbs after World War II and became automobile-dependent, retailers naturally followed them. They are often the cores of the "edge cities" [Garreau 1991] that line the freeways and include office complexes and service enterprises such as banks that surround them.

These fringe-area downtowns pose complex challenges to planners. Most are either in suburbs separately incorporated from the central city or in unincorporated county areas, and no coordination may exist between their plans and those of adjacent communities. Planning offices in those jurisdictions are often minimally staffed, and part-time elected officials may not be able to examine proposals in sufficient depth. Second, the centers' reliance on automobiles can create severe traffic congestion. Mass transit service to edge cities is minimal, and there may be no means for pedestrians to reach one center from an adjoining one. Third, such intense development puts heavy demands on inadequate water and waste management facilities.

Each addition to such a center stimulates demand for more housing and resident services in the area and turns the entire development cycle more quickly, expanding the volume of planning choices. The Mall of America in Bloomington, Minnesota, the largest such center in the nation, is both the result and the stimulus of development along the Interstate 494 strip south of Minneapolis and adjacent to the airport which the state chose to retain. Smaller communities around the nation have had Wal-Mart knocking on their doors requesting approval of a fringe-area site, to the horror of downtown merchants, and few are the places that have kept that door closed in the end.

A fourth type of commercial center is often smaller than the first and third, but like the suburban complex, owes its existence to the automobile. The *highway service strip* typically clings to major roads on the outskirts of cities, freeway interchanges, and around major airports. Common to these are automobile and truck dealers and service facilities, motels and hotels, and restaurants. General shopping centers may also be nearby. Unlike the comprehensive centers of the third type, these have grown up with no central design. Each

new Amoco station, McDonald's, and Holiday Inn added to what was already there, and they in turn attracted Texacos, Burger Kings, and Ramadas. Tangled traffic flow and visual clutter are the major results of this lack of planning. Yet, service to travelers is a vital source of revenue and jobs to many communities, and they are reluctant to restrain this market-driven development.

Fifth, the *leisure consumption zone* has appeared in many metropolitan areas in the past two decades, both as redevelopments in older districts and new placements on the growth fringes. One form of this is the "festival market," which millions of visitors to Boston's Faneuil Hall Marketplace, Underground Atlanta, and Ghirardelli Square in San Francisco have enjoyed. It may occupy one or more old buildings, perhaps erstwhile factories or warehouses, that have been remodeled just enough to accommodate shops, restaurants, and theaters within an historic ambiance. They supply a moderately affluent clientele of residents and tourists with alternatives to the traditional downtowns and the stamped-from-the-same-mold suburban malls. While they represent more imaginative design and investment, they have usually required major public subsidies as well. As many have failed as have succeeded, and so they present a higher risk that planners must later cope with a white elephant [Sawicki 1989].

Other leisure facilities consist of resort hotels, recreational and fitness centers, theaters, casinos, amusement parks, sports arenas, and boat marinas. An affluent urban population that has already invested in upscale homes now looks for additional ways to spend money, and many entrepreneurs are eager to accommodate them. Las Vegas's downtown and Strip are the grandest examples of this type (see Figure 6.3), while the Orlando area,

Figure 6.3 The world-famous Las Vegas Strip, the grandest leisure consumption zone of all. Photo by Landiscor Aerial Information.

boasting of Walt Disney World and a host of other attractions, competes strongly for the family trade. Such leisure zones have heavily impacted land values in their segments of cities and driven out homes, small businesses and even more intensive uses. Some have also drawn subsidies from state and local governments eager to entice tourists.

Times Square is being reborn in this mold also. It has been an entertainment magnet for many decades, of course, but by the 1970s was catering only to a limited-income clientele. The planners and city officials who charted its renaissance in the 1980s envisioned an extension of the midtown office cluster. As the study in chapter 1 explained, however, that never was accepted by the major investors.

> What is most remarkable about this area is that it bears no resemblance at all to the scenarios laid out by planners, civic activists, and politicians for most of the last two decades. . . . . What the shifts on 42nd Street reveal most of all is an evolution of the American city itself, from an

environment driven primarily by business and commerce to one that exists mainly for tourism, entertainment, and consumption. [Goldberger 1996]

While New York City draws more such leisure consumers than other cities, none can overlook this evolution in its economic development planning.

Two other forms of commercial activity that increasingly draw the attention of planners are on the very smallest scale: the home business and "urban farm." Residents have long used their homesites for many occupations, from music lessons and tax preparation to auto repair and animal breeding. Municipal nuisance laws regulate these to one extent or another. Some cities prohibit all commercial activity, holding that it detracts from the residential environment which that zone defines (although they may not enforce this ban diligently). Others permit home occupations that do not create noise, odors, or excessive traffic and cannot be seen by neighbors, and may charge a fee for approving them. The newest information technologies make it possible to work at home and be entirely "residence-friendly." Many central cities and suburbs have recently revised their codes toward greater tolerance of home-based businesses, responding also to the higher level of entrepreneurship in the modern economy [Freyman 1995].

The "urban farm" is gaining popularity in inner-city neighborhoods with both vacant land and a lack of supermarkets. Chicago, Los Angeles, Boston, and many other cities promote gardening with federal and local grants, enabling the producers to sell the food in neighborhood markets. A further benefit is the social cooperation that the gardening groups promote, which then are prepared to undertake other joint projects. These groups have also created jobs in marketing and food processing [A. Tyson 1996].

6.6 BENEFITS AND COSTS

No single perspective is adequate to evaluate the outcomes of these economic development efforts. The traditional and alternative strategies outlined in section 6.2 offer contrasting viewpoints from which to assess them; a project could be rated a success from one viewpoint yet seriously deficient from the other. Abundant examples could probably support any conclusion an analyst favors. Indeed, there are no fully accepted data that support any one judgment; as Molotch [1993, p. 42] observes, "The art of true-costing of development remains very much in its infancy." It may be most fruitful to begin this section with several questions that should guide an assessment.

First, has the community that one is examining obtained the most appropriate form of development for its situation and resources and yielded the best possible ratio of benefits to costs? Second, has the development plan expanded jobs and services for local residents, including realistic opportunities for the least advantaged? And third, has the decision-making process been sufficiently broad-based to take in all relevant community stakeholders yet achieve results in a reasonable period of time? Some examples will offer varied answers to these questions.

Whether development has been "appropriate" and the best use of resources depends both on the internal needs of a community and its place in the larger markets. Just after Detroit enabled General Motors to build a new plant in the Poletown neighborhood, as described above, Chrysler demanded similar aid for a new factory. Detroit officials yielded (having established a precedent that was

hard to break) and in 1992, the $1 billion plant opened after about a thousand homes and businesses had been razed. Direct public subsidies in the form of loans and grants from federal, state, and municipal sources came to $246 million [Bachelor 1994, p. 606].

These two Detroit projects, for General Motors and Chrysler, raise complex question of benefits and costs. Neither plant employs as many persons as the one it replaced, due to greater efficiencies in assembly line technology. One cannot easily measure the social impact of the destruction of the two neighborhoods. There were two clear winners, however, in the judgment of one analyst. The corporations gained new facilities at minimum cost, and both substantially increased their profits since then. Detroit public officials, as well, benefited politically from the projects. However, Bachelor points to the large and not fully determined costs that will be paid by the public over many years to come. Among them, Detroit gave up substantial revenue to cover part of the expenses, a gap which must be made up by the city's home and business owners, who will pay higher taxes or endure reduced public services [Bachelor 1994, p. 610].

The second question has acquired new urgency with the 1996 welfare reforms geared to placing clients in jobs, and with corporate downsizing putting many on the unemployment rolls at least temporarily. In 1980, one of the most depressed urban areas of the nation was the south end of New York City's borough of the Bronx. Massive federal, state, and city programs and community initiated self-help projects have partially reversed that decay. Major retail centers, industrial employers, and wholesalers have provided a stronger job base, albeit for many who live elsewhere in the region [Onaran 1994]. In 1995, a project to locate a $25 million wastepaper sorting plant in a disused railyard in South Bronx was agreed upon. The facility was intended as the first step in establishing a much larger recycling mill that would create 700 jobs along with housing, child care, and health services. The community leaders who vigorously sought this development saw it as a particularly suitable source of income for the borough's unemployed. However, such projects must be targeted at skill development if they are going to open doors to those at the bottom of the income ladder.

A responsive yet efficient process may seem a contradiction in terms, and in some instances it has been. In 1966, the U.S. Economic Development Administration (EDA) initiated a program to bring jobs to Oakland, which at that time suffered from a high unemployment rate. Its components included new hangars and an air cargo terminal for the Oakland Airport, a marine terminal and industrial park on the harbor, and small business expansion loans. Planning began with high hopes, and the EDA committed $23 million to supplement local funds. But by 1969, only $3 million had been actually spent, and very little came of the effort. The main reason was that planning and administration were divided among five federal agencies, the city of Oakland (itself fragmented between its mayor, council, and bureaucracy), the semi-independent Port of Oakland authority, and several constituent groups and would-be clients. Action on the public works program required 70 successive favorable decisions to reach completion. Although that was possible, the organizational friction slowed the pace to a crawl and finally halted it [Pressman & Wildavsky 1984, ch. 5]. Designed to be responsive to many interests, the program was in the end paralyzed by them.

A very different approach was chosen by officials in Claremont, New Hampshire (population 14,000). Much of its blue-collar industry and employment had left the city by 1993, and the central business district was largely vacant. Federal and state renewal aid had nearly dried up, so the city could not rely on that source. In response, it aggressively recruited new businesses, borrowing funds to acquire and redevelop abandoned land and buildings. The city's planner has been a major player in these actions, seeking the most appropriate firms for job expansion [Frisby 1996]. Claremont's advantage is that a few decision makers defined the city's interests and were able to seize opportunities quickly.

Economic well-being is closely tied to other aspects of planning and development. The following chapters examine choices in housing, transportation, environmental protection, and the social amenities. While they are important policy areas in themselves, each has implications for the economic base of a city as well. Home construction and remodeling is a vital source of jobs and requires a steady flow of public and private credit. In transportation, ease of access is a critical feature of communities and sites which industrial and commercial investors look for. Environmental quality has often been defined in economic terms, with a complex mix of costs and benefits. And the broader cultural amenities and quality-of-life issues affect communities' prospects for growth. These succeeding topics are thus part of the seamless web that urban planning must attend to.

FOR REVIEW AND DISCUSSION

1. For what reasons has economic development become a major task of local government planners? How compatible is this with their land regulation duties?

CHAPTER

7

Planning for Homes

7.1 GOALS OF HOUSING POLICY

The *home* is the prime symbol of personal privacy, of one's sovereignty over a piece of space. Yet, when defined as *housing*, it also becomes a major issue of responsibility of national, state, and local governments. Like other land-use issues, it is interwoven with controversial human service questions. This tension between the public and private character of personal living space creates unique political and professional responsibilities for planners. They must not only consider housing as an architectural or financial challenge but also comprehend its social, economic, and cultural meanings.

Another dimension of conflict over housing contrasts the needy with the affluent, the "shelter society" with the "post-shelter society" [Sternlieb 1986, 164]. In the first group are those whose primary needs are adequate and safe physical housing and who would lack them in the absence of outside intervention. In 1996, the U.S. Department of Housing and Urban Development reported that as of 1993, 5.3 million families lived in substandard conditions or paid more than half their income on rent. This figure had increased by 1.5

million since 1979 due to declining incomes and rising housing costs. Needs were most pronounced among elderly persons, Hispanics, and in the western part of the nation generally. This shelter society has increasingly spawned political movements with major impacts on state and local housing policies and the programs of businesses and nonprofit organizations.

The post-shelter society, however, cannot only afford a home but regards the dwelling unit as a symbol of prestige and accomplishment and, above all, as a means of capital accumulation. Its members' main fear is not the loss of home as such but the loss of property values. Not only are these two groups inherent rivals for public policy attention but they come into direct conflict over proposals to place homes for low-income persons in an established middle- or upper-class residential neighborhood.

This division between the shelter and post-shelter societies is largely spatial. A 1996 study by the Harvard University Joint Center for Housing Studies found a widening gap in housing quality between the growing number of homeowners in suburbia and the lower-income renters in central cities. Declining real incomes and numbers of affordable rental units put a tightening squeeze on the latter group. Indeed, as fringe suburban communities gain both jobs and dwellings, many older suburbs face problems of decline similar to the central cities [Humphreys 1996].

The responsibilities of government, typically spelled out in state laws, encompass both of these societies. California planning law, for example, sets a high priority on "decent housing" and "a suitable living environment for every family." To achieve this requires "the cooperative participation of government and the private sector in an effort to expand housing opportunities and accommodate the housing needs of all economic levels." [cited by Gallion and Eisner 1985, p. 316]. State and municipal building codes specify the health and safety features of dwellings. City and county plans elaborate on these responsibilities, especially in the location of residential areas. Federal policy, embodied in the Housing Act of 1937 and its successors, reinforces these mandates and has provided limited aid to implement them.

These responsibilities are embodied in three basic policy goals. First, communities seek to *establish and protect desirable residential conditions* through land-use regulation and the provision of services such as water, drainage, crime control, environmental protection, and waste management. The goal assumes that private parties will build and purchase the homes, and government concerns itself only with the conditions in which they exist. While this goal is central for the post-shelter society, such living amenities are important also to lower-income households who have found dwellings that meet their needs.

Many programs help implement this first goal. The zoning, building, and subdivision regulations mentioned in section 5.4 are most obvious. In residential areas, a common policy is to exclude, as much as possible, land uses deemed incompatible with existing homes. For a neighborhood of expensive single-family homes, thus, townhouses costing a mere $100,000 could be unacceptable. In more modestly priced areas, zoning would simply exclude factories and large stores.

A second goal is to *protect and rehabilitate the existing housing stock*. Many cities have lost serviceable older homes to decay and finally the wrecker due to lack of maintenance. Many more dwellings still standing are in danger of that fate. This occurs in scattered sites in some neighborhoods, but is most obvious in an area with large-scale deterioration. Landlords and owner occupants alike perceive that property values are declining, and if they cannot sell out, they simply cease maintaining the structures. Many causes of this decline in housing quality are beyond the immediate control of the local planning participants. For example, when a major industry closes and its employees cannot find other jobs, the surrounding residential areas are likely to suffer as well.

Communities have several means of pursuing this second goal. To strictly enforce its building code, a city may conduct regular inspections of homes. When it finds a leaking roof or unsafe wiring, it orders the owner of the building to make repairs within a set time period. If, in the owner's judgment, that dwelling is worth the investment, the repairs will be done. But another result may be abandonment, and if the building is not rescued quickly, vandals or fire may erase all value. In many large cities, the sheer number of substandard houses exceeds the resources for inspection and monitoring.

The third goal of public policy is to *expand and upgrade the housing supply for market-disadvantaged households*. This demands much more investment of financial and political resources than the first two. Since the late 1930s, much of the support for expanding housing opportunity has come from the federal government, responding to demands from urban public officials and housing-related interest groups. The forms of aid have varied: loans and grants to local housing agencies, mortgages at below-market interest rates, subsidies for construction of privately owned rental housing, and rent vouchers to lower-income persons.

In directing this flow of federal funds, local planning systems occupy the center of decision making. Federal programs have always permitted them the option of participating or not. Having received the money, planners and elected officials inherited the hard choices of how to spend it. If new homes are to be built, where? For what income levels and household types? Should home ownership be subsidized? Should the established residential patterns in the city, particularly those of race and income, be reinforced or changed by public action? And what should be done for the chronically homeless? These questions had many potential answers, each with political as well as technical benefits and costs.

Local planners need access to accurate data on their housing conditions. This is a formidable challenge in larger cities with thousands of dwellings to survey and highly transient residents. Geographic information systems, described in chapter 5, offer the best means for storing and retrieving these data if supported by a continuous means of collecting it.

The public housing project was the most common way to implement this policy in the 1940s and 1950s. Local housing authorities, arms of city governments, used federal aid and local funds to build modern apartments in place of slums and continue to manage them as landlords. Vast tracts were built in larger cities, and although most of them still provide shelter today, the quality of life in them varies widely. In general, the high-rise family dwellings are least desirable; the Cabrini-Green (illustrated in Figure 7.1) and Robert Taylor projects in Chicago are widely known symbols of the ills of the African-American urban poor. But many other developments, with lower and better-maintained buildings, have been relative successes, as long waiting lists of persons seeking to move into them testify.

Political pressures and limited budgets had much to do with the disasters of mass-housing programs. Such projects were typically located in areas of the city that were inhabited by racial minorities or otherwise undesirable to white persons. Meyerson and Banfield [1957] document how Chicago's city council placed public housing in existing African-American neighborhoods in spite of planners' efforts to disperse it around the city. Further, pressures to keep costs low led to construction of substandard buildings with minimal living amenities. In St. Louis, for example, the typical apartments were too small for the families assigned to them, and design quality in the massive Pruitt-Igoe project was so low as to make it repulsive to all but the most desperate tenants [Meehan 1979, ch. 3]. Federal rules gradually excluded households above the lowest income levels, and so denied the projects the stability that working residents often bring to an area. Viewed from the 1990s, these high concentrations of very poor people have become isolated from the employment opportunities in the region, virtually locking them in the cycle of poverty.

After viewing these experiences, Congress reshaped federal housing programs toward a wider range of approaches. The Housing Acts of 1968 and 1974 gave incentives for private construction of homes for low-income house-

Figure 7.1 The Cabrini-Green public housing complex in Chicago as it looked in the late 1970s. It is being gradually demolished. Source: American Planning Association.

holds to rent or buy, and subsidized the rents of needy families who occupied existing dwellings. From 1968 to 1985, the federal government alone spent more than $100 billion in housing assistance and state and local governments added to that sum. Yet, because the price of homes rose sharply during that period, the need remained far from met. Further policy shifts in the late 1980s and 1990s are described in a later section.

7.2 THE FALL AND RISE OF RESIDENTIAL NEIGHBORHOODS

Residential areas evolve under many interlocking influences. One might travel through a city neighborhood and see many signs of decay: abandonments, deterioration, and general disrepair. But a visit a year or two later reveals rehabilitation work going on, new homes on once-vacant lots, and fresh roofs, coats of paint, and shrubs. Conversely, a modest-cost suburban neighborhood can plunge into depression when its residents lose either the means or will to maintain its quality.

People use an informal index to rate the current desirability and future prospects of a residential area, as shown by their willingness to buy into it or upgrade their homes. This index depends on many variables: ethnicity and income of its inhabitants, physical appearance and cost of its homes, land uses in surrounding areas, physical safety, quality of schools, and distances to jobs. Some of these variables are generated within the neighborhood; others depend on external change.

Neighborhoods dominated by large multifamily structures, particularly those that are publicly assisted, are most likely to have a low desirability index, even more so when they are close to such nuisances as factories, bars, and traffic congestion. When there are no redeeming features, such as proximity to parks, lakeshores, and employment, that index will remain low. Such areas are most likely to lose current residents who can afford to live elsewhere, and attract the poorest who are most transient and likely to depend on public assistance. As housing quality declines, it becomes a "slum" or "ghetto," terms with ambiguous definitions but vivid negative images. Large areas in Detroit, for example, have been totally abandoned and some entire blocks have nothing but weeds growing on them today [Vergara 1995].

Residential areas can rise as well as fall on the index. One type of revitalization is *gentrification,* in which middle- and upper-income persons buy and rehabilitate homes in a depressed neighborhood, and if they do not live there themselves, sell or rent to others. The former residents cannot afford the higher prices or rents and so are forced to move to less desirable dwellings. This is socially controversial, in that the gentrifiers usually draw some public financial benefits which do not flow to the less affluent. Yet, the city gains tax revenue and increased housing quality, at least in the rehabilitated area. This has been common in older cities across the nation, focusing on neighborhoods close to downtown with structures that are still basically sound.

An alternative to gentrification is *incumbent upgrading.* Aid programs enable current residents to buy and/or improve their homes

and stay in the neighborhood. Generally, such persons have a high level of commitment to their area's safety and quality and resist forces that could lower its index. Essential to this restoration is a high level of public services that enhance the substance and appearance of the area's value, especially street and park maintenance, police protection, and enforcement of building codes. A later section describes specific programs that promote this upgrading.

Several studies of neighborhood improvement projects suggest that the presence of a "civil class" is vital to their initiation and success. Members of this class can be identified by their (a) commitment to the image and integrity of the neighborhood, (b) high degree of concern for their neighbors as persons and willingness to pressure them to cooperate with the projects, (c) readiness to integrate newcomers into the area, and (d) self-discipline in acting on their good intentions. Civility in this sense does not correlate closely with race, income, education, or other familiar socioeconomic indicators. All neighborhoods have varying proportions of the "civil" and "less civil." The more there are of the former, the better chance an area has to preserve its livability and to succeed in a renewal program [Clay 1979].

7.3 RESIDENTIAL DESIGN ALTERNATIVES

Public and private planners have a large repertoire of community designs from which to draw. Chapter 2 described the planned industrial towns, model tenements, and garden cities that offer some classic models. The suburban development that followed World War II further expanded the options. As planners viewed existing cities plagued by decay and new suburbs that seemingly developed at random, they often dreamed of "doing it right the next time." Their ideals blended many objectives: closeness to nature, energy efficiency, pedestrian- and child-friendliness, social cohesiveness, a mix of culture and income groups, and access to good jobs. This can be likened to a fabric into which varied strands of material are woven to produce a legible and pleasing whole. The results have been "new town" movements on various scales, sufficiently larger than the typical residential subdivision to incorporate some holistic community features. Clearly, market forces have much to do with these trends. Public policies can also affect many of these conditions, although there are limits to which such planning can be successful in the broader real estate market.

The 1960s saw the rise of such new cities as Irvine, California, (150,000 by the 1990s), Coral Springs, Florida, and Columbia, Maryland. These are holistic communities that blend residential, shopping, and employment uses, and higher- and lower-income households, using varying design concepts. Each was sponsored by a private developer and backed by a major corporation (section 4.2 notes the roles of the Irvine Company and James Rouse in the birth of Irvine and Columbia, respectively). Thus, local government authorities were only passive players in approving and occasionally modifying such plans. However, federal grants and credit backing were highly instrumental in their financing, particularly through the New Community Development Corporation within the Department of Housing and Urban Development. This program aided fifteen projects during the early 1970s, but lack of market appeal prevented most of them from expanding to their intended size.

A special form of residential governance is that which maintains a high degree of control over its immediate environment. About 32 million Americans now live within the 150,000 *residential community associations* described in chapter 3. Developers plan them holistically and use the association theme in marketing the homes. When local governments approve such a shared-property development, they require formation of this kind of association and review its rules and bylaws to ensure their conformance to law [Barton & Silverman, 1994].

More distinctive yet is the gated community, which is not only governed by a private association but also surrounded by walls and fences, with access through a guarded gate only for residents and those whom they specifically admit. An estimated four million people lived in these protected enclaves as of 1995. An example is Klahanie, Washington, east of Seattle, with nearly 10,000 middle class citizens who willingly live under tight restrictions on their property and behavior. Some, such as Canyon Lake, California, are legally incorporated as cities, while others exist as semiautonomous enclaves within other cities or counties. Such communities cannot legally exclude would-be buyers on the grounds of race or ethnicity, but their prices and social ambiance filter out people who are "different," which is exactly the intention of the developers and residents [Egan 1995].

Development of new residential communities is being reevaluated in the 1990s under conditions and values that are quite different from earlier decades. First, there is a heightened concern for the social and environmental costs of urban sprawl. As suburbs spread out unhindered except by physical barriers, travel times lengthen and the air pollution produced by the commuters' vehicles increases. Farmlands, forests, and other open spaces fill in with homes, factories, and shops to the dismay of many observers. And in this process of suburban growth, many new residents fail to connect with one another and become isolated from social and economic groups that are different from them.

A second concern is for the affordability of housing. Many households are confined to central-city locations far from job opportunities because they cannot pay for homes anywhere else. This problem is acute in such metropolitan areas as San Francisco, Los Angeles, and Washington D.C., but affects other areas in varying degrees. Part of this plight stems from private industry's inability to profitably build or remodel homes for the lower-income market, and part from the failure of public and private enterprise to maintain the existing housing stock in good condition. In some cases, government restrictions and mandates are excessive and drive up housing costs for reasons unrelated to health and safety.

For some planners, the answer to these two concerns lies in what is loosely called "New Urbanism" or "traditional neighborhood development." They base their thinking on the layout of the quintessential small town, seen in such cities as Oak Park, Illinois, Alexandria, Virginia, and Coral Gables, Florida. Their highest priority is to promote a sense of community, enabling all residents to feel linked in a network of common interests. The "classic suburb," by contrast,

> is less a community than an agglomeration of houses, shops, and offices connected to another by cars, not by the fabric of human life. . . . . The suburb is the last word in privatization, perhaps even its lethal consummation, and it spells the end of authentic civic life. [Duany & Plater-Zyberk 1992, p. 21]

A key expression of the values of New Urbanism is in the Ahwahnee Principles, authored in 1991 by planners Peter Calthorpe, Andres Duany, Elizabeth Plater-Zyberk, and others who met at the resort hotel by that name in Yosemite National Park. (Figure 7.2 sets these forth.) Several specific urban plans embody these ideals. The first of the neotraditional designs was built on 80 acres at Seaside, Florida, from a design by Duany and Plater-Zyberk. They followed this with Kentlands on 352 acres in Gaithersburg, Maryland, which incorporates homes with offices and a regional shopping mall. Late in 1995, Walt Disney Corporation began developing Celebration, a residential community with its own business district on the edge of its amusement complex near Orlando. Community design projects in such cities as Austin, Texas, and Chattanooga, Tennessee, have demonstrated that citizens take interest in traditionally styled communities when they can participate in designing them. Figure 7.3 is a design for such a development in Lino Lakes, Minnesota, a suburb of Minneapolis and St. Paul, at an interchange of I-35W. Its intent is to provide a new city center that blends medium-density housing with a commercial and civic core. In this case, the city has final control over the standards to be followed by developers, and a design review committee will monitor each segment of the project.

New Urbanists reject many of the current zoning and development regulations common to suburbia. For example, they prefer to keep residences and business in close proximity, perhaps even sharing the same buildings, to offer convenient, nonmotorized access to shopping. They favor narrow streets with sidewalks to slow vehicle movement and provide safe walking routes. Parking, if not at curbside, should be in the middle of blocks to enable stores and homes to front directly on the street. Reducing dependence on automobiles by providing ready access to public transit is another goal. The ideal seems

The Ahwahnee Principles

Preamble:

Existing patterns of urban and suburban development seriously impair our quality of life. The symptoms are: more congestion and air pollution resulting from our increased dependence on automobiles, the loss of precious open space, the need for costly improvements to roads and public services, the inequitable distribution of economic resources, and the loss of a sense of community. By drawing upon the best from the past and the present, we can plan communities that will more successfully serve the needs of those who live and work within them. Such planning should adhere to certain fundamental principles.

Community Principles:

1. All planning should be in the form of complete and integrated communties containing housing, shops, work places, schools, parks and civic facilities essential to the daily life of the residents.
2. Community size should be designed so that housing, jobs, daily needs and other activities are within easy walking distance of each other.
3. As many activities as possible should be located within easy walking distance of transit stops.
4. A community should contain a diversity of housing types to enable citizens from a wide range of economic levels and age groups to live within its boundaries.
5. Businesses within the community should provide a range of job types for the community's residents.
6. The location and character of the community should be consistent with a larger transit network.
7. The community should have a center focus that combines commercial, civic, cultural and recreational uses.
8. The community should contain an ample supply of specialized open space in the form of squares, greens and parks whose frequent use is encouraged through placement and design.
9. Public spaces should be designed to encourage the attention and presence of people at all hours of the day and night.
10. Each community or cluster of communities should have a well-defined edge, such as agricultural greenbelts or wildlife corridors, permanently protected from development.
11. Streets, pedestrian paths and bike paths should contribute to a system of fully-connected and interesting routes to all destinations. Their design should encourage pedestrian and bicycle use by being small and spatially defined by buildings, trees and lighting; and by discouraging high speed traffic.
12. Wherever possible, the natural terrain, drainage, and vegetation of the community should be preserved with superior examples contained within parks or greenbelts.
13. The community design should help conserve resources and minimize waste.
14. Communities should provide for the efficient use of water through the use of natural drainage, drought tolerant landscaping and recycling.
15. The street orientation, the placement of buildings and the use of shading should contribute to the energy efficiency of the community.

Regional Principles:

1. The regional land use planning structure should be integrated within a larger transportation network built around transit rather than freeways.
2. Regions should be bounded by and provide a continuous system of greenbelt/wildlife corridors to be determined by natural conditions.
3. Regional institutions and services (government, stadiums, museums, etc.) should be located in the urban core.
4. Materials and methods of construction should be specific to the region, exhibiting continuity of history and culture and compatibility with the climate to encourage the development of local character and community identity.

Implementation Strategy:

1. The general plan should be updated to incorporate the above principles.
2. Rather than allowing developer-initiated, piecemeal development, local governments should take charge of the planning process. General plans should designate where new growth, infill or redevelopment will be allowed to occur.
3. Prior to any development, a specific plan should be prepared based on the planning principles. With the adoption of specific plans, complying projects could proceed with minimal delay.
4. Plans should be developed through an open process and participants in the process should be provided visual models of all planning proposals.

Authors: Peter Calthorpe	Andres Duany	Stefanos Polyzoides
Michael Corbett	Elizabeth Plater-Zyberk	Elizabeth Moule

Figure 7.2 Ahwahnee Principles of Neotraditional town planning. Source: www.bizline.com/clc/ahwnprin.html

Figure 7.3 A traditional neighborhood development to be built in Lino Lakes, Minnesota, at an interchange with Interstate 35W. The intent is to give that suburb a "downtown" that incorporates medium-density housing with a commercial and civic core. Reprinted with permission of the City of Lino Lakes.

to be expressed in the Five-Minute Popsicle Rule: a child should be able to walk safely from home to buy a popsicle within five minutes [Peirce 1996a].

Calthorpe [1993] created a series of regional and neighborhood designs that pay special attention to accessibility by walking, bicycling, and public transit. In 1995, the city of Broomfield, Colorado, hired him to prepare a new master plan following New Urbanist principles. This suburb of Denver with a population of 30,000 seeks to avoid the social isolation and automobile-dependence that characterizes the typical new developments. However, Broomfield's planners must "weave new urbanism into a complex world of zoning laws, property rights, road-engineering codes, economic realities, and basic human prejudices such as opposition to living near low-income housing" [M. Howard 1996]. Viewing these conditions, many planners fear that the traditional ideals have limited application in existing cities where the problems of affordability and livability are most severe.

7.4 PUBLIC INTERVENTION IN HOUSING SUPPLY

The most pressing challenge to the public and private housing sectors targets low-income households of the shelter society who are disadvantaged by the market. The aims are to provide affordable housing in general, and to restructure land use and building regulations to make this provision less costly. Implementing these aims is controversial, due not only to the amount of money they require but also the regulatory changes they entail.

Prior to 1980, the primary support for housing programs for low-income households was the federal government, funneling its dollars through municipal housing and redevelopment agencies. Local planners chose the sites and types of dwellings aided. There was some participation by private groups, particularly for the elderly, but again the federal funds provided the bulk of the support.

1980 was a watershed, however. From then to 1988, federal spending for low-income housing assistance declined over 80% when adjusted for inflation. The Reagan administration and a conservative Congress cut these programs more sharply than any other domestic effort [Goetz 1993, ch. 1]. Consequently, state and local governments and a variety of private participants took on the planning and financing of affordable housing and have shown considerable resourcefulness. They often join forces in the community development corporations introduced in chapter 4.

The political impetus for this reorientation of housing policy has often been coalitions of activists at the city and state levels, which first lobbied successfully for public programs, and then became vehicles for planning, funding, and implementing the programs they helped to devise. Goetz [1993, ch. 6] recounts the joint experience of the Community Redevelopment Agency of Los Angeles, a municipal body, and the public-private Los Angeles Housing Partnership which aided nonprofit developers. The city had no effective housing policy of its own in 1980, but after much political conflict in that decade, it produced a cluster of programs surrounded by a politically aware alliance that monitored them and pressed for changes. Municipal planners learned to network constructively with those in the private sector.

Nonprofit organizations play several vital roles in housing development. First, they can mobilize financing from government, foundations, lending institutions, and developers using tax credit investments, and loan it to the actual producers of dwellings. Most big cities have partnerships that do this on a large scale. Second, and most common, they can acquire the land and build the homes themselves. A third function is to manage rental units or advise tenant groups in self-management. Finally, they play an advocacy role, lobbying public officials for expanded assistance [Goetz 1993, ch. 5]. Their agenda fits the community-based strategies for economic development described in section 6.2. That is, they seek to benefit the least advantaged households and neighborhoods in the housing programs they support and maximize those residents' power in the ongoing policymaking process.

New York City's Housing Partnership has sponsored modest-cost home construction by smaller neighborhood builders, most of them of color. Carlton Brown, whose company has been producing row houses on previously abandoned lots in Brooklyn, is one example. Such projects are heavily subsidized by the city and New York State, with low-rate bank mortgages also guaranteed by the state. Established builders in the area offer advice to the newcomers and a nonprofit community development corporation contacts prospective buyers, many of whom live in public rental housing [Oser 1996]. Here too, public planners at the city and neighborhood levels interact with the private entrepreneurs.

Due to the influence of the housing activists, agendas in many cities are oriented to the interests of neighborhood residents rather than the large developers who benefited from the federally financed programs. There is also a greater emphasis on rehabilitation of existing homes wherever possible and small-scale development than on large scale clearance and megaproject construction. It has made possible both *gentrification* and *incumbent upgrading*, varying with specific locations.

Local public and private agencies tap several sources of outside aid in housing development. Much of the federal assistance now flows through Community Development Block Grants, described in chapter 6, and the HOME program, enacted by Congress in 1990 to support new construction, rehabilitation, and rent subsidies. Local housing agencies determine their priorities and then receive funds which they must match on a one-to-four ratio. Community-based nonprofit developers qualify for a significant portion of these dollars, and investments by banks, foundations, and profitmaking firms often expand these resources further.

Several national linkage organizations aid housing programs and supply technical and management aid to local governments and private development enterprises. The Neighborhood Reinvestment Corporation pools government funds with contributions and private loans and transfers them to locally run Neighborhood Housing Services chapters which finance home repairs and energy-efficient improvements in more than 100 ci-

ties. The Local Initiatives Support Corporation, mentioned in chapter 6 as a backer of economic development, also supports housing programs. It has raised nearly two billion dollars to support community development corporations in distressed neighborhoods. It draws funds from major corporations, foundations, and state agencies, and arranges projects for investors who qualify for the federal low-income housing tax credit.

The Enterprise Foundation is a cluster of profitmaking and nonprofit organizations that makes loans to local agencies for affordable housing, finances home mortgages, advises developers on funding and management, and even directly builds homes in several places. A further objective of the Foundation is to assist holistic planning by local authorities and community groups, particularly on means to increase resident participation in decisions [Enterprise Foundation, 1996].

Elderly persons have benefited from many housing ventures in cities of all sizes. As people age, they decide at some point they cannot stay in the single-family home they have occupied, often for many years. Loss of mobility, fear of crime, and inability to care for a home are typical reasons to move, yet they prefer to stay close to their familiar neighborhood. Packages of funding from federal, state, city, and private sources have developed apartment buildings designed specifically for them, often with assisted-living services available. For example, the Senior Lifestyle Management Corporation has developed and currently manages many such properties around the country. The City of Chicago assisted several of its recent large projects with loans and provision of vacant land [Buchholz 1996].

Preserving the housing stock for persons at the lowest edge of the economy is also a challenge. The Tenderloin district of San Francisco stands at the western edge of an expanding downtown and was threatened with gradual demolition in the 1980s. Its dense cluster of old hotels and rooming houses shelter persons who are elderly, disabled, chemically dependent, mentally ill, and victims of AIDS. Some residents, helped by community activists, mobilized to thwart plans to obliterate these dwellings and formed the Tenderloin Neighborhood Development Corporation in 1981. Backed by federal, local, and private funds, it owned, as of 1995, ten apartment buildings that house more than a thousand persons. In addition, the corporation provides social services, medical care, job training, and even after-school programs for the more than 4,000 children who live in the district. Residents participate in building management and gain some jobs thereby. For the long term, Tenderloin has a political identity and a base of activists who stand ready to defend their homes [Robinson 1995].

As the news media make very evident, cities are places of great human need. Poverty, chemical dependency, mental illness, and criminal activity concentrate in certain neighborhoods and provide the clientele for social institutions that serve the victims. Nearly every large- and medium-sized city has a collection of missions, homeless shelters, group homes, health clinics, and halfway houses, most often on the edge of its downtown and in its inner transition zone. There are few large institutions on the scale of a half-century ago, and care is now provided in many small, decentralized facilities, often under private rather than governmental auspices. Hartford, Connecticut, for example, has an unusually large concentration of such facilities in its central area for a city of just 124,000.

From a planning standpoint, these social service facilities represent a hard dilemma. Some are in areas zoned as industrial or com-mercial, which presents few problems. Others are allowed in residential zones, usually by conditional use permit that limits their capacity and imposes other restrictions. In the latter case, they are usually not welcome neighbors, and residents often protest the granting of permits. Indeed, the neighborhoods most often chosen for these facilities tend to be economically marginal, and if there is too large a concentration, they give the area a negative image and possibly increase the dangers of living there.

Some cities have used their building and zoning codes to bar most or all service agencies or to concentrate them in limited areas. In response to a suit over such an action, the U.S. Supreme Court ruled in 1995 that cities may not use single-family zoning regulations to exclude group homes for the disabled or chemically dependent. In that case, Edmonds, Washington, had limited to five the number of unrelated residents in any home in a single-family zone. Justice Ruth Bader Ginsburg's opinion pointed to the 1988 amendments to the federal Fair Housing Act which prevents discrimination against persons with disabilities [Greenhouse 1995]. As a result, cities must show that any restrictions on such care facilities are reasonable and necessary for the disabled residents' own well being.

The need for such means of care and treatment will only increase in the future. As federal government welfare spending declines and state and county funds do not pick up the slack, there will be more privately financed activities. Religious and charitable organizations play a major role now and are flexible enough to expand services if they can attract more contributions. The locations which provide services range from church buildings to remodeled hotels, each in a location that planners must seek to harmonize with the surrounding users and uses.

A tandem strategy in expanding affordable

housing is altering land-use regulations to open more areas for such homes and possibly reduce their costs. It has long been the practice of local governments, particularly in higher-income suburbs, to use their zoning codes to prevent construction of apartments and modest-cost single-family dwellings. Responding to pressures from constituents concerned for social homogenity and property values, they set minimum lot and home sizes beyond the financial reach of a large part of the metropolitan area's residents. Such *exclusionary zoning* is entirely within their land use powers.

Efforts to expand suburban housing opportunities began in the late 1960s in California, which allowed cities to grant zoning incentives (such as higher density) to developers to build lower-cost homes. But the first major breakthrough came from the New Jersey Supreme Court, which ruled in 1975 that Mount Laurel Township's exclusionary zoning policies did not provide its fair share of low and moderate income housing and thus violated the property rights guaranteed by the state's constitution. In *Mount Laurel II* (1983) the court held that all of the state's municipalities had to modify their zoning laws to allow construction of as many as 145,000 affordable homes over the following ten years. The state legislature responded in 1985 with the Fair Housing Act that specified the means and forms of compliance with the *Mount Laurel* decisions. Each city and township must draft a plan and alter its regulations to permit a predetermined number of affordable homes within its borders. However, a municipality is also allowed to transfer up to half its "fair share" obligation to another one that is willing to take it, along with any related subsidies [Haar 1996 & Kirp, Dwyer, & Rosenthal 1995]. Newark, with a large proportion of low-income households already, benefited from many such transfers.

Although the New Jersey rulings had no legal effect in any other state, they raised nationwide concern for affordable housing. *Inclusionary zoning* consists of the methods of inducing lower-cost housing development where it would not otherwise occur, by offering developers a financial or legal incentive, zoning for homes in previously nonresidential areas, or reducing certain standards to permit homes to be sold or rented more cheaply than otherwise. A few cities chose to undertake this of their own volition; many more adopted these methods under pressure from federal agencies, state legislatures, and court rulings. Often, a developer is allowed to build expensive homes at a higher density on a parcel of land if a significant portion of the area contains lower-cost dwellings. Such density bonuses have been widely used in New Jersey to meet the *Mount Laurel* standards. Planners for cities and developers have been creative in expanding this supply, as in Yonkers, New York, illustrated in Figure 7.4. Yet, the housing stock is insufficient in many suburbs that host a growing number of jobs which pay only modest wages, a factor that businesses must consider in their location choices [Melvin 1995].

Housing costs may also be reduced by modification of local regulations and procedures. As a 1991 nationwide survey by a federal commission learned, fees and charges for permits, reviews, and inspections add a larger percentage to the cost of a small home than to a large one. Often, several local authorities must grant approval to new developments, and if they take an unnecessarily long time, that further inflates costs that builders must pass along to buyers or renters [Advisory Commission on Regulatory Barriers to Affordable Housing 1991]. Chicago sparked a residential building boom in the mid-1990s by speeding up the process of granting building permits, along with provid-

Figure 7.4 Two hundred units of public housing have been built on seven scattered sites throughout the white, middle-class areas in Yonkers, New York, as part of a federal housing remedy order. Five per cent of the units are designed for the handicapped. Photo by Oscar Newman.

technologies often provide opportunities to cut costs but must be approved before they can be legally used in construction. Many building and zoning codes have recently been liberalized to permit more manufactured homes, the segments of which are produced in a factory and assembled on the lot, rather than constructed from the ground up. These homes have long had a negative image as "mobile homes" and many communities look on them as substandard. However, an increasing number have been located on individual city lots, replacing homes that had been demolished. Indeed, plants that manufacture these have arisen in several cities and offer new job opportunities for those with low skills. These opportunities call for careful review by state and local lawmakers and planners and recognition that expanding housing opportunities takes a higher priority than preserving some marginally justified regulations.

Despite these innovations in generating affordable housing, a large stock of publicly owned and managed dwellings remain in many cities, a nagging dilemma for planners and policy makers. They have basically two options: retain them as publicly managed units with whatever rehabilitation is necessary, or demolish the worst and replace them with lower-density or scattered-site homes. A third possibility, sale of the units to private organizations or the residents themselves, is not usually feasible due to the extreme poverty of most public housing tenants.

In many cities, public housing constitutes such a large percentage of low-cost dwellings that most or all of them must be retained to minimize hardship and homelessness. Offering vouchers with which tenants can choose their own apartments is not an answer when housing markets are tight and landlords can secure nonsubsidized tenants. However, the

ing financial and tax incentives and vacant city-owned lots. As a result, the average price for a home dropped more than twenty per cent from 1992 to 1995, making many more affordable for households on modest incomes [J. Tyson 1996].

In some states, building standards are unjustifiably strict for smaller homes and for older ones that can be rehabilitated. New

U.S. Department of Housing and Urban Development (HUD) offers some funds for rehabilitation, and the medium-sized city of Chester, Pennsylvania, is using them to improve living conditions in its Ruth L. Bennett project, although reducing the density from 390 units to 269 [Stanfield 1996]. Many projects around the country desperately need upgrading, but the available funds cannot cover all of them.

A more drastic choice is to raze projects that have become too dilapidated or dangerous. In 1995 alone, 32 housing projects were slated for this, even some low-rise buildings [Gurwitt 1995]. Chester, Pennsylvania, chose this course for a project, the William Penn Homes, which had been badly designed from the beginning. In its place will be 160 garden and two-story apartments with more attractive living environments [Stanfield 1996]. Such replacement reduces the number of living units and may tighten the housing market in the rest of the city. However, it is often the case that the buildings to be razed are partly unoccupied, and little or no net loss results.

These choices typically emerge from negotiations between HUD administrators and local housing authorities and elected officials. Federal rules often put irksome restrictions on the latter, yet there is a trend toward increasing the autonomy of local decision makers. Planners at both levels realize the need for flexibility to fit unique conditions, and recognize, as did a spokesman for the Baltimore Housing Authority, that "Our buildings make no sense in 1995. . . . . . They were just not designed for poor people to have any amenities; they're vertical warehouses." [cited by Gurwitt 1995, p.19] Clearly, housing policies are in transition under the twin themes of opportunity and diversity. The political tensions that center on them will give planners abundant opportunity to sharpen their skills at advocacy and conflict management.

The economic and housing issues in this and the previous chapters are closely linked to the ways in which people access their locations. Mobility is an inherently urban problem because many people want to be in the same places, yet the ease or difficulty of access determines how successful urban plans will be. That is the focus of the next chapter.

FOR REVIEW AND DISCUSSION

1. What are the three primary goals of housing policy? To what extent are they mutually compatible?

2. Why did public housing programs at the federal and local levels take the shape they did from the 1930s to 1960s? In what ways did they succeed or fail?

3. What are the main principles of New Urbanism? How realistic are they for application to established communities with which you are familiar?

4. How have local governments and the private sector responded to the decline in federal housing aid after 1980? What challenges have they faced in achieving their goals?

5. What funding sources do housing development programs rely on today? How do the governmental, nonprofit, and business sectors cooperate in this?

6. What is *exclusionary zoning*? By what means can this be replaced with *inclusionary zoning*? How successful have these efforts been?

CHAPTER

8

Planning for Access and Mobility

8.1 THE URBAN TRANSPORTATION SYSTEM

The most distinctive feature of urban areas—their high concentration of people and their activities—also poses a vexing policy problem. Concentration easily becomes congestion, which at excessive levels frustrates the very purposes for which people come to cities. Planners realize that high traffic levels are commonly evidences of prosperity, yet when chronically above an optimum point, they choke it off.

The urban transportation system resembles housing in that it is dominated by private market choices. Altschuler [1979, p. 19] reported that governments at all levels control only about ten percent of the spending on mobility in urban areas. They have limited ability to steer the system and must thus be sensitive to the diverse demands of the transportation market. Basically, public investments consist of fixed facilities: streets and highways, rail transit networks, airports, har-

bors, and some parking space. On the other hand, most of the vehicles used are private: autos, trucks, airplanes, rail cars, ships, and bicycles. With the exception of most mass transit vehicles, therefore, the public sector provides only the infrastructures on which the private users rely.

Transportation planning is at least as complex as that for housing, due to the many modes of travel and their varied impacts on land uses. It calls for balancing the demands for highways and mass transit, for reconciling the presence of major freeways with the areas through which they pass, controlling the environment of airports and harbors, and providing for those who cannot use or afford the mobility currently for sale to them. These choices present planners with a bundle of political conflicts.

The phrase "maximum access and mobility" often sums up the goals of transportation policy. These goals have several subsidiary targets, not easily harmonized with one another: (a) the lowest possible travel time and cost to reach any given destination, (b) minimal noise levels and environmental pollution, (c) maximum safety and energy efficiency, (d) access opportunity for the disadvantaged, and (e) the most beneficial impacts on land use as defined by a community's comprehensive plans. As an example of a conflict, it is very convenient to have a major airport close to the city center, as in Boston and San Diego. But the resulting noise, air pollution, and congestion disadvantage some residents of the city while others primarily experience the benefits. In general, a city gets only as much as it pays for in terms of transportation improvements, but must decide how much is "enough" in view of other demands for investments.

Planners have long recognized that the overall vitality of urban regions depends on their transportation system. Further, their land use pattern is largely shaped by the historical development of their travel modes. Rusting railroad spurs and silted canals in older cities are still framed by obsolete factories and warehouses. The task is to match future land use needs with the ongoing choices for freeways, mass transit, airports, and freight terminals. The Regional Plan Association (RPA), a nongovernmental planning group in the New York City metropolitan area, argues that the future economic success of that area depends upon massive investments in its transportation infrastructure. The RPA recommends spending $47 billion on mobility improvements over the next 25 years. Some of that would improve transit service for the suburban commuters to Manhattan, while the suburbs need higher-capacity highway links to accommodate movement between them. Another high priority is quicker trans-Hudson freight service to access New York City's factories and docks and

maintain employment levels there [Regional Plan Association 1996].

The transportation planning process for urban areas has long been disjointed, shared by general local planners, mass transit officials, and state and federal highway authorities. Most choices on local streets and roads depend on the decision rules established by engineers and administrators in the departments of public works or transportation. Street engineers have evolved standards of traffic volumes that tell them when Main Street should be widened and where to locate a downtown bypass route. Thus, according to a study in Oakland, California, they concentrate on improving the streets that have the most traffic and construct new ones that can quickly carry motorists for longer distances. Neighborhood streets tend to be neglected, particularly where residents make no demands for improvements [Levy, Meltsner & Wildavsky 1974, p. 114]. There is no assurance, however, that these rules will harmonize with the broader development objectives that general planners pursue.

Major vehicle routes have long been the province of state highway administrators. They mapped the national interstate highway network after Congress established and financed it in 1956. Figure 8.1 depicts such an urban freeway in St. Louis. This system included inner-city and suburban segments, but the planners showed little regard for potential social and environmental impacts on the neighborhoods through which the freeways would pass. As one observer summarized this period,

For forty years, American cities and towns have had to live with the unintended consequences of transportation policies not guided by concepts of community, equity, and quality of life,

Figure 8.1   Interstate highway clogged with traffic in downtown St. Louis. Photo by East-West Gateway Coordinating Council.

but rather driven by a decision making paradigm which unconsciously assumed, *a priori*, that transportation is somehow a value free instrumentality of people's desire to get from A to B, no questions asked. [Camph, 1996]

Beginning to realize this shortsightedness after hearing many local protests, Congress in 1962 mandated a transportation planning process for metropolitan areas that took into consideration mass transit and transit-impacted development. Each region established an agency to do this, and generated the first computer models of travel patterns that identified high-priority corridors for impro-

vment. Later federal regulations gave even more emphasis to all modes of transportation, not just vehicles on highways. As computer power expanded, planners evolved more sensitive models to analyze travel behavior and forecast the facilities needed to accommodate it [Pas 1986].

The most recent mandate for urban transportation planning is ISTEA (Intermodal Surface Transportation Efficiency Act), passed by Congress in 1991 and since supplemented with federal regulations. Recognizing that decisions about modes of transportation affect much more than how people and goods are moved, lawmakers now require state and local agencies to consider air quality, historic preservation, environmental protection, and recreational opportunities in their choices. ISTEA further promotes use of a variety of modes of transportation, including bicycles and walking, and development of new technologies for using the various modes most efficiently. "From the federal point of view, ISTEA is now the nation's main metropolitan planning program, and one of the few sources of federal money going into metropolitan planning," according to a Federal Highway Administration official [Andrews 1996, p. 8]. Funding for the first six years was set at $150 billion.

Responsibility for those integrated choices rests on 340 metropolitan planning organizations (MPOs), which receive federal grants for studies and project design. They vary widely in size, composition, and level of activity, depending on the local political landscape. Generally, they involve local government executives, state and local highway and transit officials, and occasionally members of the business community and general public. The St. Louis metropolitan area's MPO, for example, includes counties in Illinois as well as Missouri and is run by a 21-member council, 14 of whom are elected city and county officials [Andrews 1996].

As planning groups, MPOs ordinarily have no power to implement their plans, relying on the highway and transit agencies for that. There is a natural rivalry between the MPOs and the state transportation departments over the final authority to choose projects for ISTEA funding. For these reasons, there is much inconsistency from one region to another, and a council may vary in its effectiveness over time. The requirement of extensive public information and participation, a necessary ingredient in 1990s planning, further complicates their job [Andrews 1996].

Most ISTEA funds have been used for highways, bridges, and tunnels. However, at least ten per cent of each state's allotment must buy "enhancements," projects that upgrade the environment around the transportation facilities. Several cities have converted abandoned railroad rights of way to bicycle or pedestrian trails. Others restored historic houses and rail stations. Highway landscaping was another common use of those dollars. As with more direct transportation projects, state and local officials select these sites according to their own criteria (some of which undoubtedly serve political ends). It is difficult to assess the program as a whole because of its varied impacts, although Walters [1997, p. 61] concludes that ISTEA "has been a better-than-adequate vehicle for getting a wide variety of transportation jobs done, from improving roads and bridges to keeping major transit systems up and running, and for forestalling any major transportation crises."

8.2 PAVING THE WAY FOR PRIVATE VEHICLES

Public rights of way for traffic have been a feature of cities since ancient times, whether to move donkey carts or war chariots. This is the *vehicle movement* sector of mobility planning: to enable people to pass through and come together in sufficient numbers to form and serve a city, yet move quickly enough to fit their purposes. To maximize both access and speed, planners over the years have resorted to bridges and tunnels, one-way streets, and bypass and limited-access roads.

Congestion is a moving target, however; it can multiply on the very roads designed to combat it. Los Angeles embarked on its massive freeway building program before World War II, but its planners found that the projected maximum traffic load for each route was reached shortly after its opening and the number of vehicles using it escalated from there. At that time, designers lacked the insight that better traffic accommodation schemes create more traffic in turn. Many metropolitan areas now experience rush-hour "gridlock" in fringe areas as well as central cities due to the suburbs' rapid growth as commercial and industrial centers. Commuting trips are now more inter-suburban and thus less oriented to the traditional downtowns. This places heavy vehicle loads on roads and intersections never designed for them.

The typical traffic plan for a city or region designates routes in a hierarchy as freeways, major and minor arterials, collector streets, and local streets, depending on the type of travel they are to serve. Each road has a designated vehicle capacity and its performance is measured by the rate of flow of vehicles at any given time. If a certain stretch of road has to operate at or above that capacity, there will be congestion and possibly dislocation of surrounding activities.

When planners consider a new development that will generate a large amount of traffic, they must forecast the number of trips, when they will occur, and which roadways they will use, and relate that to the capacity of existing means of access and any future expansion. Traffic planners have objective techniques for doing this, although such forecasts are always judgment calls to some extent. Geographic information systems are highly useful for this purpose, capable of displaying traffic counts at selected points and trip origins and destinations obtained from surveys of a large number of commuters.

Major urban highway projects were common in the 1950s through 1970s, as federal funds flowed generously to state highway agencies. The Interstate Highway program created in 1956 paid 90% of construction costs of most such freeways. In the 1990s, with such facilities in place, the major concern is maintenance and such marginal improvements in the system as are affordable. However, Boston is in the midst of rebuilding its Central Artery, which encircles downtown, plus a new tunnel under the harbor to East Boston and Logan Airport, which could ultimately cost over $15 billion. A key purpose of these projects was to replace an elevated highway that was deteriorating and hopelessly congested. Although it is designed by the Massachusetts Transportation Department, about 85% of the cost is paid by the federal government [Holmstrom 1996]. It will strongly impact that historic city in many ways which Boston and suburban planners must deal with in years to come.

The extreme cost of projects like Boston's has prompted planners and engineers to search for alternatives. Some urban areas find privately owned toll highways an attractive option. Three were in operation by early 1997, one in northern Virginia and two in southern California, one of the latter paralleling a chronically congested state freeway. While the means of financing is innovative, the public sector must still deal with the many problems that surround a major highway, not to mention the political opposition that would be likely to arise. Even for the roads that remain free, highway officials have proposed charging motorists a "congestion toll" for driving in certain areas in high-demand times, particularly when they are alone in their vehicles. This would require an automated way of identifying each car. In fact, one California private toll road, along State Route 91, charges more at peak travel times than in low-demand periods; vehicles using it carry a windshield pass that is electronically read at the tollgate, and drivers must have a prepaid toll account.

Highway planners seek to maximize the capacity of existing roads with special lanes for high-occupancy vehicles. They can be used by buses, vans, and automobiles with two or more persons. Since they are ordinarily less crowded than the unrestricted lanes, they offer incentives to drivers for ridesharing. These have had modest success on some routes, although lone drivers tend to protest the removal of a lane from their choice of route.

More technically sophisticated is the "smart highway" or Intelligent Transportation System (ITS). It uses computers that monitor traffic volumes and adjust signals, direct drivers around accidents and dispatch emergency vehicles as necessary. In preparation for the 1996 Olympic Games, Atlanta installed a $140 million system in its major freeways, with microchip sensors linked by fiber optic cables with a computerized command center. Los Angeles has installed a "smart corridor" traffic management system for the Santa Monica Freeway, the busiest in the nation. A $48 million combination of technologies enables monitors seated in City Hall to route drivers around traffic congestion and blockages [Wood 1996].

Also in the future are automated highways, guiding vehicles with on-board computers that respond to signals emitted from a control source. This technology can permit high traffic volumes to move safely and ideally would reduce the need to build additional capacity. The potential of ITS is only beginning to be realized and must be coupled with good land use and facilities planning to gain the best advantage from it. Transportation planners must work even more closely with those responsible for economic development, housing, and environmental concerns.

At the opposite end of the technological spectrum are the modest means of traffic "calming" in residential neighborhoods. In many cities, residential streets have become shortcuts for through traffic, moving at much higher than posted speed limits and posing threats to safety and neighborhood desirability. Phoenix, among many cities, has installed devices to slow such traffic and discourage through drivers from traveling them. Some simply place speed humps at chosen intervals or block an intersection diagonally, forcing all vehicles to make a right-angle turn. Others narrow the street at some points to give an obvious "slow down" signal, while small traffic circles compel the same at intersections. The overall object, says one planner, is to change the perceptions and behavior of drivers to respect the residential environment [Lemov 1996].

Another component of traffic planning is *vehicle storage*. Cars and trucks take up space at the end of their trips and may be parked in great numbers at a workplace or shopping center. Curbside parking, the simplest of all arrangements, often hinders vehicle movement and has been banned in many business districts. Off-street parking in high-use areas is expensive, and its cost must be borne by the users or someone who benefits by their presence. Some parking ramps are owned by local governments but most are private property. Clearly, no new commercial or industrial development will succeed today, in central city or suburb, without free or moderate-cost parking for employees and customers. Development regulations contain formulas for the number of required parking spaces, depending on the size and nature of a project, including those for handicapped persons as mandated by the Americans With Disabilities Act of 1990.

Another major private vehicle that has to be accommodated is the airplane, whether commercial or private, passenger or freight. Planners must always trade convenience of access for aircraft users against the noise and congestion that every major airport generates. Minnesota's rejection of a new airport for the Twin Cities, as chapter 1 related, was such a choice, in which convenience and cost factors far outweighed the greater capacity of a new facility in the ranking of those who made the decision. Totally new major airports are now rare; Denver's is the most recent.

Planners realize that siting and developing the airport itself is only part of the job; much more complex and perhaps controversial are the locations of highways, utilities, and service businesses, the environmental controls, and the limitation of residential and other development near runways. Airport operators must also work with area planners on access to and within the facility; Newark has added new transit links, and planning is underway for Orlando, San Francisco, New York's Kennedy, and Washington's Dulles Airport. Such planning is a joint operation between municipal, special district, and state authorities, and subject to the rules of the Federal Aviation Administration and other agencies. The city of Denver has a further task growing from its airport's relocation: redevelopment of the vacant Stapleton Field.

Still another type of vehicle that draws the attention of some planners is the freight train. Rail haulage of bulk cargoes and containers is at an all-time peak in some corridors, and this creates congestion at terminal cities. Long Beach shares with Los Angeles the nation's busiest seaport, yet only a single rail line connects it with the rest of the country. Port officials there, along with railroads and local governments, are planning a "rail expressway" to move shipments between docks and railyards. They must obtain the nearly two billion dollars it is likely to cost and secure the necessary right of way from local governments, and as of 1996 had received

federal grants and loans of nearly $500 million. Many other cities are looking at providing more efficient facilities to transfer cargoes between trains and trucks, realizing that lower costs and quicker movement attract business in a competitive global market.

8.3 MASS TRANSIT FACILITIES AND SERVICES

Governments, often supplemented by private organizations, provide means of moving people within urban areas. Presumably, the more persons who ride in a single vehicle, the less congestion results; a major task of transportation planners is to make these means as widely used as possible. Medium-sized and larger cities provide some form of mass transit, usually owned and operated by the local government or a special transit authority. The very largest ones have not only buses but rapid rail service, ranging from New York's extensive subway and elevated system and metropolitan rail lines to one or two light trolley lines in such cities as Portland (see Figure 8.2), San Diego, St. Louis, and Pittsburgh. The federal government began in the 1960s to pay much of the capital costs of new systems, which spurred construction in Washington, D.C., Atlanta, Baltimore, and San Francisco-Oakland. Since they generally feed into the city centers, they have had significant impact on those cities' downtown development. Very little federal money has been available in the 1990s, but most of the dollars have gone to enable Los Angeles to build one subway and two light rail lines.

Planners have learned, however, that the enormous investments that rapid transit systems require make them impractical for most metropolises. Designed to carry large volumes of traffic on fixed routes, they best serve narrow, high density travel corridors that are too congested to accommodate more automo-

Figure 8.2   A light rail vehicle in Portland, Oregon, making the sharp turn at a downtown intersection. American Planning Association file photo.

biles. New York, Chicago, Washington, and the San Francisco Bay area have these. But as suburban areas become major destinations as well as origins of commuter trips, those corridors are diffused and a steadily smaller proportion of total trips can use a fixed-route network. Some critics argue that the newer and very expensive mass transit systems fail to meet the actual travel needs of most residents; more flexible and less capital-intensive services would accomplish more reduction of congestion and air pollution [Cox 1992].

Whether needed in a strictly economic sense or not, major mass transit projects are politically popular. The Los Angeles subway project has provided some 10,000 jobs to a region that experienced a major loss of defense-related industry. Elected officials, members of Congress, and some federal and local administrators backed the project, claiming that it will give commuters an alternative to the crowded and polluting freeways.

Yet, controversy often centers on what the money could otherwise have been spent on. Local civil rights groups sued the Los Angeles Metropolitan Transportation Authority (MTA), claiming that in its attention to rapid transit it allowed the bus service, on which so many persons of color depend, to worsen. A federal judge ruled in 1996 that the agency has a legal obligation to provide all riders with fair access to mass transportation, with no discrimination as to race or national origin. In response, MTA agreed to substantially increase bus service and freeze the fare for two years [Wood 1997]. Similar disputes over priorities occur in many regions today, as well as in the halls of Washington agencies and Congress.

As planners search for other options for personal mobility, they must look at where and when people actually need to travel and at persons whose mobility is most limited by poverty or disability. One urgent task is to link inner-city residents in need of jobs with suburban employers. Conventional transit service is oriented to moving commuters into the city for work, but much less in the opposite direction. This is being remedied by a combination of public and private carriers, including the employers themselves, who may get some public subsidy as an incentive. In the Chicago region, for example, the Regional Transportation Authority carries Sears Roebuck employees from the city to the new corporate offices in a northwest suburb.

Private enterprise plays an increasing part in some forms of urban transit. Large buses, which are the mainstay of public agency systems, are not cost-effective on many inter-suburban lines. Thus a host of businesses and nonprofit organizations offer service with smaller vehicles. Typically, the public agency subsidizes their costs on desired but unprofitable routes. In this respect, government's role has shifted from being a producer of transit service to that of providing it through the most efficient means. Planners retain the task of deciding on service levels and costs, always a politically sensitive role.

Transit for persons with disabilities is another service challenge. Federal mandates for equal transportation opportunity originated in 1970, but they did not become effective until well into the following decade. By the 1990s, public and private transit systems were running buses with wheelchair lifts, and many rapid transit stations had elevator access. Added to that are special mobility services for the physically challenged who may not be able to reach a streetcorner bus stop. Each ride is subsidized with public funds, but the extent of support varies.

Some communities also pay attention to human-powered transportation, a move spurred by ISTEA grants. Designated bikeways provide incentives for recreational and work trips. Cities encourage pedestrian travel in downtown areas by providing walkways above the street or underground, linked with parking and transit facilities. Malls on streets that are closed to vehicles further encourage the use of feet on shopping trips. Much of Denver's downtown 16th Street is reserved for pedestrians, who are also attracted to its landscaping, special events, and a shuttle bus that can accommodate them for longer distances [Garvin 1996, pp. 147–148]. Less well-served are the suburban malls and commercial complexes that have no easy pedestrian connections; planners have the responsibility to design that access into them.

8.4 INTEGRATING THE TOTAL SYSTEM

Metropolitan regions have a formidable challenge in integrating their transportation plans and policies with their overall land use designs. The planning organizations that advise on use of ISTEA funds often have little power, and much depends on the willingness of autonomous officials and agencies to cooperate. Those participants, in turn, respond to political realities such as budgets, dominant interest groups, and citizen demands.

Political systems, as they contemplate transportation choices, behave in characteristic patterns, according to Altshuler [1979, p. 11]. Generally, they seek to accommodate new demand as they emerge by means, insofar as possible, that leave previous settlements. . . . . undisturbed, that involve the least possible disruption for private enterprises, and that involve the least possible inconvenience and annoyance for individuals who have built their life-styles around the expectation of system stability.

Policies thus aim to protect the status quo until it proves to be unworkable, and any adjustments typically add to, rather than replace, existing arrangements.

All transportation programs, whether of governments or private enterprises, face the economic and political realities of competition. Altshuler [1979, p. 85–94] asserted that the ideal innovation is one for which consumers will voluntarily pay a high enough price to cover its cost. Further, its costs should be diffused among many users. If restraint of some form of travel behavior, such as closing a street to traffic, becomes necessary, it is best accepted if it solves a widely recognized problem and carries little or no cost to consumers in money or travel time. Hardest of all to implement, he further states, are those innovations that impose heavy costs on commuters or interfere with their established travel patterns and which they can easily blame on the public officials who adopted them. A major restriction or surtax on downtown parking, even if a realistic way to reduce congestion, would probably fall in this latter category. For this reason, minimalist strategies such as intelligent highway systems and small-vehicle transit have become popular.

Linking transportation with larger urban designs is a strong current theme. On a small scale, Appleyard's "livable streets" concept is attractive [1981]. The residential street, as a carrier of traffic, has to be planned and managed so as to protect the social and environmental wellbeing of the persons who live on it. A neighborhood cannot survive as a desirable place to live when its streets become barriers to interaction and hazards to life and health. This concern led cities to adopt the traffic calming measures described above. Another option is the Dutch-conceived *woonerf*, a residential street that restricts motor vehicles to very slow speeds so as to protect pedestrians and minimize noise.

Calthorpe and other planners in the New Urbanism school argue for transit-oriented developments (TODs). These are large-scale urban designs that group high-density uses around major bus or rail stops. They argue that transit lines are often weakly patronized because they run through areas with low density and poor pedestrian access to stops. Further, they have little opportunity for redevelopment to increase transit use.

> The alternative is to balance these conditions with alignments that run through New Growth Areas designed for higher densities, mixed-use, and walkability. In more urban areas, neighborhoods which have these qualities should be targeted for new transit, along with areas which could redevelop [Calthorpe 1993, p. 104].

Several cities have adopted Calthorpe's TOD guidelines. The Bay Area Rapid Transit District in the San Francisco-Oakland region seeks to redevelop "transit villages" in the vicinity of several stations, replacing vast parking lots with more intense uses [Knack 1995].

Supporting this effort is the Livable Communities Initiative of the Federal Transit Administration, which is intended to enhance community life through innovations in mass transportation. It provides planning and implementation grants from the ISTEA and other funds for projects that range from walkways to transit stations that incorporate child care facilities. For example, it aided a public/

private project in downtown Cleveland that linked the new Gateway Sports Complex with a rapid transit station, and it enabled Boston to locate a health center in a bus and train station.

The holistic transportation planning envisioned by ISTEA lawmakers requires a broader constituency than that which has simply advocated increased road capacity. The latter, the "highway lobby," was dominated by construction firms, truckers, and others whose livelihood was earned in building and using roads. New coalitions have formed in the past decade to take seats around the transportation planning table, to speak for environmental, historic preservation, and outdoor recreation interests. These have halted planned freeways and bridges in such places as Atlanta and Jamestown, Virginia, and reoriented the Boston Central Artery project in several respects [Carlson 1995].

Among the most creative planning projects is LUTRAQ (Making the Land Use, Transportation, Air Quality Connection), initiated in Portland, Oregon, by a private advocacy group, 1000 Friends of Oregon. Supported by government and private funding, it sought ways to reduce travel demand and air pollution through more intensive land use and infill development in areas already served by public transit. Its work has been particularly applied to the design of a bypass road through the western suburbs and has contributed significantly to Portland's urban growth management policies described in chapters 3 and 10 [Carlson 1995, pp. 64–69].

This chapter has shown that transportation planning is an integral part of the larger urban development process. It influences the location and quality of housing, as described in chapter 7, and it has great impact on the quality of the natural environment, the subject of the next chapter. We thus have further confirmation of the wide angle vision that planners need, regardless of their employer or specialization.

FOR REVIEW AND DISCUSSION

1. What are the five "targets" that define maximum access and mobility? In what ways could they come into conflict in specific situations with which you are familiar?

2. What agencies dominate planning for transportation in metropolitan areas? What specific interests do they tend to speak for?

3. What are the major goals and provisions of the Intermodal Surface Transportation Efficiency Act? Who shares the responsibility for implementing it in specific regions?

4. What concepts and methods are used by traffic planners for streets and highways? To what extent might they overlook broader planning concerns in doing so?

5. What means are now available to improve the capacity and efficiency of existing roads? What potential is there to apply them in places with which you are familiar?

6. What rapid transit developments have taken place in recent decades? What questions and dilemmas surround choices to build major transit systems today?

9

Planning for the
Natural Environment

9.1 THE ENVIRONMENT
AS PLANNING CHALLENGE

The natural ecosystem has become a focal point for urban planning within the past generation, as Section 2.5 indicates. Planners of earlier periods tended to regard the environment as a rural or "wilderness" concern, but not applicable to city choices except perhaps in the layout of parks. The news media began to publicize environmental concerns nationally in the late 1960s, and the resulting public awareness spurred major legislation which empowered planners to incorporate ecological values.

Environmental policy now has several dimensions with distinct challenges. The first is that a city, like a human body, has a "metabolism" by which it takes in means of life support and disposes of unneeded and harmful products. In practical terms, this points to the supply of air, water, food, energy, and raw materials for manufacturing, and the safe removal or reprocessing of wastes [Wolman

1965]. While much of this exchange is conducted by the private market, it impacts how land is used and so falls under public regulations.

A second dimension is the preservation of natural areas, particularly those that have unique value for human life but are easily degraded by unwise urban expansion. These include (1) farmland that produces crops of high market value, (2) bodies of water, floodplains, wetlands, and shorelines that provide natural drainage, recharge of aquifers, and storage of floodwaters, and often serve as attractive landscapes and recreation sites, (3) sensitive land areas such as steep slopes, forests and other vegetation, and scenic views, and (4) habitats of endangered animal and plant species. A city is a human-created environment, to be sure, but it need not completely obliterate the natural conditions that preceded it.

A third and larger theme is *sustainability*, a key term in the debate over the future of the global environment.

Sustainable communities acknowledge environmental constraints—from limited groundwater and wetlands to global climate change. Current patterns of urban development and growth, and current strategies for organizing and operating human settlements, are wasteful, environmentally damaging, and ecologically unsustainable. Sustainable communities work to live within physical and biological limits [Beatley & Brower 1993, p. 16].

The practical meaning of sustainability is open to much debate. At minimum, it calls for steady reduction of air and water pollution, reduction of and recycling of wastes, more efficient use of energy and a shift to renewable energy sources, and restraint in the development of rural land. A radical view of sustainability demands major shifts in American life styles toward smaller homes, use of mass transit instead of automobiles, and reorientation of marketing toward frugality rather than consumption. While some of these policy choices are made in local communities and households, any large-scale implementation depends on choices by the national government and major corporations that compete in the global market. Yet planners recognize that even small scale choices have incremental effects on their environments, and there is growing interest in alternatives that promote sustainability while not violating the freedom of Americans to choose their life styles.

An oft-decried "sin" of cities against their environments is *urban sprawl*. This denotes the pattern of virtually unchecked suburban growth that surrounds metropolitan areas. More specifically, it is "premature leapfrog or 'highway ribbon' development or low-density scattered development that occurs beyond the current perimeter of contiguous development." [Nelson & Duncan 1995, p. 1] Often, it

encroaches upon farmland, forests, and wetlands, and it usually requires costly extension of roads, sewers, and other public services. Many regard it as visually unsightly as well, with advertising signs and parking lots.

Sprawl results from the individual choices by participants in a relatively free land market. Land costs tend to decline with increasing distance from a city center, and the resulting lower price of homes, factories, and shopping centers is a strong incentive to build farther out. Owners of fringe area land are free to sell to developers, and public officials in those counties and townships generally welcome development that expands their tax base. Unless there is an explicit policy for open space protection at some level of government, local officials have no legal grounds to deny such building applications. This freedom of choice in the market is a key reason why some observers do not object to urban sprawl; to impose government restrictions on landowners' rights hampers what they believe is the most efficient way to allocate land.

Whether unfettered market choices are indeed the most efficient is open to question. Urban sprawl has several negative effects. Low-density, fringe-area development is more costly to serve with utilities and roads, and cost allocation policies often do not lay the entire burden on those who conduct it. In many places, good farmland is lost permanently; while individual farmers may gain a comfortable retirement from the sale of their land, the nation as a whole loses that resource. Further, it can be demonstrated that sprawl has negative economic effects on the central cities that it surrounds, denying them the renewal and growth that their residents need and imposing the costs of urban decay on the entire nation [Nelson & Duncan 1995, pp. 4–8]. Far-flung development increases motor vehicle traffic with its attendant air

Figure 9.1 Geographic information systems can place pollution sources in their larger contexts. The dots indicate specific sources and the lighter circles show distances from them. Source: U.S. Department of the Interior, U.S. Geological Survey, *Geographic Information Systems.*

pollution and often contaminates waters that were previously clean. These negative effects have persuaded policy makers in many states to pursue some form of growth management.

9.2 ENVIRONMENTAL PLANNING METHODS AND GOALS

Effective planning for the urban environment begins with accurate information. The research and intelligence described in section 5.2 is vital to these choices but may be hard to obtain. Planners need access to an environmental inventory, with data and maps on the land surface, vegetation, waters, air quality, and habitats of plants and animals. Here, too, geographic information systems now available enable them to identify the specific issues of their area, whether sources of river pollution in Cincinnati, loss of wetlands around New Orleans, steep slope dangers in the Los Angeles area, or flood control for the suburbs of St. Louis. Figure 9.1 is a map in which pollution sources can be displayed in relation to their surroundings, an essential tool for regulatory actions.

Environmental data are compiled by many federal and state agencies and private organizations, and gathering, evaluating, and integrating them for a particular city or region is a major challenge. For example, the Federal Emergency Management Agency has mapped flood hazard areas for insurance purposes, and local planners have found these valuable for their own decisions as well.

Section 102(C) of the National Environment Policy Act of 1969 requires all agencies of the federal government to "include in every recommendation or report on proposals for legislation and other major Federal actions significantly affecting the quality of the environment, a detailed statement by the responsible officials on:

(i) the environmental impact of the proposed action,

(ii) any adverse environmental effects which cannot be avoided should the proposal be implemented,

(iii) alternatives to the proposed action,

(iv) the relationship between local short-term uses of man's environment and the maintenance and enhancement of long-term productivity, and

(v) any irreversible and irretrievable commitments of resources which would be involved in the proposed action should it be implemented.

Prior to making any detailed statement, the responsible Federal official shall consult with and obtain the comments of any Federal agency which has jurisdiction by law or special expertise with respect to any environmental impact involved. Copies of such statement and the comments and views of appropriate Federal, state, and local agencies, which are authorized to develop and enforce environmental standards, shall be made available to the President, the Council on Environmental Quality, and to the public. . . . , and shall accompany the proposal through the existing agency review processes."

Figure 9.2 Summary of the federally mandated process for conducting environmental impact assessments.

Federal agency geographic information systems and computer models have permitted some integration and display of data, to which local officials have access [Steffenson 1996]. However, an area like the urbanized northeastern corner of New Jersey is a single ecosystem for many purposes but is such a melange of land uses and is covered by so many different governmental authorities that keeping current a comprehensive environmental inventory like that displayed in Figure 5.1 is a major challenge.

The inventory data are essential to support several analytical techniques. Most prominent is the *environmental impact analysis,* mandated by the National Environmental Policy Act of 1969. When a project with major environmental impact is proposed, the federal government requires a study to determine its negative and positive impacts, alternatives and modifications to the projects and their likely consequences, and possible means to mitigate environmental damage. Figure 9.2 summarizes the required content of an environmental impact statement. Projects with an environmental impact on a smaller scale are examined by less formal and detailed means.

Many states and cities impose similar requirements on public and private developments over which they have control. California's Environmental Quality Act, for example, mandates a procedure by which local agencies determine, first, whether a project has sufficient impact to require a study, and second, how that study shall be conducted. Olshansky [1996] concludes that the act has broadly affected local planning agencies which, he found, devote almost one day of every work week to comply with it. However, communities vary widely in their implementation of it, and since the studies focus on individual projects, they may hinder thinking about longer-range development choices.

Environmental analyses have now been done for thousands of proposals, but they show mixed results. Certainly they have altered the outcomes of many projects and prevented some from being built at all. Yet, critics charge that studies are often perfunctory, selecting and interpreting facts to justify the project. Most are now prepared by consultants who specialize in environmental analysis and who well recognize the interests of the applicant that employed them. Planners must always assume responsibility to scrutinize the analysis and make sure it is accurate and balanced.

More specific analyses are often used to supplement general environmental impact studies. The *critical area analysis* focuses on a

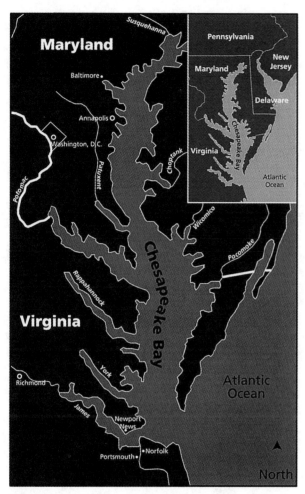

Figure 9.3 With a watershed of 64,000 square miles, Chesapeake Bay and its tributaries are vulnerable to many sources of pollution. This is a significant "critical area" requiring holistic planning. Map by Susan Deegan.

selected area prior to any development proposals for it, to enable drafting of general protective policies. For example, Maryland has designated all land within a thousand feet of Chesapeake Bay as a critical area (see Figure 9.3), and in 1972 Congress made a similar declaration for the nation's entire coastline, for which states were to set development guidelines. Planners need sufficient data to define a zone as critical and set policies suited to its unique features; these data are particularly important when landowners and developers contest these choices.

Analyses of natural and human-caused hazards are also necessary. Seismologists have mapped earthquake faults in California, Utah, and other states; using that information with maps of soil characteristics, they can anticipate damage levels in given areas. Flooding risks can be identified in hurricane-prone areas and major river valleys. Similarly, the U.S. Environmental Protection Agency has listed sites in which accidents involving hazardous wastes could pose threats to surrounding residents.

Such analyses depend to an important extent on subjective judgments as well as measurable quantities. Estimates of risk and cost can be challenged by experts with different assumptions or methods, and any citizen can contest a conclusion in legislative bodies and courts. These analyses have been used by groups to delay unwanted projects, and frequently a project's sponsor has scaled down or canceled it. In general, the use of environmental analyses has increased citizen awareness of the need to anticipate long-term effects and to identify the human and natural stakeholders in any choice.

9.3 END PRODUCTS OF THE URBAN METABOLISM

Government plays three basic roles in managing waste products of urban activities: preventing or mitigating pollution on specific sites and larger waterways and airsheds, restoring areas that were polluted in the past, and storing or treating the wastes that are currently being produced. Waste, conceived broadly, is any product that is perceived as having no further use and that must be removed from human contact. It is the end product of the urban metabolism cycle described by Wolman [1965]. This includes household sewage and garbage, chemicals emitted by industrial plants and motor vehicles, dust and soot, and radioactive substances. Each enters the biosphere and poses a potential hazard to humans whenever concentrations rise above some minimal level. In addition, waste reduces the economic and esthetic value of a contaminated area.

Efforts to prevent and mitigate pollution focus on the nation's waters, air, and soils. Planning and administration of water quality programs involves a network of federal, state, and local agencies within a legal framework of federal mandates [Arrandale 1994]. One such challenge is to regulate stormwater. Rain that flows off lawns, roofs, streets, parking lots, and construction sites carries a variety of contaminants into lakes, rivers, and groundwater aquifers, and local agencies are on the front line of defense. Cities and industries must obtain permits from EPA and state agencies for such water flows, which must also meet certain standards. Thus a planner who examines a proposal for a new factory or shopping center must ensure that the runoff from its site will not exceed the criteria for rate of flow or pollutant content.

A similar network of laws and agencies monitors the flow of sewage and hazardous wastes into waters. In many suburbs and urban fringes, on-site systems such as septic tanks treat household wastes. One task of their planners is to determine when the density becomes great enough to mandate connection of homes to sewers, which is a major cost for residents and communities. As population grows, treatment plants need expansion, and the once-abundant federal aid has been only partially replaced by revolving loan funds within each state. Thus, while generalist planners are not directly responsible for clean water, their choices on urban

expansion must be related with the choices of others who keep watch on a community's sanitary needs.

Air quality is another planning challenge, reflecting the fact that pollutants move easily across and between regions. The 1990 Clean Air Act set strict standards for local authorities and businesses to reduce pollutants. The Los Angeles area claims a significant reduction in its notorious smog levels due to state and regional agency programs affecting motor vehicles and major industries. Its South Coast Air Quality Management District has also targeted volatile chemicals used by businesses, such as paints and cleaning fluids, and presses for reductions in their use or better containment of their fumes. But these measures roused strong opposition from industries that use such chemicals and would find it expensive to alter their processes. In fact, many companies have moved from the Los Angeles area to more permissive places in the Western states or Mexico. For this reason, the District eased up on the restrictions recently, because of concerns about lost jobs. As that region's suburbs grow and commuters travel ever longer distances to work, planners may find it impossible to reduce pollution levels to their preferred targets.

Pollution of soils is likewise an intergovernmental concern. Strict state and federal laws limit disposal of wastes, even used motor vehicle oil, into the ground. These regulations are only effective, however, when local officials diligently enforce them. For example, a major source of contamination is leaking tanks beneath gasoline stations and refueling facilities. Many states conduct regular inspections of these tanks, and mandate replacement and cleanup when leaks are found.

Public policy responses to such wastes are fragmented, but fall into two broad categories: first, to dispose of or recycle such wastes after they appear; and second, to reduce their volume through planning for the efficient use of land and facilities. The first task is by far the larger, but the latter offers planners more room for innovation. Much environmental policy making is done by a complex of federal and state agencies, with a supplemental role for those at the local and regional level.

Solid wastes management is the immediate job of local officials, for whom federal and state policies call for a hierarchy of choices. The primary goal is *source reduction*, by which households and businesses are encouraged to reduce the volume of trash they produce. Second, local governments promote recycling of paper, metals, plastic, and glass by collection and marketing efforts. Third, they burn combustible wastes to produce steam or electric power, resulting in a much smaller volume of ash.

Landfills are the last resort, to contain only that which cannot be reduced by the above means. According to one study, the percentage of trash going to landfills dropped from 83% in 1985 to 62% in 1993. The number of landfills has fallen by more than half, as the small town dumps were replaced by large depositories that take wastes from many sources and are designed to prevent escape of gases and liquids [Arrandale 1996].

Sites for recycling, burning, and deposit of wastes are highly sensitive to the political process in that nearby residents typically protest their location or continued operation. One of the most prominent of these is the Rocky Mountain Arsenal, within fifteen miles of downtown Denver, which has stored plutonium for several decades. A gradual cleanup of the buildings, ultimately to cost more than $5 billion, is under way, and remaining stocks of that highly toxic element will be either shipped out or stored in vaults on the site. Many residents of the area fear, however, that

an accident could spread the plutonium downwind and poison many of the two million persons in the region [Brooke 1996]. Individuals and groups readily file lawsuits over such sites, claiming personal injury and lost property values, and judges often lack clear medical and economic evidence for deciding for either party. Federal, state, and local legislators hesitate to settle such conflicts, fearing voter reprisal no matter which side they favor.

Increasingly, these large waste facilities are privately owned and operated. Their sites and activities are jointly regulated by EPA, the relevant state agency, and the city or county in which they are located. Their interlocking administrative process requires joint planning, yet lacks a single locus of responsibility. Sunland Park, New Mexico, is a low-income city that borders El Paso, Texas, and contains the Camino Real landfill, its state's largest. Although it generates much-needed jobs, a vocal community group wants it closed. The city approved its location, but has little control over its operations [Rosell 1996]. This is a likely model of controversies to come in many places.

To restore areas that have been polluted in the past is a very site-specific task for which local public and private planners have a major responsibility. Section 6.4 described efforts to restore urban brownfields to industrial use. However, these sites could also be made suitable for residential, recreational, and other uses. The most heavily polluted sites in the nation have been identified by EPA for cleanup under the Superfund program, set up by Congress in the Comprehensive Environmental Response, Compensation, and Liability Act of 1980. Many of these are urban and thus of concern to local planners. The Love Canal (in Niagara Falls, New York) controversy of the late 1970s first dramatized this issue in the national media and alerted residents and officials to the dangers of similar sites in their own communities [Levine 1982].

Superfund is an ambitious program of identifying and cleansing such hazardous sites, but over the years it has cost far more than was anticipated, and much high-priority work yet needs to be done. For example, a site near Pottstown, Pennsylvania, is leaching toxic chemicals into the Schuylkill River from which that city takes its drinking water, and 2,800 people live within a mile of that source. As of 1996, EPA lacked the funds to remove and burn the wastes [Cushman 1996]. Local planners and officials find their choices on such polluted lands and their surroundings shaped by federal action or inaction in many such cases. In one response, city, state, and business leaders in Wichita, Kansas, cooperated on a cleanup effort to bypass the lengthy and expensive Superfund procedures. A pool of hazardous industrial chemicals was discovered under a large area of the city's center in 1988. City Manager Chris Cherches negotiated an agreement with area corporations and federal and state agencies to make a determination of legal liability and to supply funds. By 1992, cleanup was under way and commercial redevelopment had begun [Rosegrant 1992].

Planners and public officials have often cooperated with business and citizen groups in environmental renewal. The Duwamish Coalition is a broad alliance of governmental units, corporations, unions, and environmental groups that is reclaiming polluted industrial land in a Seattle river corridor to create jobs and restore some natural conditions. Its projects range from ecological research on specific contaminants to financing cleanup by individual businesses [Duwamish Coalition 1996]. Citizen organizations have also been active in pressuring public agencies to undertake cleanup projects and in monitoring their

progress. Save the Bay is such a group, formed in 1970 to track the restoration of Narragansett Bay, Rhode Island. As it lobbied for legal changes, it also challenged local zoning and subdivision decisions and prepared a manual to inform citizens on land-use issues and methods [Goslant 1988].

Of growing concern in the 1990s has been the fact that many of the nation's high-polluting industries and waste sites are located near the residences of lower-income people of color. This is partly because the cheapest places to live are in the least desirable (and often the dirtiest industrial) neighborhoods. Too, such persons often lack the political power to resist new sitings of such facilities. It was revealed in 1992, for example, that the most contaminated zip code area (90058) in California is in south central Los Angeles, inhabited largely by African-Americans. The Altgeld Gardens housing project, on Chicago's far south side, has an entirely Black population and is surrounded by hazardous-waste landfills, incinerators, and heavily polluting industries [Bullard 1994].

Recognizing this bias in land use choices, residents of such areas have turned it into a civil rights issue with protests and lawsuits. In 1993, EPA studies confirmed that racial and ethnic minorities are disproportionately exposed to most hazardous emissions. President Clinton issued an executive order the next year that cleanup of minority neighborhoods be given a higher priority in EPA choices, with residents playing a strong monitoring role. The U.S. Department of Housing and Urban Development followed with an environmental justice strategy to deal with these issues and with such localized concerns as lead paint in older homes.

It is important to view environmental threats to living areas holistically. Usually when officials and other nonresidents view depressed neighborhoods, they concentrate on what is most visible: the polluting factory, garbage dump, or incinerator. To be sure, residents are conscious of smoke and foul odors which make them and their children ill. However, a recent study found that many who live in such "environmentally devastated neighborhoods" are even more concerned about crumbling buildings, trash-strewn lots, streets and sidewalks in disrepair, and noise from many sources. Their most relevant environment is that which is very close to them and is marred by ugliness, disease and violence [Greenberg & Schneider 1996]. To target equally the multiple hazards that degrade their living environments requires great sensitivity by planners.

As a result of these concerns, planners and public officials encounter more challenges in their already difficult choices of sites for incinerators, sewage treatment plants, and garbage transfer stations. When more affluent and white citizens successfully play NIMBY (Not In My Back Yard) on behalf of their neighborhoods, such facilities may not be built at all. Indeed, existing ones may be overloaded, increasing the threat to those living near them. The only long-run answer is to reduce overall loads of pollutants and wastes, and to design treatment facilities to be more environmentally benign. In such actions, federal and state agencies must take the lead due to their greater legal and financial resources.

9.4 PROTECTING CRITICAL LANDS AND WATERS

We can categorize critical areas in several groups, each with unique planning challenges. Shorelines and bodies of water need to be protected against inflows of pollution and against developments that degrade their wildlife habitat and scenic beauty and deny public access. Many cities allowed industrial and transportation facilities along their river banks over the years, which was quite logical in the mindset of the industrial age. Now, as riverside location is no longer necessary, their abandoned sites call for redevelopment, from the decaying warehouses and piers on New York City's Hudson River shore to a disused steel mill on Lake Michigan in Chicago. Nonindustrial uses are now usually preferable for riverfronts. For example, an organization called Riverfront Recapture is lobbying and raising funds for recreation sites along the Connecticut River at Hartford. Both banks of this corridor offer major opportunities for holistic planning and bringing together the public and private sectors in financing, design, and operations [Hamilton 1996].

On a much larger scale is the work of state coastal protection agencies and the local agencies under their supervision. The overall intent is to protect coastlines from degradation, prevent damage to structures from storms, and allow public access to beaches and scenic areas. For example, landowners are increasingly prevented from building on and near beaches that are threatened with erosion. South Carolina encountered a major legal battle in 1986 when its coastal commission denied David Lucas the right to build on two lots he owned on an offshore island. It cited state policies to protect endangered species and limit construction on areas vulnerable to beach erosion and storm damage. Lucas sued, claiming that the state had taken his property without compensation, contrary to the Fifth Amendment to the U.S. Constitution (an argument similar to that of the Dolans, cited in Chapter 1). The U.S. Supreme Court agreed with Lucas that he was potentially entitled to compensation (*Lucas v. South Carolina Coastal Council*, 1992), and a settlement out of court awarded him $1.575 million for the lots.

Figure 9.4 Urban encroachment on wetlands challenges planners and developers to make them compatible, as at the Fallbrook project at Laguna Creek in Sacramento County, California. Reprinted with permission of MacKay & Somps, Civil Engineers and Land Planners.

State protective programs have achieved many of their objectives, despite the Lucas decision. At the very least, development projects along shores are subject to more intense public attention and official evaluation. They work best when citizens and property owners perceive the restrictions to be in their own long-term best interests. Recent hurricanes that destroyed billions of dollars worth of property along the Southeast and Gulf coasts dramatically demonstrated the costs of rebuilding homes, businesses, and access roads and thus the wisdom of seashore building limits. Especially where the rules are strictly defined, local planners and officials have a

strong legal base on which to rest their comprehensive plans and regulations [Burby & Dalton 1994].

Wetlands, variously defined as swamps, marshes, bogs, and tidelands, attract developers who find them cheap to buy and fill. These lands, however, are valuable in themselves as water cleansing and retention areas and wildlife habitat. Figure 9.4 illustrates a California development that avoided wetland destruction. Through Section 404 of the Clean Water Act of 1972, Congress gave EPA and the Army Corps of Engineers jurisdiction over such areas, and the Corps must grant a permit before filling can take place in any but the smallest wetlands. State environmental agencies often supplement this protection with their own regulations. Local planners with wetlands in their communities must comply with these restrictions in comprehensive plans and development approvals. In practice, the Corps has routinely granted permits for small filling projects (up to ten acres) if isolated from other bodies of water. This has aroused opposition from those who argue that many small developments have added up to very large net losses of wetland.

In cases where filling is allowed, the developer must ordinarily create new wetland to replace the loss, often on another part of the same site. This mandate has also created *mitigation banks*, by which a landowner may establish a new offsite wetland area or restore one that has been degraded. Thus a builder who is allowed to fill in five acres at one site contributes money to restore five acres or more at another location. Private entrepreneurs as well as public agencies sponsor these. A 1992 survey indicated that 46 such mitigation banks existed in 18 states [Salvesen 1995]. Thus planners must give attention to their location and management and to whether the mitigation adequately compensates for the original loss.

Wildlife habitat poses the newest critical area challenge to planners. The federal Endangered Species Act and related state statutes mandate local habitat protection, which is most controversial at the fringes of urban expansion. These concerns are widespread, differing only in the names of the species whose habitats are threatened, but the San Diego case in chapter 1 offers one of the more prominent examples. Early in 1997, the San Diego City Council approved a plan to acquire and protect as much as 2,400 acres of natural habitat land within the city limits at a cost of $60 million or more. This is a major political victory for the growth-limitation forces [Ayres 1997].

Another success story is being written in the Balcones Canyonlands Conservation area on the edge of Austin, Texas. The intent is to withhold from development about 70,000 acres of hills and canyons that shelter several endangered species. The city of Austin and Travis County have purchased part of that, and as much more has been donated by private landowners. This is doubtless a factor in that region's quality of human life as well, in view of its rapid economic development. If efforts like Austin's and San Diego's are to succeed, local planners and lawmakers must have strong evidence that such habitat is essential and outweighs the legal claims of landowners to alter it. Following the principles which the U.S. Supreme Court stated in *Dolan v. City of Tigard* (see section 1.2), governments may have to purchase some lands outright to secure adequate protection.

A final type of critical area is high quality agricultural land near cities which is attractive for urban development. Although the United States has abundant cropland, there are long-range concerns for its protection in a world threatened by famines. Since the 1960s, when this became a widespread concern, most states have adopted programs to reduce development pressures on farmers. Figure 9.5 depicts a farm on the edge of Richmond, Virginia, the future of which depends on public policy. A few states and counties purchase the development rights of metropolitan area farmers, assuring that the land will remain agricultural until they choose otherwise. In the past 20 years, such buyouts have preserved 450,000 acres in 18 states [Feder 1997]. Counties and suburban cities also have agricultural or rural zones that limit urban growth; these are by their nature less permanent, however.

Figure 9.5   Farms remain, although in decreasing number, in the shadow of urban developments; this is near Richmond, Virginia. Source: U.S. Department of Agriculture.

A method increasingly used to save rural open spaces is *cluster zoning*. It has been common for rural townships and counties near metropolitan areas to zone land in very large lots, typically five acres or more. This allows farms and woodlands to be converted to low density residential use. An oft-favored alternative is to zone a given area for smaller lots, grouped in clusters, and reserve larger parcels in which no development takes place. Thus a section of land that might be zoned to accommodate fifty homes, spread across its entirety, could instead be subdivided to place the fifty homesites on a third of the area and leave the rest vacant [Arendt 1994]. This method has been used in the Connecticut

River valley in that state, Lancaster County, Pennsylvania, and the city of Brookfield, Wisconsin, among other places.

Private organizations also play a major role in preserving open and natural areas. *Land trusts* are nonprofit groups, formed at the state and regional levels, that obtain by purchase and gift parcels that are particularly worth saving from development. Such groups have acquired urban land for parks, protected lake fronts, and preserved farms, forests and wetlands. Landowners receive tax abatements or deductions either for donating property outright or for donating the development rights, an attractive incentive to those whose land has appreciated greatly in value.

As of 1996, more than 1,100 such trusts have preserved about four million acres. These efforts are supplemented by the Trust for Public Land, a national nonprofit agency that works with local governments to buy land for parks and open space. Trust officials can purchase a site quickly when it is on the market and a city or county lacks funds to acquire it at the time, and it then holds the land until public acquisition is possible. Its field offices also work with community groups, foundations, businesses, and individual donors of land and money [Trust for Public Land, 1996].

9.5 GROWTH MANAGEMENT POLICIES AND POLITICS

The entire package of policies for open space preservation and limitation of urban sprawl is commonly referred to as *growth management*. In its many forms, communities seek to control the type, location, pace, and sequencing of new development on urban fringes and to assure that when it occurs, it has adequate utilities, roads, schools, and other necessary services. Many legal and planning tools are used to this end, each with certain strengths, weaknesses, and implications for political conflict.

The most comprehensive means of growth management are the regional plans that place enforceable limits on development in defined areas. The most successful of these are based on state programs; section 3.6 described the efforts of Oregon and Florida to mandate the preparation and enforcement of local plans that meet common standards. As of 1995, thirteen states had comprehensive growth legislation for all or critical parts of their territory. They varied widely in the strength of their provisions and in the vigor of enforcement [Nelson & Duncan 1995, ch. 2].

Armed with its state granted powers, Portland, Oregon, has arguably the strongest met-ropolitan growth management program. It maintains an urban growth boundary, outside of which only rural land uses and previously existing homes are permitted. Because the region is growing rapidly and land costs are rising, there are strong pressures from development interests to expand the urban zone. However, the municipal plans emphasize higher density growth inside that line to accommodate the new residents. Local zoning ordinances and other planning choices must conform to the state policies, and disputes over specifics are settled by the state's Land Conservation and Development Commission [Oregon Department of Land Conservation and Development 1995; P. Lewis 1996, chs. 4 & 6]. Although these policies are supported by many developers, political disputes still center on the sufficiency of land for urban expansion in the foreseeable future.

Orlando also has such a boundary, as required by Florida's growth mangement policy. However, its growth pressures are even more intense than Portland's, and much of the development up to now has been in suburban Orange County. Its once-dominant citrus industry is in rapid decline, opening up large tracts for urban uses. As large as the task of channeling growth is, even greater is that of servicing the growth that has already occurred with highways, sewers, and schools. And as those amenities are provided, they set the stage for further expansion. Many Floridans want to protect their open spaces but the political capacity to do so may be seriously inadequate [Roy 1996].

Petaluma, California, attracted national attention in 1972 by enacting a policy of allocating only 500 residential building permits a year. If more applications were submitted, a rating scheme based on design qualities and availability of public services was used to set priorities. Its council also set a long-range population ceiling of 55,000. The purpose was to make sure that the growth rate did not exceed the city's ability to finance capital improvements. Although it was challenged in court by development interests as restricting the constitutional right of movement, a U.S. appeals court upheld it. The program remains in effect today, and Petaluma's population was about 43,000 in 1991 [Nelson & Duncan 1995, pp. 107–108]. It has been copied by other communities, mainly metropolitan suburbs, but most have not imposed as strict a limit on growth.

The transfer of development rights is a less sweeping means of limiting growth. It occurs when a local government permits owners of land on which it wants to restrict development, usually cropland or sensitive areas, to sell the rights to develop it to owners in other areas where development is permitted. For example, Montgomery County, Maryland, allows farmers in that quickly suburbanizing area to sell rights to build housing units to other landowners, who are then able to exceed the normal density limits for their subdivisions. This effort has enabled the county, located between the cities of Washington and Baltimore, to preserve many farms and thus the open space that residents enjoy seeing [Nelson & Duncan 1995, pp. 48–49].

In a few instances, local authorities have directly purchased these development rights with no transfer intended. In 1996, voters in Dunn Township, on the edge of Madison, Wisconsin, approved a property tax increase to finance such purchases. Such a program is a politically workable means to maintain urban growth boundaries, since these transfers and sales are voluntary by landowners. However, its success also depends on the price paid for the rights and the property's attractiveness in the larger land market. It clearly requires that planners target the most valu-

able lands for protection, which in turn assumes that they have chosen the appropriate areas for the growth that will occur. A metropolitan strategy is also imperative; it may avail little if one village or township restrains growth but an adjoining one undergoes more development as a result.

Growth management is, like zoning, a signal to many interests of the benefits and evils of public intervention into private property choices. Much of the environmental and growth management regulation has been lobbied for by citizen groups at the national, state, and local levels. For example, the pioneering Oregon policy was promoted by 1000 Friends of Oregon, which continues to interpret it and influence the local planmaking so crucial to its implementation. Indeed, it grew well beyond that number of members and has its own planning staff to back up the public agencies' work. Similar "1000 Friends" organizations now exist in several other states. Rhode Island's Save the Bay, described above, has also been a model for other groups.

Opponents of growth management programs are also well organized in many places. Among them are the groups of developers and property owners who value their traditional freedom to use their land as they choose. From this ideological base, Oregonians in Action has attacked the position of 1000 Friends of Oregon and the policies it supports. Montanans for Property Rights argues against land use controls in such areas as the west entrance to Glacier National Park, a high-demand region for resort and vacation-home growth and the businesses that serve them.

The larger question at stake is the "takings issue" and the extent of property owners' rights. The U.S. Constitution stipulates that government may not take private property except for public use and without fair compensation. This clearly applies to the outright acquisition of land, when a unit of government compels a sale by right of eminent domain, as for a highway. Open to argument, however, is when a regulation of land use which reduces its current or future value becomes a taking. Recall the Dolans' hardware store in chapter 1: the city of Tigard granted them the permit to expand, but required them to grant part of the property for a pathway and flood control. This reduced the usable portion of their land with no compensation, to serve what the city defined as a public purpose. The Supreme Court's decision for Dolan indicated that regulation can in some circumstances become taking.

The central concern of those in the *property rights movement* is that a few landowners are forced to pay for benefits that the entire nation or community enjoys. If they are prohibited from draining a swamp or building homes on the habitat of a rare bird, an unjust burden is thrust on them. This is entirely apart from whether the given parcel is in fact a swamp or the bird actually nests there (which can also be questioned). Since this is a right guaranteed in the Constitution, landowners also fear that the failure to challenge violations can let it become a dead letter. They deeply distrust planners and government "bureaucrats" who, in their eyes, can do little that is right. Their primary weapons are lawsuits and legislative lobbying, and the Republican Party in particular has taken up their cause.

This issue has drawn the attention of federal and state lawmakers. Several states require "takings impact analyses" as part of environmental regulations to ensure that property owners' interests are considered. A bill passed the U.S. House of Representatives in 1995 (but was not acted upon by the Senate) to require the federal government to reim-burse landowners when wetlands or endangered species laws reduced their land values by forty per cent or more. Doubtless, these efforts, together with recent court decisions, have made local planners more sensitive to the impacts of their choices on landowners.

Taken together, the courts have established three general tests for determining whether a given regulation imposes a burden that could be called a taking [Duerksen & Roddewig 1996]. Most simply, if the owner is left with no economic use for the property, a taking has indeed occurred. If there is some use, deemed "reasonable" in the specific circumstances, no compensation is probably due.

Second, there must be a valid public purpose to justify the regulation. The original zoning laws were upheld in the 1920s because courts deemed that local governments' police powers authorized them to seek orderly land uses. These accepted purposes include protection of open space and environmentally sensitive areas, defined as essential to the larger public interests. Some courts, in specific cases, have compared the overall public benefit to the loss that landowner underwent and upheld the regulation when it judged that the former was greater.

The third test focuses on how the government action was imposed on the private property. Courts have usually allowed the taking of parts of privately owned parcels for public access, such as the trail and floodplain on the Dolans' site. However, the message from *Dolan* and similar decisions is there must be a sufficient relationship between the needs created by the building project and the portion of land that is so taken. In this case, the Supreme Court questioned whether the mere enlargement of a hardware store warranted the claim of a bike path corridor. If the city needs that corridor to complete its trail network, the majority of justices implied, it should purchase the land outright from the Dolans.

Basically, there is no single criterion to determine whether a taking exceeds constitutional limits. Federal and state court decisions reflect the many diverse situations they deal with [Wise & Emerson 1994]. Planners and legislators must study previous decisions in cases similar to theirs and use their best judgment, aware that any future court ruling could compel them to rewrite their policies.

There are several means by which planners can protect their policies against takings claims. First, they must ground their land-use and environmental regulations on sound analysis of data and comprehensive planning. Judges insist that communities make informed and rational choices that are rooted in an established public interest. If, for example, a study shows that a proposed home development would thrust too heavy a traffic burden on narrow roads, a city could deny it or require a lower density that would be less profitable to the builder. But to be "arbitrary and capricious" in their decisions is one of the worst sins that planners can commit.

Second, they should be sensitive to economic impacts of their regulations on property owners and be ready to modify the rules where it would not materially weaken their policies. In some cases, compensation may be justified, while in others, they could negotiate an alternative solution. A city in Tigard's situation should be prepared to negotiate some incentives with an applicant to avoid a lawsuit.

In a larger sense, planners should anticipate future takings challenges and discern where more positive tools of control would be helpful. The transfer of development rights, described above, is a workable alternative in some situations. A developer may forego

building in a sensitive area if granted additional leeway on another project.

A final question for this chapter, leaving the legal questions behind, concerns the outcomes of the past several decades' efforts at urban growth management. Here too, the evidence is mixed and subject to many interpretations. Urban sprawl has certainly continued and no one can say with confidence what it would look like today without the restrictions on it. Evidence from three areas in southern California suggests that even cities with growth limiting policies have not actually curbed it much. The regulations contain enough loopholes and exceptions to allow developers to win approval for many of their projects. However, those policies have steered the growth in more desired directions, such as infill construction in Santa Monica and Santa Barbara. Thus the regimes supporting growth have had to adjust to new resident expectations [Warner & Molotch 1995].

A recent analysis of California's efforts to limit urban growth discerned several lessons [Bank of America 1996]. In general, "the engine of sprawl is fueled by a mix of individual choices, market forces, and government policies, most of which have only become more entrenched over time." In particular, growth control policies by individual cities are futile, since they tend to deflect it into less regulated communities or farther out in the fringe area. Further, there are too many disincentives to use more efficiently the urban land that is already developed, particularly the brownfields noted in chapter 6.

What is needed instead, argue the authors of the Bank of America paper, is a comprehensive metropolitan strategy for where and when development should occur that all local authorities buy into. Supporting this must be a financing structure that imposes on fringe area construction its full marginal costs, so it does not enjoy a special advantage over inner-city redevelopment. This is workable, in turn, only if a private constituency supports sustainable communities, a broad alliance of businesses, environmentalists, community leaders, public officials, and homeowners who realize the stakes in their choices. Oregon, as noted above, appears to have many of these necessary ingredients.

Chattanooga and Hamilton County, Tennessee, have drawn national attention for such a holistic coalition for sustainable development. Among the projects of the past ten years are the introduction of electric transit vehicles, redevelopment of polluted industrial zones, treatment of wastewater through constructed wetlands, recycling of solid wastes, an expanded park and greenway system, and the protection of the Tennessee River Gorge. Planners and officials in several agencies and private firms mobilized their skills and financial resources to link the environmental goals with the imperatives for economic development [Chattanooga/Hamilton County, Tennessee 1996]. Thus, there are models from which other communities can learn, even though no experience can ever be exactly copied with success.

We have seen that the natural environment is an essential ingredient in that elusive concept, "urban quality of life." A sustainable community is one in which all residents can live in some kind of harmony with their surroundings. This has a counterpart in the social and cultural environment. Planners create and sustain many conditions for existence, and they must take care that they benefit every group. Many of the issues already discussed—jobs, homes, and transportation—also impact this quality of life. Chapter 10 addresses several cultural influences for which the planning process also has some responsibility.

FOR REVIEW AND DISCUSSION

1. What meanings could *sustainability* have in an urban context? Why is it difficult to agree on a single definition or application?

2. What are the evidences of *urban sprawl*? How much has occurred in metropolitan areas with which you are familiar?

3. What are the main sources of air, water, and soil pollution in urban areas? What role can planners play in their control or curtailment?

4. What goals does the Superfund program have? What factors have prevented it from fulfilling them to this point?

5. What legal and planning tools are used to protect critical areas from development and abuse? In what ways are these tools limited in their effectiveness?

6. What is the major point of contention of the property rights movement? How valid is its claim that landowners should be compensated when environmental regulations cause a loss of value?

CHAPTER

10

Planning the Cultural Landscape

10.1 CULTURAL MEANINGS AND PLANNING CHOICES

Land-use choices often have cultural meanings beyond the tangible structures they produce. A city's identity is rooted not only in its citizens' homes, workplaces, and physical environment but also in its history, in the places where people gather for edification and enjoyment, and in the symbols that give significance to their lives. Planners and politicians can easily overlook and degrade these features' place in the urban environment if they limit their vision to the technical issues of where to build and at what cost.

This chapter focuses on several examples of this concern: preservation and enhancement of historic buildings and sites, places for recreation and cultural growth, sports facilities, schools, and libraries. These might be seen as the distinct ingredients of a city's culture, to be then woven into a larger fabric. Then the attention turns to the broader issues of urban design, seeking a view of that fabric as

a whole. Although such designing occurs within a stream of distinct choices, they come together in shaping the qualities that many citizens want to find in their communities.

10.2 HISTORIC PRESERVATION

Our society requires tangible evidence of years and lives gone by. This demand is strong today because we are experiencing rapid change in life styles as well as the built environment. Preservation of historic structures and sites has gained markedly in the priorities of urban planners since Congress passed the Historic Preservation Act of 1966. Lynch [1972, p. 57] provided an eloquent rationale for it.

The contrast of old and new, the accumulated concentration of the most significant elements of the various periods gone by, even if they are only fragmentary reminders of them, will in time produce a landscape whose depth no one period can equal. . . . . The esthetic aim is to heighten contrast and complexity, to make visible the process of change. The achievement of the aim requires creative and skillful demolition, just as much as skillful new design.

That act set up the National Register of Historic Places and mandated that federal agencies consider the effects on such places of the projects they finance. It further emphasized the responsibility of state and local governments and the private sector to carry out the purposes of the act in their own areas, and provided grants for a share of the costs of approved projects. They cover not only individual buildings and sites but also areas and districts that contain unique and valuable evidence of human experience and accomplishment. Great age or beauty is not necessary; railroad stations and waterworks have qualified where significant to local history.

Local and state government officials have guided many historic preservation projects, although most financing has come from profit-seeking investors, individual property owners, and local and national foundations. Often, cities create special zoning districts that restrict alteration of designated structures. Charleston, South Carolina, enacted the first preservation ordinance in the nation in 1931, designating the boundaries of a historic district, requiring permits for alterations of existing structures and design of new construction, and creating a Board of Architectural Review to pass on all proposals. The city of San Jose, California, one of the state's oldest, also has a historic preservation policy, based on a resources inventory taken in the 1970s and 1980s. The city planning department must review all development requests to ensure they are consistent with this policy [San Jose, City of 1994]. A private nonprofit corporation, the Preservation Action Council

of San Jose, provides valuable support to the city's efforts by informing property owners and the public of the need to protect sites that embody its 150 years of history.

Historic districts are sometimes designed to attract large numbers of visitors, and thus include interpretive centers and the inevitable parking lots. Atlanta has developed such facilities around the boyhood home of Dr. Martin Luther King, Jr. and the Ebenezer Baptist Church, where he and his father preached. His tomb is there as well, along with a museum. Extending west from those sites is Auburn Avenue, the "Sweet Auburn" that was for decades the center of African-American business during the era of segregation. It is thus not just a geographic location but anchors a period in time that Whites and Blacks alike do well to remember.

A leading private organization in this field is the National Trust for Historic Preservation. It owns some buildings of particular historic value; Figure 10.1 is one example. The Trust's staff members also help local communities to identify valuable sites and to choose how to protect them. One such project is the National Main Street Center, which enables them to revitalize their traditional business districts. Another program works with real estate firms in the marketing of historic homes, seeking to promote a commitment to their preservation by buyers and sellers.

Landmark protection can also promote economic development. Several of the 19th century cloth mills in Lowell, Massachusetts, have been converted to office and residential space. Other mill buildings are part of a National Historic Park that lets visitors view their ancestors' harsh working conditions. Across the nation, formerly vacant hotels, offices, and factories now contain apartments, art galleries, and festival markets; their devel-

Figure 10.1   The Gaylord Building in Lockport, Illinois, was built in 1838 for the construction of the Illinois and Michigan Canal that linked Chicago with the Mississippi River. It is now owned by the National Trust for Historic Preservation and houses an art gallery and restaurant. Photo by Hedrick Blessing.

opers have benefited from generous tax credits and low-interest loans.

The politics of historic preservation can be as heated as that over other planning issues. When a developer wants to build on a site such as Civil War battlefield, new battles are sure to begin. In 1993, Walt Disney executives announced plans to build a massive theme park which opponents claimed would de-

secrate the site of the 1862 Second Battle of Manassas (or Bull Run), in Prince William County, Virginia. Although comprehensive local plans allowed such development, nearby residents carried their opposition into court, concerned also for the sprawl, traffic, and pollution the park would produce. Disney surrendered, fearing damage to its corporate image, but the county still must decide what development to allow there if any [Gallagher 1995].

A second problem is that the wishes of the owners of historic structures may not coincide with the community's concept of preservation. For example, old churches in many parts of the country are designated historical landmarks and so cannot be altered or demolished. In some cases, their congregations are growing but local protective ordinances prevent them from enlarging their structures. Other congregations are small and find maintenance a heavy burden and would like to replace their buildings, but are legally barred from doing so [Dunlap 1997]. Similarly, landowners in a historic district may be prevented from choosing the most economically rewarding uses for their property. Thus, historic preservation is not in the immediate financial interest of everyone.

10.3 PLANNING FOR PARKS AND CULTURAL AMENITIES

Parks and recreational open space present another planning challenge. The objective here is not the protection of nature as such but the opportunity for people to enjoy the outdoors either actively or passively. Serious attention to park planning began in the 1850s, when New York City acquired the land that is now Central Park. Its purpose, as explained by its designer, Frederick L. Olmsted, was to afford the growing urban masses some contact with nature and fresh air. This occurred well before the establishment of city planning in general. Later in that century, large park systems and parkways were established in Boston, Chicago, and Philadelphia, drawing on Olmsted's inspiration.

Park and recreational site planning is of high priority for communities today. The National Recreation and Park Association has set recommended standards for park types and sizes relative to population. For example, it calls for a minimum of 6.25 acres of developed open space per thousand persons, to include facilities for specific sports such as tennis and baseball. It envisions a hierarchy of park types, from the small "tot lots" with play equipment, up through neighborhood, community, and regional parks with progressively larger areas and a wider choice of activities. Trails for hiking, biking, and rollerblading are popular, and some cities require them in new subdivision layouts. Passive recreation areas, limited to trails, are also popular for wetlands and woods that are set aside for critical-area protection [Kaiser, Godschalk & Chapin 1995, pp. 388–392].

Many communities have a special body charged with advising or policy making on parks and recreation. It may be a voluntary commission, answerable to the city council, or an elected board governing a park district that is separate from other local authorities. Both seek to determine citizens' interests and needs and develop plans and programs to meet them; the park boards have the legal power to implement them as well. Members have to be sensitive to issues of safety and security, particularly in inner-city neighborhoods, and fit programs and facilities to the needs of families, the elderly, and persons with disabilities. It is also common to require developers of large subdivisions to dedicate land for parks, and to levy a park dedication fee on smaller developments to finance acquisition of sites elsewhere.

Cities have learned to create parks in even unpromising locations. San Antonio has a river flowing through its downtown that was for many years both a flood hazard and a collector of garbage. By 1941, it had turned a 1.8 mile stretch into the Paseo del Rio, a pair of tree-shaded walkways now lined with shops, cafes, galleries, and hotels, and is one of the city's most celebrated showplaces. It required a substantial investment, however, including voter-approved bond issues. As a choice site for further investment, it has come to serve more and more residents and tourists alike [Garvin 1996, pp. 53–54].

Other means of recreation are also in demand by an affluent society. Cities are building community centers with gymnasiums, indoor and outdoor pools, ice arenas, and exercise rooms, often in conjunction with meeting spaces, libraries, and municipal offices. Public marinas, golf courses, and ski facilities increasingly compete with private clubs. Neighborhood gyms and courts for basketball nurture the next century's Michael Jordans and help keep energetic youths out of trouble. Spectator sports demand stadiums for professional, amateur, and school competition. Whether these facilities are the highest priority for investment of public funds is a perennial question, and some communities enter into partnerships with private companies for joint financing and management.

Community cultural centers, typically art galleries, auditoriums, theaters, and museums, command attention for their economic as well as esthetic values. A host of new galleries have been built recently, reflecting both the proliferation of artists in many media and the wealth and sophistication of devotees and collectors. Such large-investment projects are typically joint ventures, in which local or state government provides incentives to giving by foundations, community organizations, and wealthy patrons.

Arts-centered development coalitions have emerged in many cities to promote these facilities [Whitt 1987, ch. 7]. With the decline of their traditional industries, the promoters of growth see benefits in the production and enjoyment of the visual and performing arts. Many of these new facilities have been lo-

cated in older downtown areas, a boost for their stores and hotels as well. A depressed area of central Newark now boasts the New Jersey Performing Arts Center, built at a cost of $165 million. The hope is not only to provide an alternative to Manhattan for music and dance enthusiasts but also to enhance that city's image and draw additional development downtown. The state even built a new exit ramp from Interstate 280 to serve the site [MacFarquhar 1997].

On a less grand scale, planners in Peekskill, New York, have actively marketed vacant downtown space for living and working studios and granted special zoning conditions for them. Since 1991, it has used Community Development Block Grant funds for rehabilitation, and drawn about eighty artists to what had been a fading business area. Providence, Phoenix, and St. Paul have also been leaders in attracting artists downtown [Schamess 1996]. An influx of younger and less affluent artists has revived activity and land values in many urban neighborhoods, such as Wicker Park on Chicago's northwest side.

The public library is another essential in the cultural life of cities. Governed by a city or county agency or a semi-independent library board, a system typically consists of a central facility along with any number of neighborhood branches. While some big-city libraries are strapped for funds, others now operate in impressive new structures. Chicago, San Francisco, Denver, Phoenix, and San Antonio recently completed new central libraries that not only house books and videos and access points for the Information Highway but also provide a dramatic symbol of the city's commitment to culture [Jordan 1996].

Schools, from early childhood centers to universities, are also major landmarks in cities and towns. Planning for them is done by specialized educational authorities, such as school boards and university regents. Yet their location, size, means of access, and surrounding recreational facilities command attention by planners in city and county governments, who have to approve their site plans and the public improvements that serve them. The neighbors of a new high school, for example, are naturally concerned about how the buses will reach it, where the athletic fields will be, and how it will affect their own security. Many disused school buildings have been turned to other uses, such as apartments and nursing homes, and require more explicit government attention. A college or university site multiplies these concerns by many times. Suburban campuses pose heavy traffic burdens, with demands for nearby housing and convenient transit service. Several large city downtowns have acquired campus sites in new or recycled buildings, serving not only commuters but also those who work in the area and seek to advance their education with late afternoon and evening classes.

It is also vital that the specialized authorities responsible for these services share projections of growth with city and county planners in their area. As cities like Las Vegas, Phoenix, San Jose, and their suburbs grow rapidly, their school authorities must have classrooms in place when new residents move in. This requires reserving locations well in advance, determining a street pattern, and assuring that water and sewer pipes will be in the ground.

10.4 URBAN DESIGN: INTEGRATING THE CITY'S SIGHTS AND SPACES

The overall character of the city is culture in the largest sense, the fabric into which are woven the amenities discussed in this chapter. But it also encompasses all the planning choices in the previous chapters, to become what is ideally a pleasing and workable whole. *Urban design* is thus the conscious linking of structures, spaces, and movements with the purposes and values of the human beings who live and work in that environment. Those values are basically the four outlined in chapter 2: esthetic, functional, social, and ecological. Such design is akin in purpose to architecture, but applied on a series of larger scales, from the city block to the neighborhood, corridor, district, and region.

Planners and architects who consciously practice urban design work with several elements: the built structures, which may range from individual homes to high-rise office buildings; the spaces between those structures; means of access to and through them; landscaping and natural features; signs that direct and portray; and environmental standards relating to water, energy, and wastes. They also build in the subjective messages that these elements send to people who live, work, play, shop, and travel through there. This is a complex task, not least because their constituents find many different meanings in those elements.

The historic city plans described in chapter 2 paid attention to this task in various ways. When L'Enfant planned Washington, D.C., to resemble a grand European capital, he intended that Americans visiting that city view their nation as equal if not superior to the English and French. By contrast, when Pullman laid out his factory town on the edge of Chicago, he wanted his employees to view their working and family lives as seamless, each supporting the other. Howard's garden city took a third direction: to demonstrate that the pursuits of city and country are compatible and to give residents the ambiance of both. More oriented to a concept of 20th century technology was Le Corbusier's city of towers, which would have obliterated all evidences of earlier living styles.

Plans made today are less oriented to grandeur or social idealism and certainly are more modest in geographic scope. Most bow to such economic and technical criteria as "highest and best use" and "maximum accessibility." A visit to a major airport presents one with such an image. Yet, many planners remain concerned with the social consequences of their craft, particularly the long-range and intangible effects that cannot be represented in a blueprint or budget.

Design at the block and neighborhood levels can take many forms, depending on the market that a particular architect or developer targets. Most single-family suburban neighborhoods are monotonously familiar, even though financially successful. More interesting are efforts to renew older districts and fill in vacant spaces. The replacement of public housing in Chester, Pennsylvania, described in section 7.4, calls for application of all that decades of experience with failed projects has to teach.

An essential aim of small-scale design is public safety. In view of high urban crime rates and resident fears of violence, planners can no longer dismiss this as merely a police concern. They have learned that security depends also on the ways in which buildings and spaces are laid out. Oscar Newman, a planner with long experience, examined the reasons why public housing projects are so crime ridden. He found part of the answer in their lack of "defensible space," areas which residents perceive to be their own and thus guard from unwanted and dangerous intrusions. Unwise physical design contributes to alienation, indifference to one's surroundings, and outright fear, an outcome which earlier housing planners failed to anticipate. To Newman [1973, p. 3], defensible space is

a surrogate term for the range of mechanisms—real and symbolic barriers, strongly defined areas of influence, and improved opportunities for surveillance—that combine to bring an environment under the control of its residents. [It] is a living residential environment which can be employed by inhabitants for the enhancement of their lives, while providing security for their families, neighbors, and friends.

Newman's concepts have since been applied in many locations. For example, when a new public housing development was placed in a middle-income neighborhood in Yonkers, New York, complying with a court order, it provided for maximum resident view of, and responsibility for, its entryways, yards, and even garbage cans (see Figure 7.4 for an example). To the surprise of the project's bitter opponents, the new tenants adopted the law-abiding behavior of their more established neighbors. Crime did not increase nor did the area's property values decline [Newman 1995].

The theme of defensible space is central to that of the traditional neighborhood developments described in section 7.3. Andres Duany and his collaborators believe that the most secure environment is the one in which residents and users feel the strongest commitment to one another as persons. For example, they design houses with front porches and line streets with sidewalks to encourage residents to pay close attention to who may be passing through or stopping. They want to make the entire neighborhood "defensible space" through a sense of mutual interest.

Law enforcement officials have recently added their voices to the concern for defensible space. A national program inspired by Newman's work, Crime Prevention Through Environmental Design (CPTED) directs attention to the security effects of walkways, building entries, illumination, parking areas, and landscaping. Planners are increasingly requiring development applications to maximize the visibility and safety of users. Proper placement of lights, vegetation, and access doors will reduce a building's vulnerability to burglary and vandalism. Basically, every space open to public access should be under someone's view and control.

CPTED principles also call for traffic controls in residential neighborhoods. Projects in Hartford, Portland, Oregon, and Minneapolis included traffic diverters at intersections that force drivers to make a right-angle turn, making alleys into cul-de-sacs, and otherwise discouraging easy escape from crime scenes. Essentially, such programs aim to reduce crimes of opportunity; in practice, though, they may simply channel crime into less-protected areas.

Much urban design effort focuses on downtown public spaces, since these are especially visible and often criticized. Many areas around high-rise buildings are shunned except by those who have to cross them. Goldsteen and Elliott [1994, pp. 9 & 2] argue, however, that these spaces are

> major functional and visual factors in the well-being of American urban structures. From village to metropolis, our dwelling places are embedded in networks of open spaces that strongly influence our work and our leisure, and they largely determine the way we view our everyday environment and ourselves. . . . . . . The physical environment so strongly affects the economic and social behavior in cities that deteriorating spaces can cause building and land values to plummet.

Dramatic outdoor spaces, like Union Square in San Francisco, the Gateway Arch in St. Louis, and San Antonio's Paseo del Rio, give both definition to the city and a place to meet and walk. If people perceive a space to be safe and friendly, they will come; but a dangerous place will repel visitors and become even more so. Project for Public Spaces, a nonprofit corporation of scholars and designers, aids cities in their design of gardens, fountains, sculptures, and comfortable places to sit that add a vital social as well as esthetic dimension. They have learned, for example, that simply providing benches and flower planters does not draw visitors; someone must take responsibility for an area's cleaning and security and respond to changing public needs and conditions. Often, this is a joint public-private endeavor, depending on actual ownership of the location [Davies 1985].

Indoor public space, whether private or government owned, further adds to an area's vitality. Inner-city shopping malls can be distinctive when compared with the more standardized suburban centers. San Diego's Horton Plaza and community theater complex is likened by imaginative observers to an Italian hill town. St. Paul's Town Square not only houses three floors of shops and offices but also an indoor public park on the top level. The dramatic interior space of the State of Illinois Building (Thompson Center) in Chicago and the restored Old Post Office in Washington, D.C., illustrate this potential on a grand scale.

Corridors for travel also call for careful design. Even bridges can add design attractiveness, as the Central Avenue crossing of the Salt River in Phoenix in Figure 10.2 shows. Chicago recently redesigned its famous State Street to be more congenial to pedestrian traffic and thus attract shoppers to its remaining retailers. Figure 10.3 shows a new subway entrance and street lights that seek to recall a past elegance. Previous chapters have traced the struggles to redefine New York's Times Square and the 42nd Street corri-

Figure 10.2   Central Avenue Bridge over Papago Freeway in Phoenix, with distinctive balustrade and light standards. Photo by Dennis McClendon.

Figure 10.3   When Chicago recently refurbished State Street, it constructed subway entrances that recalled a more elegant era of design. Photo by Richard Sessions.

dor. This is likewise a design question: what is the area to mean, to New Yorkers and visitors? The gaudy signs and flashing lights that have long marked that district invite them, "Come here for some fun! You're a long way from Canarsie or Cedar Rapids!" It is also a long way, culturally, from Sixth Avenue with its rigidly posed office towers and well disciplined executives and computer programmers. To design that small segment of New York is to contribute to a definition of the

whole city. While stakes are lower in smaller cities, planners still realize that a noteworthy downtown shopping street or humanely equipped park is an asset that defines their character as well.

The architecture of public buildings goes even farther to define neighborhoods and communities. Schools, city halls, courthouses, stadiums, even prisons and waste treatment facilities project images of our common social values. Dattner [1995] argues that school placement and architecture teaches lessons about how important education is, whether children are truly welcome and safe there, and how the learning they get there relates to the real life of the community.

Ultimately, all public structures and spaces should send clear messages about the civility and public spiritedness necessary to maintain a democratic civilization. Dattner [1995, ch. 2] is particularly impressed with another New York City project: Riverbank State Park. When the city required a new sewage treatment plant on the Hudson River shore in the 1960s, it filled 28 acres of riverfront, but later capped it with athletic fields, picnic grounds, an amphitheater, and community gardens, reached by decorative bridges over Henry Hudson Parkway. After it opened in 1993, three million persons visited it in the first year. It presents a creative approach to the LULU problem described in earlier pages, demonstrating that planners can indeed serve the less pleasant public functions in a way that also enhances the qualities of urban living.

Coherent urban design on a larger scale is much less common today. Some of the most creative work is that of the New Urbanists described in section 7.3. To be successful on that scale requires substantial financial as well as architectural resources; the Walt Disney Corporation's new Celebration in Florida enjoys both and has a good chance of reaching the intended population of 20,000. However, critics note that it will be a very distinct community, under the governance not of an elected council but of homeowners' and shopkeepers' associations. The cultural and design integrity will be protected by strict rules which the associations enforce. While critics complain that it cannot be a "real city," there are apparently many who are eager to buy into that version of Utopia.

The survey of major planning issues is now complete. Basically, it has demonstrated where we are today in terms of the choices made and results from them. The final concern of this book is the likely directions of future development. Since all planning is about the future, we need to fix in our thinking the major trends and forces for which planners will be accountable and which will constrain the world that planners seek to shape. Chapter 11 will provide that survey and the challenge to the planning community to rethink its procedures and as well as its policies.

FOR REVIEW AND DISCUSSION

1. What are the common rationales for preservation of historic buildings and districts? What political and practical difficulties does this often present to planners and public officials?

2. What are the commonly agreed upon standards for the size and type of public parks? How do you believe the need for parks and recreation facilities is changing today?

3. What are the arguments for expanding arts facilities and libraries today? How high a priority do you believe these ought to have in cities with many pressing public needs?

4. How is *urban design* generally defined today? What are the political limits to planners' efforts to provide coherent designs for significant parts of cities?

5. By what means can good design reduce the likelihood of crime in an area? How successful is this likely to be in the long run?

11

Planning for the New Century

11.1 THE CHOICES AHEAD

The planning profession was in its infancy at the end of the 19th century, yet there was an abundance of planning for American cities. Builders, financiers, architects, and politicians all carried visions of what their cities could become. Growth was virtually a religion, and they were its priests and prophets. But as chapter 2 recounted, they faced the conflict of three basic values: esthetic, functional, and social (the distinctly ecological value came later). To what extent, they had to ask, do we want our cities to be beautiful? to be places to make money? to promote solidarity and community? Even at that time, the more sensitive growth boosters had to admit that those values may not be fully compatible.

The cities look very different now, but the questions remain. As Campbell [1996, p. 296] foresees them,

> in the coming years, planners face tough decisions about where they stand on protecting the green city, promoting the economically growing city, and advocating social justice. . . . . . These

conflicts go to the historic core of planning, and are a leitmotif in the contemporary battles in both our cities and rural areas.

Campbell calls these goals the "planner's triangle," a juxtaposition of conflicts, to be sure, but also an opportunity for joining interests. With skillful intervention, they can bring participants together and help design projects that serve all three aims.

This chapter examines four key concerns that will hold the attention of planners in the early decades of the 21st century.

1. *As the Information Revolution progresses at an increasing pace, how will cities enable their businesses and residents to take best advantage of the technological resources for prosperity and opportunity?*

2. *As cities become more diverse in culture and life styles, how can they be made secure and congenial places for families with children, the elderly, women, immigrants, persons with disabilities, and others who have been in some way disadvantaged by the social systems?*

3. *As urban settlements spread farther and*

wider and produce more waste products, how can they exist in reasonable compatibility with the natural ecosystems?

4. How can the entire planning process be made both competent and responsible as it wrestles with these questions, encompassing the larger publics and interests yet sensitive to the "small" concerns of people in their own lives and neighborhoods?

11.2 CITIES IN CYBERSPACE

Cities have always been centers of information. Their very reason for existence from earliest antiquity was to communicate, about trade, war, governing, religion, customs, and new inventions. But that information had always, until the coming of the telegraph, arrived in the city by physical means. After the mid-19th century, electrical and electronic messages swelled this volume, and much more is now being transmitted and stored in digital form than in print. Cities are points of origin, switching and destination for communications, and they provide jobs for many who generate, process, and use information as well as those who maintain the instruments and networks.

This fact has not been of central concern to planners, as their concerns are defined here. Telephone wires and microwave transmission facilities are privately owned and are regulated by state public service agencies and the Federal Communications Commission. Local authorities needed only allow the utility companies to string wires above or under the ground and grant permits for signal transmitters and receivers. It was easy to regard these as technical matters, properly left to engineers.

Graham and Marvin argue that *telematics,* the "services and infrastructures which link computer and digital media equipment over telecommunications links," [1996, p. 2] is no longer a mere technical issue that planners can ignore. Rather, its stakes touch deeply the economic and social futures of cities and the ways in which land will be used in the 21st century.

How do cities and urban life interrelate with the proliferation of electronic networks?. . . . . What happens to cities in the shift away from an economy based on the production and the circulation of material goods to one based more and more on the circulation and consumption of symbolic and "informational" goods? How are cities to sustain themselves economically given that more and more of their traditional economic advantages seem to be accessible, "online," from virtually any location?. . . . . . How are social power relations and the traditional social struggles within cities reflected in the new era of telecommunications? What is the relevance of telecommunications for burgeoning current debates about the "environmental sustainability" of industrial cities? [Graham & Marvin 1996, p. 4]

We cannot now answer these questions, but they will be definitively anwered by coalitions of corporations, investors, entrepreneurs, and political leaders over the coming decades. If professional and citizen planners are to contribute their holistic viewpoints to this debate, they must be sufficiently informed on the potentials and dangers. In the terms with which this book opened, the vision and imagination that planners put to work must encompass the virtual realms of electronics and cyberspace.

Planners will certainly make more decisions on the location of telecommunications facilities. No city can attract the typical high technology-using employer without sophisticated fiber-optic cable and high-capacity wireless links. Telephone cell sites have very specific locational requirements, and their an-

Figure 11.1   As more and more antennas are needed for wireless communication, municipal water tanks become favored places to site them. They pose legal and esthetic problems, however. Photo by AT&T Wireless Services.

tennae, whether on free-standing towers or attached to other structures, come under zoning standards (see Figure 11.1). However, under the federal Telecommunications Act of 1996, cities cannot simply exclude them outright. Placement of fiber-optic cables in streets and other corridors to serve businesses and homes is proceeding rapidly, and local authorities have a strong incentive to plan this network to supply maximum coverage. Overall, planners must be proactive in determining how to accommodate the current technologies and in reserving capacity for the personal communications systems that will be widely used [Covington 1996].

Telematics will also impact the shape of metropolitan areas and travel patterns within them. Some forecasters expect many companies to move to small towns and rural areas, since they don't need an urban physical location to do business by telephone or internet. A major travel agency based in Philadelphia moved its reservation center to Linton, North Dakota, to reduce labor costs. This trend would bode ill for the economic prospects of many cities. Other observers do not expect most firms to follow suit, however, since so many companies favor urban locations with their more skilled work forces, close access to customers, ease of face to face communications, and living amenities for executives. Even if the latter forecast is more accurate, it is likely that major shifts between metropolitan areas and between central cities and their suburbs will continue [Atkinson 1996].

Very likely, as well, is the placement of "teleports" in downtowns and suburban edge cities—terminals for high-volume cable and satellite communications that can serve many enterprises in one location. Graham and Marvin [1996, pp. 349–354] report that these have been established in New York City as well as several European locations. In the United States, these will be primarily privately sponsored, but cities, counties, and states can support and promote them as stimuli for high-technology development. In these efforts, cities and states will continue to vie with one another for the prize employers and offer whatever incentives the market appears to demand.

11.3 FAMILY AND COMMUNITY IN A MULTICULTURAL AGE

High technology will certainly provide more advancement opportunities for the well educated, but there is no assurance that those prospects will extend to everyone. Nor can we be sure that they will be congenial for anyone, whether affluent or not. There is abundant documentation of the wide gap that now exists between rich and poor, between young people who can look forward to high living standards and those who seem trapped in a culture of poverty. Graham and Marvin [1996, p. 37] are concerned that information systems can enable affluent neighborhoods to become fortresses, shut off from the poor and deviant. People who can work, shop, and socialize electronically will come to believe they need have little concern for those who are not succeeding. As a result, social and economic polarization could well increase with dire political consequences as well. Certainly those who will lack access to the terminals of the information society face very limited prospects. We may well ask what it will profit a city to have the "best-in-the-world" teleports, yet keep a quarter of the population living below the poverty line.

Urban planners have displayed social concerns since the days of the housing reformers, as chapter 2 demonstrated. Every city has groups of persons who are marginalized for reasons based primarily in social structures or personal handicaps. While those sources are beyond the professional scope of the planners' endeavors, some disadvantages can be mitigated by public action. These range from community business enterprises, described in chapter 6, to transportation from inner cities to suburban jobs, as noted in chapter 8, to provision of safe living environments, touched on in chapter 10. Expansion of housing opportunities, job-creating business incubators, and control of neighborhood pollution sources add to the list.

A vision for the future must take a holistic view of distributing advantages. The community-based organizations and public-private partnerships which often appeared in these pages empower the disadvantaged to act on their own behalf, defining their needs, gathering resources, and carrying out their plans. They have been most successful when backed by the planning resources of governments and large enterprises, not dictating to them but empowering them. The challenge is to put information technology to work for them, enabling them to generate new ideas, build competence in inventing and applying, and forge global links with suppliers and customers, just as most major corporations do now. Peirce & Marshall [1996] tell of a data management center established in a low-income housing complex in Washington, D.C. An effort of Hamilton Securities, a banking firm, it trains residents for jobs requiring computer skills, which can be performed there in the Edgewood Terrace homes. Such integration of training and work within a living environment offers a challenge to planners and architects.

Planners must give increasing attention to the elderly in the 21st century. Many of them are not disadvantaged today, thanks to Social Security and the American Association of Retired People, but they do have special needs for housing, health and personal care, transportation, and recreation. This is most true for the growing numbers who are over 80 and are gradually losing their vitality. Many communities make special provision to meet varied needs for senior housing today, ranging from apartments in which they can live independently to intensive-care homes. Blacksburg, Virginia, with a population of 35,000 and about 1,750 retirees, has made special efforts to become "senior friendly." Its comprehensive plan has a goal of attracting retirees to the city as a means of economic growth, with special provisions in the zoning code for senior housing [Knack 1996]. One economic challenge is to provide needed living facilities for the low-income elderly, who cannot afford typical nursing home care without public assistance. A second, however, is to enable those who are healthy and vigorous to contribute services to their community, perhaps through child care, tutoring, advising organizations, and other ways that employ the skills and knowledge they have gained over a lifetime.

Some observers have raised the issue of gender in planning choices, which they believe disproportionately reflect a masculine outlook. Reese and associates [1996] argue that lower-income women and their dependent children have been particularly disadvantaged by city conditions that limit their living options and make it more difficult and expensive to find child care, nearby jobs and shopping, and health care. More women should participate in planning at the neighborhood and citywide levels to inject those concerns, they maintain. Most helpful would be zoning and development policies that allow mixed uses of space, placing modest-cost homes in the same building or block with community centers, shops, parks, and day care centers. These would be highly defensible spaces to reduce the danger of assault and robbery that keeps many inner-city families in fear. Much of the New Urbanism agenda, described in chapter 7, addresses these concerns.

11.4 HOW GREEN CAN THE CITY BE?

"Sustainable development" is an ambiguous term, as chapter 9 demonstrated. Lacking clear standards for what should be sustained, and to what degree, there is no logical resting point for political debates over it. Surely the evolving bargains over what the "growing city" and the "just city" should look like will also set the criteria for the "green city."

Planners will confront several emerging issues along the way. The urban/rural boundaries, once rather sharp, will continue to blur as more and more residents of the "countryside" will earn their living in "urban" ways, either by physical or electronic commuting to workplaces. We have seen how resort areas, such as Cape Cod, the entire Florida coastline, and the Lake Tahoe region, have gained permanent residents and thus experience pressures for sewers, roads, and city services. Even Three Forks, Montana, at the point where the Missouri River is formed from three tributaries, is in this category. Its population of 2,000 has jumped 50% in six years, with most of the new migrants from elsewhere in Montana. Two faculty members from Montana State University in Bozeman, 35 miles away, prepared a study of the community and its options for the future, and there is serious discussion of hiring a city planner [Wilkinson 1996].

Three Forks's situation is similar to many other communities, within an attractive natural environment, near an interstate highway, and enjoying a small town atmosphere that growth will not immediately obliterate. For such regions the relevant planning area must take in whole counties, watersheds, and regions. Local officials must devise means of networking: Three Forks with Bozeman, the entire Missouri headwaters area, and relevant state agencies. Similarly, the citizen groups that monitor and guide this planning should be organized so as to consider all stakeholders in the region. Planners in each metropolitan area must be able to communicate with officials in the outlying counties and townships that are just beginning to urbanize, even when the latter don't want to think about growth. This may not require new governing institutions if the existing ones are well linked by the very information technologies that are spurring their growth.

A further set of ecological issues arises from long-term climatic changes. The global atmosphere is steadily warming, evidence strongly indicates, although scientists disagree over how much is humanly caused and how much is a naturally cyclical trend. An obvious effect is rising of ocean levels, which has particularly affected the East Coast. A recent study by Rutgers University scientists portrays the average ocean level eight inches higher in 2046 than now and the shoreline several yards farther inland; storms battering the New Jersey beaches will be far more destructive than today. They recommended that governments stop protecting beaches and repairing storm damage to buildings, and instead abandon a wide shoreline area as a buffer from the rising waters. This was not well received by resort owners and local officials, whose most valuable property lies in this coastal margin. Yet, there is no agreement on how to pay the inevitable costs of future storm damage [Hanley 1996]. Far-seeing planners cannot ignore this issue, however. The "green city" must seek a compatible interface with its natural forces.

Inland urban areas will also experience the effects of climate change. In one common projection, the nation will become hotter and drier with obvious impacts on water supply and vegetation. This will dictate planning choices on issues ranging from building insulation to drought-tolerant landscaping to water conservation. While such environmental challenges have a long-term buildup, a destructive flood or succession of very dry years will create public calls for immediate new policies. Certainly the recent and very costly storms on the East Coast have contributed to what acceptance the Rutgers report has had thus far.

11.5 WHO SHALL BE IN CONTROL?

This survey of issues that planners need to anticipate and the public to act upon points to a final question: who shall take the lead in deciding? Chapters 3 and 4 described the "cast of thousands" that take part in planning. As this process responds to uncounted local conditions and choices, it becomes highly fragmented.

> Cities are built and maintained by a host of agents: families, industrial firms, city bureaus, developers, investors, regulatory and subsidizing agencies, utility companies, and the like. Each has its own interests, and the process of decision is fragmented, plural, and marked by bargaining. . . . .
>
> [They] do not control city development in any directed, central fashion. Typically, they are single-purpose actors, whose aim is to increase their profit margin, complete a sewer system, support the real estate market, or maintain a taxation system [Lynch 1981, pp. 40–41].

These competing players in planning politics will have strong incentives in the future to pursue cooperative strategies. Evidence is mounting that urban regions will prosper or lag in the global economy according to how they build and apply their human and technological resources. Investors are not limited by national boundaries in choosing to build, employ, and market, and thus look for places which stimulate a high level of performance. Kanter [1995, pp. 30–31] argues that three resources are essential to a region's success: concepts (the intellectual bases for innovation), competence (the capacity for high-value and efficient production), and connections (the high-volume information links with the rest of the world). "Cities specialize in using those assets to link the local population to the global economy. Thus they develop prominence in one of three generic ways: as *thinkers, makers,* or *traders.*" She cites three regions that exemplify each asset: Boston, Greenville-Spartanburg, South Carolina, and Miami, respectively.

To develop these assets requires extensive cooperation between business, government, and civic institutions. In 1996, the U.S. Department of Housing and Urban Development began promoting the "metropolitan regional strategy" concept, through efforts to enhance and promote the unique resources of each region in a globally competitive arena. In addition to Kanter's examples, Akron, Ohio, has built a leading industry in polymer products, Seattle dominates in aircraft and computer software, and Philadelphia has expertise in health services and biomedical products. Each region's key players would mobilize its local resources for further advancement, while federal agencies shape their programs and policies to aid its success [Peirce 1996b].

This extends further the partnerships described in earlier chapters for the wide variety of urban development efforts already underway. A vital role for planners in the private sector as well as government is to identify the highest priorities for public investment; the telematics capability noted above is an essential. Another is to speed the movement of people and goods, whether by an international airport, mass transit, an efficient harbor, or rail/truck cargo transfer. One reason for the movement behind a new Minnesota airport (recall the case in chapter 1) was to open the region to greater global passenger and freight volumes which in turn would draw investors. Kanter [1996, ch. 12] credits several such partnerships with enhancing their region's global competitiveness.

Planning strategies must not be limited to high-level corporate perspectives in pursuing the "growing city." A metropolis cannot view itself as successful if an underclass does not find opportunities to succeed, or if growth occurs in ways that further degrades its environment. One example of a socially holistic partnership is that between the University of Illinois at Urbana-Champaign and East St. Louis, Illinois. That city's 35,000 residents are among the nation's poorest and lack the money and political connections to revive on their own. Faculty and students joined with residents in the East St. Louis Action Research Project for housing rehabilitation, cleanup of waste-filled vacant lots, and neighborhood redesign. Remedying the decay that accumulated over decades will take many years, but the very fact that an effort has begun gives hope [Reardon 1997, p. 241].

The issues in this chapter illustrate the contrary trends toward the coalescing and diffusing of authority over urban areas. As Lynch [1981] perceived, governments at all levels, economic and financial power centers, community based organizations, and social movements make up a complex web of power. It has many nodes, each a site at which autonomous decisions can be made, yet the interconnecting strands enable them to bargain, agree, and take common action. This web, however, also has access points that give opportunities for citizens who assert themselves for a cause. The community-based organizations that appear so often on these pages, such as the one enabling contractors of color to build modest-cost homes in Brooklyn (see section 7.4), found and used such "political spaces."

The rearranging of urban authority leads to a further concern for planners. The "space-dependent social and economic policies," identified in chapter 1 as part of the domain of planning as defined in this book, are enlarging in scope. To link disadvantaged teenagers with electronic networks is a social mandate for the future, for example. Planners enter the picture as they choose sites for terminals and the infrastructures that connect them, perhaps an inner-city high school, neighborhood library branch, or training center in a disused factory. Whether zoning codes allow multiuse buildings in which single mothers may conveniently access child care, grocers, and clinics may affect their chances of escaping welfare dependency.

This "spreading" of policy may reduce the distinctiveness of the planning endeavor. Certainly it differs sharply from the various missions of George Pullman, Daniel Burnham, and the Levitt brothers. Professional and citizen planners who continue to focus on land use must extend their attention into these related domains and take in a wider span of information. Many of the works cited in this book illustrate how the field has broadened. They depend so heavily on new data and reconsidered understandings of the communities for which they plan that they are most in danger when they stop learning. In contrast to the highly unitary visions of L'Enfant, Howard, and Le Corbusier, who assumed they knew that all that could be known about city building, today's planners interweave their ideals with the ever-emerging realities of urban life.

Chapter 1 introduced planning as the product of vision and imagination. It does not simply spin plans out of thin air. Rather its vision sweeps across the real world of cities, eager to learn what goes on in them. Its imagination then constructs what can be done with them—what citizens acting together can do to render them green, growing, and just.

FOR REVIEW AND DISCUSSION

1. What technological facilities are needed to enable urban regions to be economically competitive in the 21st century? Who should be responsible to provide them?

2. What challenges to planning will be posed by the increasing diversity in urban populations? How can these challenges be met?

3. Why are urban/rural boundaries likely to be less sharp in coming years? What means will be necessary to guide development around and along them?

4. For what reasons are cooperative planning strategies essential for future political and economic development? What authorities and institutions must participate in them?

Appendix

CASE STUDIES IN PLANNING

Those who want to learn "how things really happen" in urban planning do well to examine the good case study literature of the field. The following 25 citations include some "classics" from several decades ago and some relatively new ones (publishers of the books are listed in the References section). Some books consist of a single case while others offer a collection from one or several cities. They also provide some interpretation of the case(s) within a conceptual framework that could be elitist, pluralist, neo-Marxist, or regime-oriented. They cover different policy areas, from housing, transportation, and neighborhood renewal to comprehensive planning. Readers should take care to distinguish between the objective facts of a case and their possible interpretations, and may want to draw alternative judgments and conclusions.

These books certainly do not exhaust the list of good case studies. Many have been published in professional and scholarly periodicals, some of which are cited in the foregoing pages. The *Journal of the American Planning Association,* a quarterly, and *Planning,* which appears monthly, are good sources of this type. Occasionally, a national newspaper like the *New York Times* presents one in a longer article. Increasingly, the Internet provides cases also; see for example the Civic Practices Network at <http://www.cpn.org>.

Alan A. Altshuler, *The City Planning Process* [1965]. Four cases, two each from Minneapolis and St. Paul, emphasize the political context in which planners must operate and which they must understand if they would be successful.

Richard F. Babcock & Charles L. Siemon, *The Zoning Game Revisited* [1985]. Eleven cases from around the country describing political and legal conflicts over land use regulation. The authors, both attorneys, played a personal role in most of them.

Edward C. Banfield, *Political Influence* [1961]. Six cases from Chicago, all but one concerning land use, illustrating that planning influence in a large metropolitan area is exerted by many players, and government is the process of concerting that influence.

Phil Brown & Edwin J. Mikkelsen, *No Safe Place* [1990]. Community efforts to identify and clean up a toxic waste dump in Woburn, Massachusetts, within the larger context of industrial land pollution and public health.

Robert A. Caro, *The Power Broker* [1974]. A sequence of megaprojects in the life of Robert Moses, powerful planner of public improvements in the New York City region, whose political astuteness brought to reality his enormous ambition and deep-seated biases.

Robert A. Catlin, *Racial Politics and Urban Planning: Gary, Indiana 1980–1989* [1993]. How a city with an African-American majority experienced economic decline and the resulting political and social turbulence.

Mario Cuomo, *Forest Hills Diary: the Crisis of Low Income Housing* [1974]. The struggle to locate a housing project in a middle-class Queens neighborhood, by the recent governor of New York. He was then an attorney who was asked by the mayor to mediate the dispute.

Robert A. Dahl, *Who Governs? Democracy and Power in an American City* [1958]. Classic analysis of decision making in New Haven, including its large scale urban renewal programs, which portrayed the city's political system as pluralistic.

Susan S. Fainstein et al, *Restructuring the City: The Political Economy of Urban Development* [1983]. Cases from New Haven, Denver, New Orleans, Boston, and San Francisco demonstrate the interpenetration of governments and capitalist economic enterprises in determining the use and re-use of city land.

Bernard J. Frieden, *The Environmental Protection Hustle* [1979]. The politics and economics of growth limitation programs in several California suburbs, with their built-in biases and effects on housing supply and costs.

Chester W. Hartman, *The Transformation of San Francisco* [1984]. The conflict between city planners, developers, and residents over the rebuilding of a low-income neighborhood on the edge of downtown.

Bryan D. Jones & Lynn W. Bachelor, *The Sustaining Hand: Community Leadership and Corporate Power* [1986 or 1993 ed.] Conflicts over siting of automobile plants in Detroit, Flint, and Pontiac, which demonstrate the constraints on public officials in making industrial location decisions.

David L. Kirp, John P. Dwyer & Larry A. Rosenthal, *Our Town: Race, Housing, and the Soul of Suburbia* [1995]. The nationally watched struggle that focused on opening Mount Laurel and other New Jersey suburbs to modest-income housing, and its varied results.

Adeline G. Levine, *Love Canal: Science, Politics, and People* (1982) The first major confrontation over buried toxic wastes in a residential community, illustrating the follies of unwise planning, the reluctance of public officials to take responsibility for their errors, and the vigorous efforts of residents to secure remedial action.

Larry S. Luton, *The Politics of Garbage: A Community Perspective on Solid Waste Policy Making [1996].* How Spokane, Washington, struggled to build a waste-to-energy facility in the midst of technological uncertainty, citizen fears, and intricate federal and state regulations.

Peter Medoff & Holly Sklar, *Streets of Hope: The Fall and Rise of an Urban Neighborhood* [1994]. Experiences of the Dudley Street Neighborhood Initiative in Boston, in which residents organized to claim the power and resources to renew their homes, streets, and businesses.

Eugene J. Meehan, *The Quality of Federal Policymaking: Programmed Failure in Public Housing* [1979]. The many federal and local governmental choices that led to both the failure of the Pruitt-Igoe housing project in St. Louis and the relative success of several other efforts.

Martin Meyerson & Edward C. Banfield, *Politics, Planning, and the Public Interest* [1957]. The struggle between the Chicago Housing Authority and the city council over the location of public housing sites, the outcome of which was the racial ghettoes that stand today.

Ross Miller, *Here's the Deal: The Buying and Selling of a Great American City* [1996]. Decades of effort by city officials and big-name developers to renew a block in the heart of Chicago's Loop, which produced to date only three acres of empty space.

John H. Mollenkopf, *The Contested City* [1983]. The national-local coalitions that sponsored extensive inner-city rebuilding in Boston and San Francisco.

Jeffrey Pressman & Aaron Wildavsky, *Implementation* [1973, 1979, or 1984 ed.] Efforts by federal and local officials to stimulate economic development in Oakland by funding job-creating projects, and the reasons for their near-complete failure.

Jim R. Rooney, *Organizing the South Bronx* [1994]. Successful efforts by low-income citizens in organizing to secure affordable housing in that depressed borough of New York.

Gregory D. Squires, *Unequal Partnerships: The Political Economy of Urban Development in Postwar America* [1989]. Cases from 12 large cities that explore the influences and outcomes of economic development efforts, arguing that the economic dominants have benefitted much more from them than ordinary city residents.

Randy Stoecker, *Defending Community: The Struggle for Alternative Redevelopment in Cedar-Riverside* [1994]. How residents mobilized to halt expansion of a Minneapolis "new town in-town" into a low-income neighborhood and secure its renewal.

J. Allen Whitt, *Urban Elites and Mass Transportation: The Dialectics of Power* [1982]. The successful effort to build the San Francisco area's rapid transit system (BART) and the lack of success in doing so in the Los Angeles region, analyzed from the elitist, pluralist, and neo-Marxist perspectives.

HOW TO RESEARCH AND WRITE A CASE STUDY IN PLANNING

The learning advantages from reading and analyzing other scholars' case studies can be multiplied by researching and writing one's own. Here are some guidelines on how to do this in the study of planning politics.

First, find a "case." Decision making events in urban planning are continuous, and in a larger city or region many controversies present themselves at any one time. The best ones, however, are those which illustrate the major themes in this book: value conflicts, interactions of governments and nongovernmental participants, goal setting, policy implementation, and the dynamics of urban change. In some, the contest will be open and vivid, while in others it will be in muted tones and require more sensitive perception.

The second step is to discern the key issues at stake. They can be legal, economic, social, environmental, or interpersonal, but more often several of these are wrapped together. Within these issues are one or more basic values, as chapter 2 demonstrated.

Third, it is necessary to identify the participants, with their goals, interests, and degree of power or influence. Chapters 3 and 4 catalogued the most common groups, but it is not an exclusive list. Again, the researcher must recognize the less obvious ones as well as those "out front."

After that, the major events must be chronicled. They can initially be listed in the order in which they occurred. For example, a developer makes a proposal, and a week later the city council approves it. However, the relationship between events may be more complex, since cause and effect do not flow in perfect order.

Last, the outcomes of the case demand explanation. Even if it has not been concluded at the time of writing, one can still analyze progress up to that point. This too can be challenging: one outcome may have several antecedents, and any given action several results. "Outside" influences, not immediately within the scope of a controversy, are common. The explanation can refer to larger theoretical issues such as elitism versus pluralism, or it can approach the outcome in terms of the organizational forces, economic imperatives, or global influences at work. Political factors, such as strong leaders, partisan rivalries, and election prospects may also be present. Most cases offer latitude for two or more reasonable explanations.

What information sources are most useful for this? Data are where one finds them, but not all data are equally valid or useful. Generally, more than one source is necessary to approach balance and accuracy. Newspapers and other periodicals often report events from a "here and now" perspective, which is helpful to a chronology, but they often lack depth and comprehensiveness. Documents and reports, such as minutes of city council meetings, are more official but tend to omit political factors. Statistics can be useful when the debate concerns measurable factors such as housing units or land values.

In most situations, the researcher needs to supplement the above with more personal sources: interviews with participants, surveys of residents, and on-site observations of key events. Some excellent cases have been produced by persons who took part themselves, as interns, citizen activists, or journalists. To be sure, none of these will be completely objective and the analyst does well to watch for other perspectives. Students have to decide for themselves what their opportunities and time constraints are and set their research priorities accordingly. In all stages of the inquiry, they must keep their central questions clearly in mind so as to recognize what data will be most important to obtain.

Finally, analysts must decide how objective to be about their work. Scholarly dicta call for scrupulously factual analyses, not initially seeking to justify or condemn the outcome of any of the participants. They may properly make judgments afterward, as the facts support. Yet it is possible to hold and express preferences and still do honest work. Such normative conclusions can bring out valuable dimensions of the case. The case studies cited above do present judgments, many of which are open to debate by others who interpret the evidence from different perspectives.

Glossary

Brownfield: abandoned industrial site likely to have ground pollution that is a deterrent to redevelopment.

Capital improvement plan: schedule of major governmental construction and improvement projects, with the means of paying for them.

Citizen participation: the formal and informal means by which persons not in official positions can take part in or influence governmental decision making.

Cluster zoning: practice of grouping new developments in rural areas into relatively small parcels to preserve significant open spaces.

Coalitional politics: shifting alliances among power holders, who create patterns of cooperation and conflict over major public issues.

Command and control centers: major metropolitan areas in which are made the strategic economic and political decisions which affect the nation and world.

Comprehensive plan: holistic statement of the development policies of a city, county, or region, with applications to specific parcels of land.

Developer: Private entrepreneur that plans and undertakes a construction project; typically profit making, although nonprofit developers exist.

Ecological values: concerns for air, soil, and water quality and the protection of natural environments; ecosystem integrity a key term.

Empowerment zone: urban area defined as depressed and thus made eligible for special government assistance for economic development in the form of tax breaks and subsidies. Similar to **enterprise zone.**

Environmental impact analysis: study of anticipated environmental impacts of a major development project, with potential means of minimizing environmental consequences. Often expressed in an **environmental impact statement.**

Esthetic values: values related to the visual and sensual properties of the built environment and their impact on its inhabitants; beauty a key term.

Exclusionary zoning: practice of zoning residential areas exclusively for large lots and homes, thus excluding those with lower incomes.

Functional values: values related to the accumulation of wealth and the means to carry on productive enterprises; efficiency a key term.

General purpose government: unit of local government with broad powers in public services and regulations, including land use control; includes cities, villages, boroughs, counties, towns, and townships.

General obligation bonds: means of governmental borrowing of funds by which repayment is guaranteed by the full tax base of the unit.

Gentrification: process by which more affluent persons buy into a depressed neighborhood and their improvements raise property values and rents such that former residents are economically excluded.

Geographic information system: means of linking land use data with specific locations and displaying them graphically.

Greenlining: practice of making loans to declining or high-risk neighborhoods in order to stimulate their renewal.

Growth management: policies for limiting the type, pace, location, and sequencing of urban expansion and protecting open space.

Historic preservation: maintenance or restoration of structures and districts of historic significance; legal provisions restricting alteration and encouraging investment in such efforts.

Inclusionary zoning: methods of inducing lower-cost housing development in areas where it would not otherwise exist.

Incumbent upgrading: neighborhood renewal process which enables current residents to remain.

Land trust: nonprofit group that obtains land or development rights for preservation as open space, parks, farms, and other uses.

LULU (Locally Unwanted Land Use): land uses with

features such as noise, odors, ugliness, and health and safety hazards that are objectionable to members of the public, who resist their siting.

Metropolitan area: contiguous urban region that includes one or more central cities, the county or counties in which located, and surrounding counties that are urbanized and linked economically with the core city or cities.

Neighborhood: residential area within a governmental unit that has some distinct identity to its inhabitants and observers; may be designated by law for citizen participation purposes.

New town: urban settlement built according to a unitary plan that incorporates housing, business, employment, and other elements; may be sponsored by government or private enterprise.

New Urbanism (or Traditional Neighborhood Development): design philosophy intended to create strong sense of community by incorporating features of traditional small towns.

Planned unit development: total plan for an area in which the developer negotiates a land use design that deviates from strict legal standards in return for additional public advantages.

Planning: process of making and implementing decisions about land use and space-dependent social and economic policies.

Planning commission: board composed of nonspecialist citizens and/or elected officials who study the planning choices to be made by their local government and advise lawmakers on them.

Politics: the process of managing or steering the common life of a society.

Power: the means by which one person or group secures an action or outcome in a conflict situation that would not otherwise come about.

Power structure: regularized exercise of power within a social system.

Property rights movement: mobilized citizens concerned for protecting their land from government regulations that would reduce its value or utility.

Redlining: refusal of lenders to provide credit in neighborhoods defined as declining or high-risk, thus further promoting decline.

Regime: the informal arrangements by which public bodies and private interests function together in order to make and carry out governing decisions.

Residential community association: a "private government" that exerts legal control over the owners of condominiums, townhouses, and cooperatives which hold some or all of their property in common.

Revenue bonds: means of goernmental borrowing of funds by which repayment is guaranteed only by the income derived from the funded project.

Shelter society: persons whose primary need is adequate and safe housing and would lack them without outside intervention.

Social values: values rooted in the interactions that citizens have with one another and the degree of fairness and justice that mark them.

Special purpose government: unit of local or regional government that is responsible for one or a few related functions and is independent of the general purpose governments in the area; may be called authority, board, council, commission, or district.

Tax-increment financing: means of subsidizing desired development by dedicating future property taxes to pay for improvements on the developed site.

Telematics: information technology that links computers and media in global networks.

Urban place: a nonagricultural settlement of sufficient size, density, and heterogeneity to pose regular choices about the use of land.

Urban sprawl: pattern of unchecked urban expansion; typically low density development that occurs beyond the current boundary of settlement.

Valued environment: place that holds personal meaning for a group of people, who may act to enhance or protect it.

Zoning: classification of permitted and prohibited land uses, applied to each parcel of land.

References

Abbott, Carl. "Five downtown strategies: policy discourse and downtown planning since 1945." *Journal of Policy History* 5:1 (1993) 5–27.

Abbott, Carl, Deborah Howe, & Sy Adler, ed. *Planning the Oregon Way: a Twenty-Year Evaluation.* Corvallis: Oregon State University Press, 1994.

Abeles, Peter L. "Planning and Zoning." Charles M. Haar & Jerold S. Kayden, eds. *Zoning and the American Dream.* Chicago: APA Planners Press, 1989. 122–153.

Advisory Commission on Regulatory Barriers to Affordable Housing. *"Not In My Back Yard" Removing Barriers to Affordable Housing.* Washington: U.S. Department of Housing and Urban Development, 1991.

Altschuler, Alan. *The Urban Transportation System: Politics and Policy Innovation.* Cambridge: MIT Press, 1979.

Andrews, James H. "Metro power." *Planning* 62 (June 1996) 8–12.

Angotti, Thomas. "New York City's '197-a' Community Planning Experience." and "Red Hook: Memoirs of a Planner." Pratt Institute Graduate Center for Planning & the Environment, 1996. <http://www.pratt.edu/picced>

Apgar, Sally. "Setting the stage." *Minneapolis Star-Tribune*, February 5, 1996.

Appleyard, Donald. *Livable Streets.* Berkeley: University of California Press, 1981.

Arendt, Randall. *Rural by Design.* Chicago: American Planning Association, 1994.

Arrandale, Tom. "A guide to environmental mandates." *Governing*, March 1994, 73–86.

Arrandale, Tom. "The immortal landfill." *Governing*, December 1996, 45–48.

Atkinson, Robert. "The rise of the information-age metropolis." *The Futurist*, July-August 1996, 41–46.

Axelrod, Donald. *Shadow Government.* New York: Wiley, 1992.

Ayres, B. Drummond, Jr. "San Diego backs 'model' nature-habitat plan." *New York Times*, March 20, 1997.

Babcock, Richard E. & Charles L. Siemon. *The Zoning Game Revisited.* Boston: Oelgeschlager, Gunn & Hain, 1985.

Bachelor, Lynn W. "Regime maintenance, solution sets, and urban economic development." *Urban Affairs Quarterly* 29: 4 (June 1994) 596–616.

Bachrach, Peter & Morton Baratz. "Decisions and non-decisions: an analytical framework." *American Political Science Review* 57 (September 1963) 632–642.

Banfield, Edward C. *Political Influence: A New Theory of Urban Politics.* New York: Free Press, 1961.

Bank of America. "Beyond sprawl: new patterns of growth to fit the new California." 1996. <http://www.bankamerica.com/community/>

Bartik, Timothy J. "Strategies for economic development." J. Richard Aronson & Eli Schwartz, ed. *Management Policies in Local Government Finance, 4th ed.* Washington: International City/County Management Association, 1996. 287–312.

Barton, Stephen & Carol Silverman, eds. *Common Interest Communities: Private Governments and the Public Interest.* Berkeley: Institute of Governmental Studies Press, 1994.

Baum, Howell. *Planners and Public Expectations.* Boston: Schenkman, 1983.

Baumbach, Richard O. Jr. & William E. Borah. *The Second Battle of New Orleans: A History of the Vieux Carre Riverfront Expressway Controversy.* University AL: University of Alabama Press and the National Trust for Historic Preservation, 1981.

Beatley, Timothy & David J. Brower. "Sustainability comes to Main Street." *Planning* 59 (May 1993) 16–19.

Berger, Renee. "People, power, and politics." *Planning* 63 (February 1997) 4–9.

Berry, Jeffrey M., Kent E. Portney, & Ken Thompson. *The Rebirth of Urban Democracy.* Washington: Brookings Institution, 1993.

Betancur, John J., Deborah E. Bennett, & Patricia A. Wright. "Effective strategies for community economic development." Philip W. Nyden & Wim Wiewel, ed. *Challenging Uneven Development.* New Brunswick NJ: Rutgers University Press, 1991. 198–224.

Bollens, Scott A. "Restructuring land use governance." *Journal of Planning Literature* 7 (February 1993) 211–226.

Borgsdorf, Del. "Charlotte's city within a city." *National Civic Review* 84 (Summer–Fall 1995), 218–224.

Boyer, M. Christine. *Dreaming the Rational City: The Myth of American City Planning.* Cambridge: MIT Press, 1983.

Brooke, James. "Plutonium stockpile fosters fears of 'a disaster waiting to happen'." *New York Times,* December 11, 1996.

Brown, Phil & Edwin J. Mikkelsen. *No Safe Place: Toxic Waste, Leukemia, and Community Action.* Berkeley: University of California Press, 1990.

Buchholz, Barbara B. "Building apartments for the low-income elderly." *New York Times,* October 20, 1996.

Buder, Stanley. *Pullman: An Experiment in Industrial Order and Community Planning 1880–1930.* New York: Oxford University Press, 1967.

Bullard, Robert D. "Environmental justice for all." Robert D. Bullard, ed. *Unequal Protection: Environmental Justice and Communities of Color.* San Francisco: Sierra Club, 1994. Chapter 1.

Burby, Raymond J. & Linda C. Dalton. "Plans can matter! The role of land use plans and state planning mandates in limiting the development of hazardous areas." *Public Administration Review* 54 (May/June 1994) 229–237.

Burnham, Daniel H. & Edward H. Bennett. *Plan of Chicago.* New York: DaCapo Press, 1970. (Original edition published by the Commercial Club of Chicago, 1909).

Calavita, Nico. "Vale of Tiers." *Planning* 63 (March 1997) 18–21.

Calthorpe, Peter. *The Next American Metropolis: Ecology, Community, and the American Dream.* New York: Princeton Architectural Press, 1993.

Campbell, Scott. "Green cities, growing cities, just cities? Urban planning and the contradictions of sustainable development." *Journal of the American Planning Association* 62 (Summer 1996) 296–312.

Camph, Donald H. "Transportation, the ISTEA, and American cities." 1996. <http://www.transact.org/mono/city.html>

Carlson, Daniel, with Lisa Wormser & Cy Ulberg, Surface Transportation Policy Project. *At Road's End: Transportation and Land Use Choices for Communities.* Washington: Island Press, 1995.

Caro, Robert A. *The Power Broker: Robert Moses and the Fall of New York.* New York: Random House, 1974.

Catanese, Anthony J. *The Politics of Planning and Development.* Beverly Hills: Sage Publications, 1984.

Catlin, Robert A. *Racial Politics and Urban Planning: Gary, Indiana 1980–1989.* Lexington: University of Kentucky Press, 1994.

Caves, Roger W. *Land Use Planning: The Ballot Box Revolution.* Newbury Park CA: Sage Publications, 1992.

Chattanooga/Hamilton County, Tennessee, 1996. <http://www.sustainable.doe.gov/ss/pti>

Chicago, City of, Departments of Environment and Planning and Development. *Brownfields Forum: Recycling Land for Chicago's Future. Final Report and Action Plan.* Chicago, 1995.

Clavel, Pierre. *The Progressive City: Planning and Participation.* New Brunswick: Rutgers University Press, 1986.

Clay, Philip L. *Neighborhood Renewal: Middle-class Resettlement and Incumbent Upgrading in American Neighborhoods.* Lexington MA: Lexington Books, 1979.

Covington, William. "Wireless world." *Planning* 62 (December 1996) 8–12.

Cox, Wendell. Address to Ohio Transportation Users Conference, Columbus OH, 1992. <http://www.il.net>

Crenson, Matthew A. *Neighborhood Politics.* Cambridge: Harvard University Press, 1983.

Cuomo, Mario. *Forest Hills Diary: The Crisis of Low-Income Housing.* New York: Vintage, 1974.

Cushman, John H. Jr. "Program to clean toxic waste sites is left in turmoil." *New York Times,* January 15, 1996.

Dahl, Robert A. *Who Governs? Democracy and Power in an American City.* New Haven: Yale University Press, 1958.

Dattner, Richard. *Civil Architecture: The New Public Infrastructure.* New York: Mc Graw Hill, 1995.

Davies, Stephen. "Managing downtown public spaces." *Technology Review* 88 (August–September 1985) 18–25, 60–61.

Duany, Andres & Elizabeth Plater-Zyberk. "The second coming of the American small town." *Wilson Quarterly* (Winter 1992): 19–50.

Duerksen, Christopher J. & Richard J. Roddewig. *An Introduction to Takings Law and the Historical Background of Takings.* <http://www.webcom/~pcj/duerk.html>

Dunlap, David W. (1996a) "Lawyers who mold the shape of a city." *New York Times,* February 25, 1996.

Dunlap, David W. (1996b) "Developers' hazard: legal hardball." *New York Times,* December 8, 1996.

Dunlap, David W. "Church v. State: landmark case." *New York Times,* February 2, 1997.

Duwamish Coalition, *Land Use Challenges: Preserve and Reclaim Industrial Land.* 1996. <http://www.ci.seattle.wa.us>

Egan, Timothy. "Many seek security in private communities." *New York Times,* September 3, 1995.

Ehrenhalt, Alan. "Cooperate or die." *Governing,* September 1995: 28–32.

Eisinger, Peter K. *The Rise of the Entrepreneurial State.* Madison: University of Wisconsin Press, 1988.

Enterprise Foundation, 1996. <http://www.entrprisefdn.org>

Fainstein, Susan S., Norman I. Fainstein, Richard Child Hill, Dennis Judd & Michael Peter Smith. *Restructuring the City: The Political Economy of Urban Redevelopment.* New York: Longman, 1983.

Feder, Barnaby J. "Sowing preservation." *New York Times,* March 20, 1997.

Fischer, Hank B. *Evaluating Public Policy.* Chicago: Nelson-Hall, 1995.

Fishman, Robert. *Urban Utopias of the Twentieth Century.* New York: Basic Books, 1977.

Freyman, Russ. "Regulating the tiniest business." *Governing,* September 1995: 46–48.

Frieden, Bernard J. *The Environmental Protection Hustle.* Cambridge: MIT Press, 1979.

Frieden, Bernard J. & Lynne B. Sagalyn. *Downtown, Inc.: How America Rebuilds Cities.* Cambridge: MIT Press, 1989.

Frisby, Michael K. "Tired of promises, New Hampshire town rebuilds on its own." *Wall Street Journal,* February 20, 1996.

Gallagher, Mary Lou. "Taking a stand on hallowed ground." *Planning* 61 (January 1995) 10–15.

Gallion, Arthur B. & Simon Eisner. *The Urban Pattern: City Planning and Design. 5th ed.* New York: Van Nostrand Reinhold, 1985.

Garreau, Joel. *Edge City: Life on the New Frontier.* New York: Doubleday, 1991.

Garvin, Alexander. *The American City: What Works, What Doesn't.* New York: McGraw Hill, 1996.

Goetz, Edward G. *Shelter Burden: Local Politics and Progressive Housing Policy.* Philadelphia: Temple University Press, 1993.

Gold, John R. & Jacquelin Burgess. "On the significance of valued environments." John R. Gold & Jacquelin Burgess, ed. *Valued Environments.* London: George Allen & Unwin, 1982: 1–9.

Goldberger, Paul. "The new Times Square: magic that surprised the magicians." *New York Times,* October 15, 1996.

Goldsteen, Joel B. & Cecil D. Elliott. *Designing America: Creating Urban Identity.* New York: Van Nostrand Reinhold, 1994.

Goslant, Kim Herman. "Citizen participation and administrative discretion in the cleanup of Narragansett Bay." *Harvard Environmental Law Review* 12 (1988): 521–568.

Graham, Stephen & Simon Marvin. *Telecommunications and the City: Electronic Spaces, Urban Places.* London: Routledge, 1996.

Greenberg, Michael R., Frank J. Popper, & Bernadette M. West. "The TOADS: a new American urban epidemic." *Urban Affairs Quarterly* 25 (March 1990) 435–454.

Greenberg, Michael R. & Dona Schneider. *Environmentally Devastated Neighborhoods: Perceptions, Policies, and Realities.* New Brunswick: Rutgers University Press, 1996.

Greenhouse, Linda. "Local bars to group housing are lowered by high court." *New York Times,* May 16, 1995.

Gurwitt, Rob. "The projects come down." *Governing,* August 1995, 16–21.

Haar, Charles M. *Suburbs Under Siege: Race, Space, and Audacious Judges.* Princeton: Princeton University Press, 1996.

Hall, Derek. "Valued environments and the planning process: community consciousness and urban structure." John R. Gold & Jacquelin Burgess, ed. *Valued Environments.* London: George Allen & Unwin, 1982: 172–188.

Hamilton, Robert A. "In Hartford, the river beckons again." *New York Times,* April 7, 1996.

Hanley, Robert. "Drawing lines in the shore's sand." *New York Times,* October 24, 1996.

Hartman, Chester W. *The Transformation of San Francisco.* New York: Rowman & Allenheld, 1984.

Hoch, Charles. *What Planners Do: Power, Politics, and Persuasion.* Chicago: Planners Press, 1994.

Holmstrom, David. "Help and hope for the inner city." *Christian Science Monitor,* August 25, 1994.

Holmstrom, David. "The big dig." *Christian Science Monitor,* October 30, 1995.

Howard, Ebenezer. *Garden Cities of Tomorrow.* London: Faber & Faber, 1965.

Howard, Malcolm. "Cities plan to build a sense of community." *Christian Science Monitor,* March 11, 1996.

Humphreys, Brian. "US rich/poor divide extends to housing in cities, suburbs." *Christian Science Monitor,* June 25, 1996.

Hunter, Floyd. *Community Power Structure.* Garden City NY: Doubleday, 1963.

Imbroscio, David L. "Nontraditional public enterprise as local economic development policy: dimensions, prospects, and constraints." *Policy Studies Journal* 23:2 (Summer 1995) 218–230.

Jacobs, Allan B. *Looking at Cities.* Cambridge: Harvard University Press, 1985.

Jackson, Kenneth T. *Crabgrass Frontier: The Suburbanization of the United States.* New York: Oxford University Press, 1985.

Johnson, Kirk. "Where a zoning law failed, seeds of a New York revival." *New York Times,* April 21, 1996.

Jones, Bryan D. & Lynn W. Bachelor. *The Sustaining Hand: Community Leadership and Corporate Power.* 2d ed. Lawrence: University Press of Kansas, 1993.

Jordan, Anne. "Library renaissance." *Governing,* January 1996, 20–25.

Kaiser, Edward J., David R. Godschalk & F. Stuart Chapin, Jr. *Urban Land Use Planning,* 4th ed. Urbana: University of Illinois Press, 1995.

Kanter, Rosabeth Moss. *World Class: Thriving Locally in the Global Economy.* New York: Simon & Schuster, 1995.

Kirp, David L., John P. Dwyer, & Larry A. Rosenthal. *Our Town: Race, Housing, and the Soul of Suburbia.* New Brunswick: Rutgers University Press, 1995.

Klobuchar, Amy. *Uncovering the Dome.* Prospect Heights IL: Waveland, 1982.

Knack, Ruth Eckdish. "BART's village vision." *Planning* 61 (January 1995) 18–21.

Knack, Ruth Eckdish. "Gray is good." *Planning* 62 (August 1996) 20–24.

Knox, Paul L. "Globalization and urban economic change." *Annals of the American Academy of Political and Social Science* 551 (May 1997) 17–27.

Kraus, Keith. "*Dolan v. City of Tigard:* Property owners win the battle but may still lose the war." *Journal of Urban and Contemporary Law* 48 (Summer 1995) 275–296.

Le Corbusier. *The City of Tomorrow.* Cambridge: MIT Press, 1971. (First published in French, 1924; translation into English by Frederick Etchells, 1929.)

Leicht, Kevin T. & J. Craig Jenkins. "Three strategies of state economic development: entrepreneurial, industrial recruitment, and deregulation policies in the American states." *Economic Development Quarterly* 8 (August 1994) 256–269.

Leitner, Helga & Mark Garner. "The limits of local initiatives: a reassessment of urban entrepreneurialism for urban development." *Urban Geography* 14:1 (1993) 57–77.

Lemov, Doug. "'Calming' traffic." *Governing,* August 1996. 25–27.

Leonard, Paul A. "Debt management." J. Richard Aronson & Eli Schwartz, ed. *Management Policies in Local Government Finance, 4th ed.* Washington: International City/County Management Association, 1996. 313–338.

Levine, Adeline G. *Love Canal: Science, Politics, and People.* Lexington MA: Lexington Books, 1982.

Levine, Marc V. "The politics of partnership: urban redevelopment since 1945." Gregory D. Squires, ed. *Unequal Partnerships: The Political Economy of Urban Redevelopment in Postwar America.* New Brunswick NJ: Rutgers University Press, 1989. 12–34.

Levy, Frank S., Arnold J. Meltsner, & Aaron Wildavsky. *Urban Outcomes: Schools, Streets, & Libraries.* Berkeley: University of California Press, 1974.

Lewis, Paul G. *Shaping Suburbia: How Political Institutions Organize Urban Development.* Pittsburgh: University of Pittsburgh Press, 1996.

Lewis, Sylvia. "Tough love works in Newark." *Planning* 59 (October 1993) 24–29.

Luton, Larry S. *The Politics of Garbage: A Community Perspective on Solid Waste Decision Making.* Pittsburgh: University of Pittsburgh Press, 1996.

Lynch, Kevin. *Good City Form.* Cambridge: MIT Press, 1981.

Lynch, Kevin. *What Time is This Place?* Cambridge: MIT Press, 1972.

MacFarquhar, Neil. "Downtown Newark gambles on the arts." *New York Times,* January 14, 1997.

Marris, Peter. *Community Planning and Conceptions of Change.* London: Routledge & Kegan Paul, 1982.

McHarg, Ian L. *Design With Nature.* Garden City NY: Doubleday/Natural History Press, 1971.

Medoff, Peter & Holly Sklar. *Streets of Hope.* Boston: South End Press, 1994.

Meehan, Eugene J. *The Quality of Federal Policymaking: Programmed Failure in Public Housing.* Columbia: University of Missouri Press, 1979.

Melvin, Tessa. "Using zoning to spur lower-priced housing." *New York Times,* April 16, 1995.

Meredith, Robyn. "Motown enters the zone: U.S. program helps return industry to an inner city." *New York Times,* April 11, 1997.

Metropolitan Council. *Growth Options for the Twin Cities Metropolitan Area.* Saint Paul: Metropolitan Council, 1996.

Meyerson, Martin & Edward C. Banfield. *Politics, Planning, and the Public Interest.* New York: Free Press, 1957.

Miller, Ross. *Here's the Deal: The Buying and Selling of a Great American City.* New York: Alfred A. Knopf, 1996.

Minton, Eric. "Plunging into the mainstream." *Planning* 58 (August 1992) 18–23.

Mollenkopf, John H. *The Contested City.* Princeton: Princeton University Press, 1983.

Molotch, Harvey. "The political economy of growth machines." *Journal of Urban Affairs* 15:1 (1993) 29–53.

Myerson, Allen R. "O governor, won't you buy me a Mercedes plant?" *New York Times,* September 1, 1996.

Nelson, Arthur C. & James B. Duncan, with Clancy J. Mullen & Kirk R. Bishop. *Growth Management Principles and Practices.* Chicago: Planners Press, 1995.

Newman, Oscar. *Defensible Space: Crime Prevention Through Urban Design.* New York: Macmillan, 1973.

Newman, Oscar. "Defensible space: a new physical planning tool for urban revitalization." *Journal of the American Planning Association* (Spring 1995) 149–155.

North Carolina, State of. *North Carolina Consolidated Plan, Community Development Strategy.* 1995. <http://www. commerce.state. nc.us/>

Olshansky, Robert B. "The California Environmental Quality Act and local planning." *Journal of the American Planning Association* 62 (Summer 1996) 313–330.

Onaran, Yalman. "The Bronx." *Christian Science Monitor,* June 1, 1994.

Oregon Department of Land Conservation and Development. *Oregon's Statewide Planning Program.* 1995. <http://darkwing.uoregon.edu/>

Oser, Alan S. "Building homes, and skilled developers, in Brooklyn." *New York Times,* February 11, 1996.

Pagano, Michael A. & Ann O'M. Bowman. *Cityscapes and Capital: The Politics of Urban Development.* Baltimore: Johns Hopkins University Press, 1995.

Pas, Eric I. "The urban transportation planning process." Susan Hanson, ed. *The Geography of Urban Transportation.* New York: Guilford Press, 1986, Chapter 3.

Peirce, Neal R.(1996a) "Giving neighborhoods a real chance." *National Journal,* April 13, 1996. 836.

Peirce, Neal R. (1996b) "Visions of a new urban policy." *National Journal,* October 26, 1996. 2302.

Peirce, Neal R. & Alex Marshall. "Where there's a wire, there's a way." *Planning* 62 (July 1996) 4–8.

Perrenod, Virginia M. *Special Districts, Special Purposes: Fringe Governments and Urban Problems in the Houston Area.* College Station: Texas A&M University Press, 1986.

Perry, Clarence A. Planning a city neighborhood from the social point of view. *Proceedings of the National Conference of Social Work.* Chicago: University of Chicago Press, 1924.

Peterson, Paul E. *City Limits.* Chicago: University of Chicago Press, 1981.

Pressman, Jeffrey L. & Aaron Wildavsky. *Implementation.* (3d ed.) Berkeley: University of California Press, 1984.

Putnam, Robert D. "Bowling alone: America's declining social capital." *Journal of Democracy* 6 (January 1995) 65–78.

Rapoport, Amos. *Human Aspects of Urban Form.* Oxford: Pergamon Press, 1977.

Ravetz, Alison. *Remaking Cities: Contradictions of the Recent Urban Environment.* London: Croom Helm, 1980.

Reardon, Kenneth M. "State and local revitalization efforts in East St. Louis, Illinois." *Annals of the American Academy of Political and Social Science* 551 (May 1997) 235–247.

Reese, Laura, Robin Boyle, Colleen Croxall, & F. Elaine Martin. "The feminization of urban planning and community development." Paper delivered at the 1996 annual meeting of the American Political Science Association, August 29–September 1, 1996.

Regional Plan Association. *A Region at Risk: Executive summary of the Third Regional Plan for the New York New Jersey-Connecticut Metropolitan Area.* 1996. <http://maestro.com>

Rider, Robert W. "Local government planning: prerequisites of an effective system." *Urban Affairs Quarterly* 18 (December 1982): 271–280.

Riposa, Gerry. "From enterprise zones to empowerment zones." *American Behavioral Scientist* 39 (March/April 1996) 536–551.

Robertson, Kent A. "Downtown redevelopment strategies in the United States." *Journal of the American Planning Association* 61 (Autumn 1995) 429–437.

Robinson, Tony. "Gentrification and grassroots resistance in San Francisco's Tenderloin." *Urban Affairs Review* 30 (March 1995) 483–515.

Rooney, Jim. *Organizing the South Bronx.* Albany: State University of New York Press, 1995.

Rosegrant, Susan. "Wichita confronts contamination." John F. Kennedy School of Government Case Program, Harvard University, 1992.

Rosell, Ellen. "The Sunland Park/Camino Real partnership: landfill politics in a border community." *Policy Studies Journal* 24 (Spring 1996) 111–122.

Rosenbaum, Nelson. "Growth and its discontents: origins of local population controls." Judith V. May & Aaron B. Wildavsky, ed. *The Policy Cycle.* Beverly Hills: Sage Publications, 1978: 43–61.

Rothblatt, Donald N. "Swimming against the tide: metropolitan planning and management in the United States." *Planning Practice and Research* 7 (Spring 1992).

Roy, Roger. "Orlando: too much of a good thing." *Planning* 62 (March 1996) 4–9.

Rubin, Herbert J. "Renewing hope in the inner city: conversations with community-based development practitioners." *Administration & Society* 27 (May 1995) 127–160.

Salvesen, David. "Banking on wetlands." *Planning* 61 (February 1995) 11–15.

San Jose, City of. *City of San Jose Historic Resources Inventory.* 1994. <http://www. preservation.org>

Sawicki, David S. "The festival marketplace as public policy." *Journal of the American Planning Association* 55:3 (1989) 347–361.

Sayre, Wallace S. & Herbert Kaufman. *Governing New York City.* New York: W. W. Norton, 1965.

Scavo, Carmine. "The use of participative mechanisms by large US cities." *Journal of Urban Affairs* 15:1 (1993), 93–109.

Schamess, Gil. "Lofty plans for artists." *Planning* 62 (August 1996) 16–18.

Schattschneider, E. E. *The Semi-Sovereign People.* New York: Holt, Rinehart & Winston, 1960.

Scherer, Ron. "Cities put smut business in its place." *Christian Science Monitor,* November 6, 1995.

Schultz, Stanley K. *Constructing Urban Cuture: American Cities and City Planning, 1800–1920.* Philadelphia: Temple University Press, 1989.

Scott, Mel. *American City Planning Since 1890.* Berkeley: University of California Press, 1969.

Sengupta, Somini. "Meshing the sacred and the secular." *New York Times,* November 23, 1995.

Spaid, Elizabeth Levitan. "How one city survives base closing." *Christian Science Monitor,* March 25, 1996.

Squires, Gregory D. (ed.) *Unequal Partnerships: The Political Economy of Urban Development in Postwar America.* New Brunswick: Rutgers University Press, 1989.

Stanfield, Rochelle. "Block by block." *National Journal,* July 8, 1995, 1763–1766.

Stanfield, Rochelle. "Communities reborn." *National Journal,* Jume 22, 1996, 1370–1374.

Steffens, Richard. "What the incubators have hatched." *Planning* 59 (May 1992) 28–30.

Steffenson, John. "Uncle Sam, map maven." *Planning* 62 (July 1996) 14–17.

Steinhauer, Jennifer. "When shoppers walk away from pedestrian malls." *New York Times,* November 5, 1996.

Stephens, G. Ross. "The least glorious, most local, most trivial, homely, provincial, and most ignored form of local government." *Urban Affairs Quarterly* 24 (June 1989) 501–512.

Sterngold, James. "Foiling the best laid plans." *New York Times,* September 17, 1995.

Sternlieb, George. *Patterns of Development.* New Brunswick: Rutgers University Center for Urban Policy Research, 1986.

Stevens, William K. "Salvation at hand for a California landscape." *New York Times*, February 27, 1996.

Stoecker, Randy. *Defending Community: The Struggle for Alternative Development in Cedar-Riverside*. Philadelphia: Temple University Press, 1994.

Stone, Clarence N. *Regime Politics: Governing Atlanta, 1946-1988*. Lawrence: University Press of Kansas, 1989.

Trust for Public Land, 1996. <http://www.igc.apc.org/tpl>

Tuan, Yi-Fu. *Topophilia*. Englewood Cliffs NJ: Prentice-Hall, 1974.

Turner, Robyne S. "Intergovernmental growth management: a partnership framework for state-local relations." *Publius* 20:3 (1990) 79-95.

Tyson, Ann Scott. "Urban farms: how green is my barrio." *Christian Science Monitor*, December 4, 1996.

Tyson, James L. "How Chicago sparked family-housing boom." *Christian Science Monitor*, March 4, 1996.

Vergara, Camilo Jose. *The New American Ghetto*. New Brunswick: Rutgers University Press, 1995.

Wallis, Allan D. "Governance and the civic infrastructure of metropolitan regions." *National Civic Review* 82 (Spring 1993) 125-139.

Walters, Jonathan. "Tightening the screws on 'takings'." *Governing*, August 1994, 18-20.

Walters, Jonathan. "A guide to playing the highway game." *Governing*, February 1997, 61-66.

Warner, Kee & Harvey Molotch. "Power to build: how development persists despite local controls." *Urban Affairs Review* 30 (January 1995) 378-406.

Warren, Elizabeth. *Chicago's Uptown*. Chicago: Loyola University Center for Urban Policy, 1979.

West, Harry & Zach Taylor. "Stimulating civic change in metropolitan regions." *National Civic Review* 84 (Summer-Fall 1995) 225-238.

Whitt, J. Allen. "The arts coalition in strategies of urban development." Clarence N. Stone & Heywood Sanders, ed. *The Politics of Urban Development*. Lawrence: University Press of Kansas, 1987. Chapter 2, 144-156.

Whitt, J. Allen. *Urban Elites and Mass Transportation: The Dialectics of Power*. Princeton: Princeton University Press, 1982.

Wilkinson, Todd. "Rural Montana rewrites myth of yuppie sprawl." *Christian Science Monitor*, October 10, 1996.

Williams, Oliver P. & Charles R. Adrian. *Four Cities*. Philadelphia: University of Pennsylvania Press, 1963.

Wirt, Frederick M. *Power in the City: Decision Making in San Francisco*. Berkeley: University of California Press, 1974.

Wirth, Louis. "Urbanism as a way of life." *American Journal of Sociology* 44 (July 1938): 1-24.

Wise, Charles R. & Kirk Emerson. "Regulatory takings: the emerging doctrine and its implications for public administration." *Administration & Society* 26 (November 1994) 305-336.

Wolman, Abel. "The metabolism of cities." *Scientific American* 213 (September 1965) 179-205.

Wong, Kenneth K. & Paul E. Peterson. "Urban response to federal program flexibility: politics of Community Development Block Grant." *Urban Affairs Quarterly* 21 (March 1986) 293-309.

Wood, Daniel B. "Cities design smart highways; next, smart drivers." *Christian Science Monitor*, December 16, 1996.

Wood, Daniel B. "City buses are newest vehicle to help inner-city workers." *Christian Science Monitor*, February 6, 1997.

Index